CHILTON'S Repair and Tune-Up Guide

Corvair
1960–69

ILLUSTRATED

Prepared by the

Automotive Editorial Department

CHILTON BOOK COMPANY
RADNOR, PENNSYLVANIA

Copyright © 1971 by Chilton Book Company
Chilton Way, Radnor, Pa. 19089
Published in Radnor, Pa., by Chilton Book Company
and simultaneously in Ontario, Canada,
by Thomas Nelson & Sons, Ltd.
All rights reserved
ISBN 0-8019-5607-2
ISBN 0-8019-6691-4 pbk.
Library of Congress Catalog Card No. 70-161623
Manufactured in the United States of America
67890   09

Contents

Chapter 1 Identification and Maintenance 1
    Introduction, 1   Maintenance, 4
    Model Identification, 1

Chapter 2 Tune-Up and Troubleshooting 10
    Tune-Up, 10   Troubleshooting, 23

Chapter 3 Engine 37
    General, 37   Engine Inspection and Servicing, 43
    Engine Removal, 37   Engine Assembly, 52
    Engine Disassembly, 41

Chapter 4 Fuel System 56
    General, 56   Fuel Pump, 74
    Carburetors, 56   Air Injection Reactor (A.I.R.), 75

Chapter 5 Electrical System 81
    Battery and Charging System, 81   Starter, 99

Chapter 6 Power Train 105
    Clutch, 105   Transmission, 108

Chapter 7 Rear Axle and Suspension 126
    Description, 126   Differential, 132
    Maintenance, 126

Chapter 8 Brakes 140
    General, 140

Chapter 9 Suspension and Steering 149
    Front End, 149   Front End Alignment, 156
    Steering, 153

Although information in this guide is based on industry sources and is as complete as possible at the time of publication, the possibility exists that the manufacturer made later changes which could not be included here. While striving for total accuracy, Chilton Book Company can not assume responsibility for any errors, changes, or omissions that may occur in the compilation of this data.

1 • Identification and Maintenance

Introduction

The Chevrolet Corvair, manufactured from 1960 through 1969, was General Motors first attempt to reclaim the sales lost to foreign car makers. The Corvair was the first General Motors car powered by an air-cooled, rear-mounted engine. This six-cylinder, horizontally opposed engine was used on all models. The power train is rear-drive, through a transaxle and either an automatic or a standard transmission.

Model Identification

The chief model and series differences are as follows.

1960: Four-door sedan and coupe, 500 (Standard) or 700 (Deluxe) series.

1961: Four-door sedan and coupe and Lakewood station wagon (500 and 700 series), Corvair 95 and Greenbrier vans.

1962, 1963: Four-door sedan and coupe (500 and 700 series), Monza coupe (900 series), Corvan and Greenbrier vans.

1964: Four-door sedan and coupe (500 and 700 series), Monza (900 series), and Monza Spyder (600 series), Greenbrier van.

1965-1969: Four-door sedan and coupe (Standard), Monza four-door sedan and coupe, Corsa coupe and convertible.

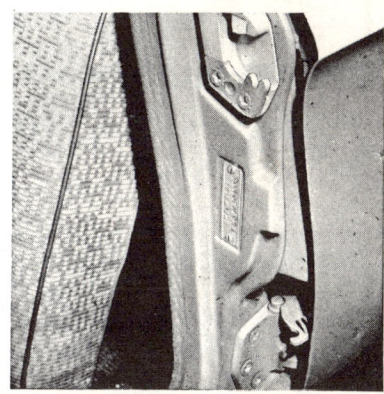

Serial number tag located on left front lock pillar

Vehicle Serial Number: Left front door lock pillar.

Engine Number: Top of engine block (crankcase) forward of oil filter adapter.

Engine number stamped on top of engine block, immediately forward of generator-oil filter adapter

IDENTIFICATION AND MAINTENANCE

Serial Number Location

1960-64—Left front door hinge pillar.
1965-69—Left-hand top of frame side rail rearward of battery bolts.

Engine Identification Code

1960-64—Top of engine block forward of generator-oil filter adapter.
1965-69—Top of engine block behind oil pressure sending unit.

No. Cyls.	Cu. In. Displ.	Type	1960	1961	1962	1963	1964	No. Cyls.	Cu. In. Displ.	Type	1965	1966	1967	1968	1969
6	145	M.T.	YH, V	YH, V	YH, V	V	V	6	164	M.T., AC, w/ex. EM			QM		
6	164	M.T.						6	164	PG, AC, w/ex. EM			QO		
6	145	A.T.	W, ZL	W, ZL	W, ZL	W	W	6	164	HP, PG, w/ex. EM			QP		
6	164	A.T.						6	164	HP, MT, AC, w/ex. EM			QS		
6	145	4 Spd., TC	YR	YR	YR	Y		6	164	M.T.	RA	RA	RA		
6	145	M.T.	YC	YC	YC	YC	YC	6	164	HP	RB	RB			
6	164	M.T.						6	164	M.T., AC	RD	RD	RD	RM	RM
6	145	M.T., AC	YL	YL	YL	YL	YL	6	164	HP, AC	RE	RE	RE		
6	164	M.T., AC						6	164	PG	RF	RF	RF	RF	RF
6	145	M.T., HP, AC	YM	YM	YM	YM	YM	6	164	PG, HP	RG	RG	RG		
6	164	4 Spd., TC	Y, YN	Y, YN	Y, YN	YN	YN	6	164	PG, AC	RH	RH	RH		
6	145	M.T., HP						6	164	PG, HP, AC	RJ	RJ	RJ	RJ	RJ
6	164	M.T., HP	ZB	ZB	ZB	Z	Z	6	164	TC	RK	RK	RK	RK	RK
6	145	A.T.	ZJ	ZJ	ZJ	ZD	ZD	6	164	M.T., SHP	RL	RL			
6	164	A.T.						6	164	PG, SHP	RM	RM			
6	145	A.T., AC	ZF, ZK	ZF, ZK	ZF, ZK	ZF	ZF	6	164	SHP, w/ex. EM	RN	RN			
6	164	A.T., AC						6	164	AC		RQ			
6	145	A.T., HP	ZG	ZG	ZG	ZG	ZG	6	164	M.T., HP, w/ex. EM		RR			
6	164	A.T., HP						6	164	w/ex. EM	RS	RS	RS	RS	
6	145	A.T., HP, AC	ZH	ZH	ZH	ZH	ZH	6	164	M.T., HP		RT			
6	164	A.T., HP, AC						6	164	PG	RU	RU	RU		
6	145	A.T.						6	164	PG, w/ex. EM	RV	RV	RV	RV	RV
6	164	A.T.						6	164	HP, w/ex. EM		RW	RW		
								6	164	PG, SHP, PG, AC		RY			
								6	164	HP, PG				RE	RE
								6	164	PG, SHP, w/ex. EM	RX		RX		
								6	164	SHP, AC			RZ		

AC—Air conditioned.
HP—High performance.
SHP—Special high performance.
PG—Powerglide transmission.
M.T.—Manual transmission.
TC—Turbocharged.
w/ex. EM—With exhaust emission.
A.T.—Automatic transmission.

IDENTIFICATION AND MAINTENANCE

Transmission Serial Number: Left side of case.

Differential Serial Number: Right-hand side of housing, near oil pan flange.

Powerglide transmission unit number stamped on right hand side of casting between forward and middle pan mounting bosses

Differential number stamped on lower left side of casting

Conventional transmission unit number stamped on side of upper left differential mounting boss

Capacities

YEAR	MODEL	ENGINE CRANKCASE (Qts.) ADD 1 Pt. FOR NEW FILTER	TRANSMISSIONS Pts. TO REFILL AFTER DRAINING Manual 3-Speed	4-Speed	Automatic	DRIVE AXLE (Pts.)	GASOLINE TANK (Gals.)	COOLING SYSTEM (Qts.) WITH HEATER
1960	All	4	2	—	8	3	11	Air Cooled
1961-63	500, 700, 900	4	3	3¾	13	3★	14	Air Cooled
	1200	4	3	3¾	13	3★	18.6	Air Cooled
1964	All except below	4	2¼	3¾	13	4½	14▲	Air Cooled
1965-68	All	4	3	3¾	13	4	14	Air Cooled
1969	All	4	3.7	3.7	13	2.7	14	Air Cooled

▲—Station Wagon or truck; 18½ gal.
★—1963—4½.

Maintenance

General

The Corvair is an unusual automobile and requires special maintenance and service techniques. Procedures which are useful but not critical on other cars are very important on the Corvair because of its many unique features.

The Corvair engine's design is duplicated by no other American automobile presently in existence, so that new maintenance techniques must be learned. The engine is an air-cooled flat-six; therefore, special attention must be paid to air flow through the shrouds and ducts. Specialized air flow areas such as the cylinder head fins and the oil cooler must be kept free of dirt at all times to ensure proper engine cooling. Cleanliness, important only for appearance on other engines, is a necessity on the Corvair.

The rear-drive arrangement of the Corvair necessitates long, complex linkages from the driver's controls to the engine and transmission. These linkages must be more carefully maintained than the shorter linkages of other cars, in order to prevent minor problems, which could be misinterpreted as more serious drive line problems, from occurring.

Engine Oil

The Corvair engine, even more than other engines, requires close control of the crankcase oil for efficient operation and long service. In all internal combustion engines the crankcase oil serves as a coolant as well as a lubricant. In the Corvair's air-cooled engine, the oil is a more critical factor than usual in cooling the engine parts. The "flat-six" arrangement of the cylinders brings them closer to the level of the crankcase oil for ease of lubrication, but the level and the condition of the oil should be closely checked, preferably every time the gas tank is filled.

Engine oil itself does not wear out in operation but becomes contaminated with other substances from the heat and chemistry of combustion, so that its ability to lubricate and protect is weakened. Gasoline from the combustion chambers, water from condensation, and acids from combustion combine in old oil to dilute it and to corrode engine parts. Combustion causes formation of varnish and carbon particles, which collect on engine parts as sludge and may plug critical oil passages. Use of the proper grade of oil and frequent changes of the oil will help to prevent engine problems

directly linked to lubrication, such as valve wear, overheating, and excessive blow-by (crankcase vapor pressure from ring leakage).

Filtration is the greatest single factor in maintaining oil condition. Oil and air filtration are both important. The oil filter prevents dirt in the oil from continuing through the oil system, and the air filter prevents dirt from entering the engine in the first place. A surprising amount of the foreign matter in used engine oil has its origin in the air rather than in the combustion process or in engine friction.

Types of Engine Oil

The crankcase oil specified for normal operation in the Corvair engine is SAE 30 (or multigrade) weight. Grades as low as SAE 5 or 10 are acceptable for extremely cold conditions, but the engine should not be run with such oil for long periods or at high speed.

If the lowest anticipated temperature during the interval in which the oil will remain in the crankcase is:	The following SAE viscosity oils are recommended:	Multi-Viscosity oils recommended:
32° F	SAE 30	SAE 10W—30
—10° F	SAE 10	SAE 10W—30
Below —10° F	SAE 5W	SAE 5W—20

CAUTION: Operation with SAE 10W above 60° F is not recommended.

"MS" or "SD" type oils are recommended for the Corvair engine because of the high degree of protection provided by these oils against scuffing and corrosion. Less protective oil types, such as "MM" or "SC" are acceptable providing they are not used under driving conditions for which they are not suited.

CAUTION: With an engine known or suspected to have been run for a long time with non-detergent oil, do not change to high-detergent oil; "dirt seals" in the engine will be removed by the detergent oil and high oil loss and possible bearing failure may result.

Checking the Oil

Check the oil every time you buy gas and add oil whenever the level falls to the "ADD" mark on the dipstick.

NOTE: Do not overfill the crankcase; excess oil will be forced out the filler pipe and into other areas, such as the distributor drive tower, which fouls the points and spark plug wires and coats the engine with oil.

Changing the Oil

The oil should be changed every 4,000-6,000 miles, or less under hard or dusty driving condi-

IDENTIFICATION AND MAINTENANCE

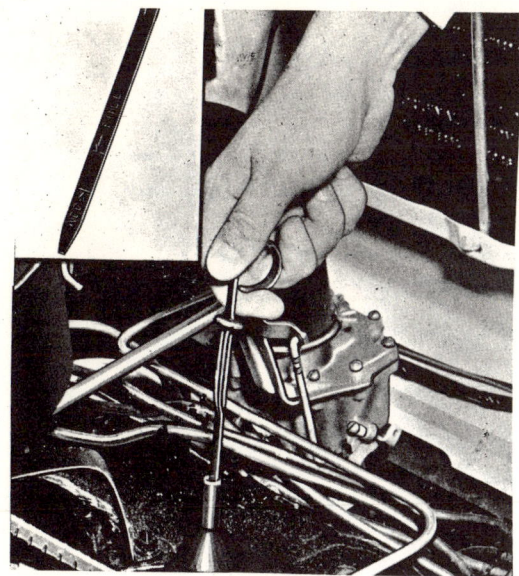

Checking engine oil level

Oil filter

tions. Immediately before draining the oil, the engine should be warmed up to ensure that as much foreign matter as possible is in suspension when the oil is removed. The use of flushing oil before draining is permissible so long as the engine normally is run with detergent-type oil.

Place the car on a lift, or drive it onto ramps so that it will be elevated and level.

NOTE: Corvair "95" vans have jacking pads with holes to accept the pin of a scissors jack.

Remove the crankcase drain plug, toward the rear of the crankcase, and allow the oil to drain out completely. Replace the drain plug and add new oil (approximately 4½ quarts when replacing the filter), after servicing the oil filter and oil cooler as described below.

Oil Filter

The engine is equipped with a cartridge type oil filter located at the rear center of the engine. At least every other oil change, unscrew the filter cover, remove the old filter cartridge, wipe out the casing, and install a new cartridge.

NOTE: Be careful not to spill oil on surrounding engine shrouds or crankcase surfaces; engine heat will cause smoking and odors in the engine compartment. Also, spillage on the blower belt or pulley could cause slipping or deterioration of the belt.

Oil Cooler

The Corvair engine is equipped with an airflow type oil cooler. Remove the access cover to the cooler (at the rear side of the engine) and remove any dust or dirt with a brush or an air hose, at every other oil change.

Manual Transmission and Differential Lubrication

The Corvair transmission and differential are bolted together in a "transaxle" with no separate shafts or linkages to divide the transmission case from the differential carrier. A manual transmission and its mating differential share gear lubricant through passages left open around the mainshaft of the transmission. The two units should be checked for lubricant level and topped off separately, using the filler plugs half-way up the case on each unit.

NOTE: On 1964 models, a rear axle dipstick is provided for checking lubricant level.

Check the transmission and rear axle at every chassis lubrication and add SAE 80 multi-purpose gear lubricant if necessary. Preferably

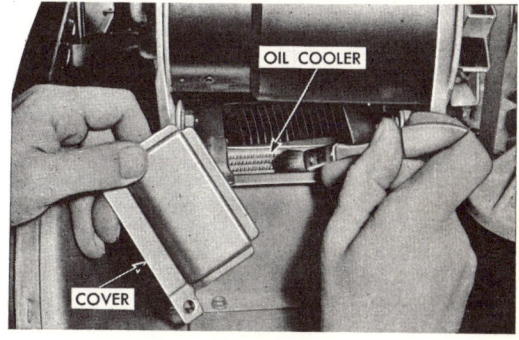

Oil cooler access hole cover

IDENTIFICATION AND MAINTENANCE

Removing foreign matter from oil cooler

Checking automatic transmission lubricant level

check the level when the engine and drive train are warmed up—the level should be up to the base of the filler hole. When cold—½" below this level.

NOTE: Limited slip differential should use only the special grease for this type differential. Units of this type are identified by a tag on one bolt; use of normal lubricant will not damage the unit but will keep the limited-slip feature from functioning.

When necessary for overhaul, or every 10,000 miles, drain both the transmission and rear axle units by opening the bottom drain plugs in each, and refill with approximately 4½ pints of the appropriate lubricant per unit.

NOTE: Do not overfill the transmission or differential units. A good procedure is to fill the unit with lubricant until it runs out of the filler hole, wait about one minute to ensure an accurate check, then install the plug.

Automatic Transmission Lubrication

On a vehicle equipped with an automatic transmission, the rear axle (differential) is the same type as that for a manual transmission, except that the seals in the front of the differential prevent exchange of lubricant and transmission fluid across the mating surfaces.

Check the transmission fluid every time you buy gas and add one pint of Type A transmission fluid when the indicated level on the transmission dipstick is at or below the "ADD" mark.

NOTE: Automatic transmissions are sensitive to dirt of any kind. Be careful to keep dirt out of the filler pipe when checking fluid.

It usually is not necessary to drain and fill the automatic transmission. However, if necessary for overhaul, drain the unit through the lower vent union and fill with six pints (if the converter was not drained) or 13 to 14 pints (if the converter was drained) of fluid.

Chassis Lubrication

The Corvair chassis is equipped with standard grease fittings at various chassis joints. Wipe each fitting with a rag before use, to avoid injecting dirt into the joint under grease pressure. Inject grease into the joint with a hand or pneumatic gun until grease being expelled from the joint looks clean, indicating that the old grease has been expelled.

NOTE: When lubricating a front ball joint, do not force lubricant out through the rubber seal; inject only enough to fill the joint.

Wipe away any heavy accumulation of grease to prevent its dripping onto the brake drums or pavement.

The Corvair Sports Wagon and commercial van models have additional lubrication points. Do not neglect the pedal shaft, clutch control cross-shaft and shift linkage fittings.

Steering Box

When lubricating the chassis, remove the filler plug on the steering box and refill if necessary with chassis or gear grease, to the base of the filler hole.

Front Wheel Bearings

Often neglected until they are on the brink of failure, these bearings can be made to last indefinitely if they are repacked periodically. Once a year, pull each front wheel and clean and repack both front wheel bearings as described in Chapter Nine.

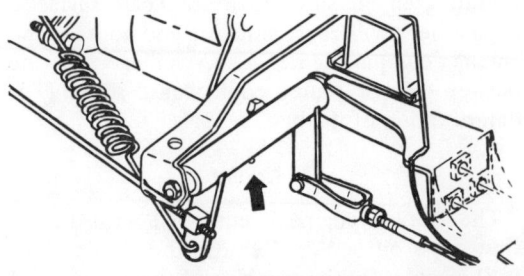

Clutch control cross-shaft

IDENTIFICATION AND MAINTENANCE

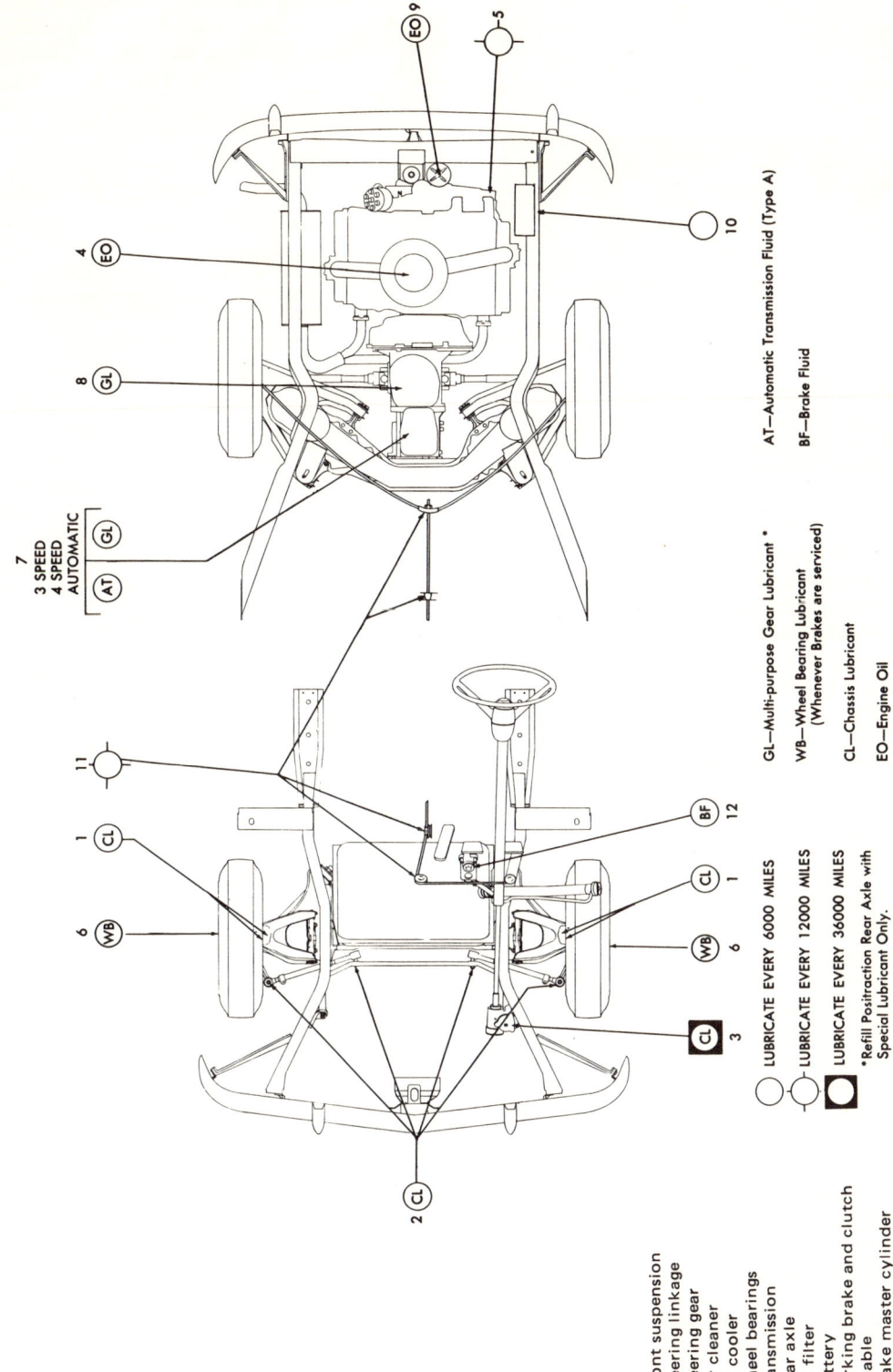

AT—Automatic Transmission Fluid (Type A)

BF—Brake Fluid

GL—Multi-purpose Gear Lubricant *

WB—Wheel Bearing Lubricant
(Whenever Brakes are serviced)

CL—Chassis Lubricant

EO—Engine Oil

LUBRICATE EVERY 6000 MILES
LUBRICATE EVERY 12000 MILES
LUBRICATE EVERY 36000 MILES

*Refill Posistraction Rear Axle with Special Lubricant Only.

1 Front suspension
2 Steering linkage
3 Steering gear
4 Air cleaner
5 Oil cooler
6 Wheel bearings
7 Transmission
8 Rear axle
9 Oil filter
10 Battery
11 Parking brake and clutch cable
12 Brake master cylinder

IDENTIFICATION AND MAINTENANCE

Air Conditioning System

On a Corvair equipped with air conditioning, check the refrigerant level at every oil change, or more frequently during the hot months. A sight glass is located on the dehydrator unit at

Steering gear filler plug

the right side of the engine compartment; this glass should show clear fluid at all times. If any significant bubbles or dirt are visible, or if the glass is empty, take the vehicle to a dealer or air conditioning facility to have the system inspected and recharged.

Air Cleaners

Corvair vehicles are equipped with one of two main types of air filters. The first type has a washable polyurethane element and was the principal air cleaner from 1960 to 1963, and on later turbocharged vehicles. The second type has a disposable paper element. An oil-bath "precleaner" was offered in addition to the paper element for use in extremely dusty areas.

Neglected air cleaners can cause contamination of the crankcase oil from atmospheric dirt as well as carburetor trouble from air restriction. Many high-speed performance and mileage problems can be traced to dirty air filters.

Polyurethane Element

Remove this element from its support and clean it in kerosene or alcohol. Squeeze the element gently to remove the solvent; do not wring it or shake it. Dip or wipe the element in light engine oil and squeeze out the excess.

Replace the element in its support and install the air cleaner on the engine. Make sure the element fits tightly in the casing top and bottom so that no air can bypass the filter.

Paper Element

Remove and check the paper element periodically (at every tune-up or oil change). Heavy discoloration indicates that the element is clogged. Shine a light bulb or strong flashlight at the inner surface of the element; if the light cannot penetrate the paper of the element, the filter cartridge should be replaced.

Oil-Bath Precleaner (Optional)

Empty the oil from the casing and wipe casing out at every oil change. Wash the filter

Removing element from support

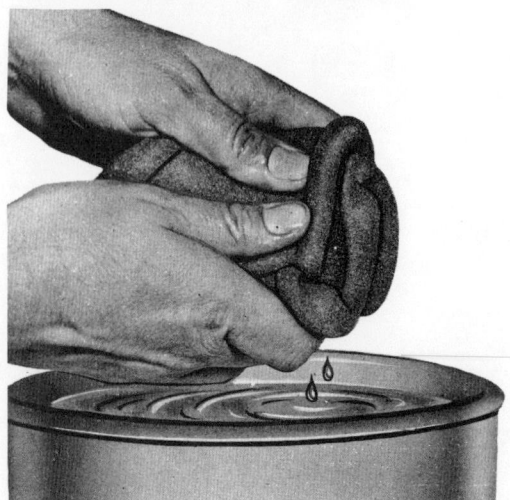
Cleaning element

element in solvent and let it dry. Wet the element with heavy oil; pour a pint of heavy oil into the casing and replace the element and its cover.

IDENTIFICATION AND MAINTENANCE

Blower Belt

The rubberized belt driving the accessory and blower system is perhaps the most important small item on the maintenance check list. This belt drives the blower which supplies cooling air to the engine; if it breaks the engine will overheat and serious damage can result.

Check the belt for wear and tension periodically; specified belt tension is 50-60 lbs. Approximately 3/8" deflection of the belt under 15 lbs. pressure between the idler pulley and the blower pulley is an acceptable maximum limit. To adjust the belt, loosen and adjust the idler pulley.

NOTE: This belt is so important to engine cooling and electrical system operation that a spare belt should always be carried. If, during operation, any indication of belt failure is evident (charging light on, engine overheating), stop the vehicle *at once* and investigate.

2 • Tune-Up and Troubleshooting

Tune-Up

Tune-up procedures normally include cleaning and regapping the spark plugs, setting or replacing contact points, checking the distributor cap and rotor, setting the ignition timing, setting the valve clearance (lash), and adjusting the carburetors. Carburetor adjustments are in Chapter Four.

Ignition

Corvairs are equipped with a common single breaker point distributor ignition system. The distributor is located at the right rear of the engine, and is easily accessible. Its location and wiring arrangement are illustrated. The distributor rotor and cam rotate clockwise.

A breaker-point ignition system operates as follows: a set of contact points in the distributor, next to a six-sided cam, is geared directly to the crankshaft of the engine, so that the cam makes one revolution for every two revolutions of the crankshaft (matching the incidence of the compression or power stroke in a four-cycle engine). When the points in the distributor are closed, they complete a 12-volt DC circuit (the "primary" circuit) which is wired to the spark coil (a set of two concentric windings electrically isolated from each other). The low-voltage primary winding induces a high voltage in the secondary windings; when the points are opened by a lobe of the distributor cam, the induction circuit collapses and high voltage secondary current (as high as 18,000 volts) is re-

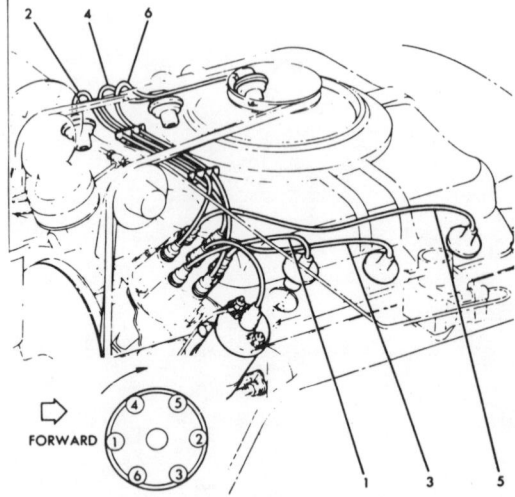

Distributor, spark plug wires installed

leased to flow back into the distributor at the center of the cap and be sent out to each cylinder's spark plug in turn by the distributor rotor.

Ignition Timing

The timing of each ignition impulse would not change in relation to the position of the crankshaft and pistons (because of the linkage of the distributor to the crankshaft), were it not for the advance (or retard) units fitted to the distributor. These units change the moment a secondary current is generated (point opening) by changing the radial position of the contact points relative to the cam. This is done by rotating the breaker plate on which the points are mounted with or against the direction of

TUNE-UP AND TROUBLESHOOTING

rotation of the cam. Higher engine speed or advanced throttle position necessitates a different timing, usually more advanced, to increase the "head start" the spark needs over the fuel mixture.

Three types of timing control devices are fitted to Corvairs:

1. Vacuum advance, a diaphragm unit which advances the spark when a reduced vacuum from the intake manifold signals an opening throttle plate and thus a greater volume of fuel mixture.

2. Centrifugal advance, a system of spring-loaded weights on the distributor shaft which advance the spark when flung out by centrifugal force as the engine speeds up.

3. Pressure retard (on turbocharged cars only), a diaphragm unit which acts against the centrifugal advance when a positive pressure in the intake manifold signals the activation of the turbocharger.

Maintenance

Many ignition difficulties can be avoided with a little regular attention to the surface cleanliness of the distributor cap, wires, and spark coil. Electricity will flow along the line of least resistance, and if moisture and dirt collect on the surfaces of the ignition parts, short circuits (especially in the secondary wiring) can result.

Periodically wipe the distributor cap and the coil top clean with a rag moistened with solvent. Pull each spark plug wire through a rag to remove any film of oil and dirt and check for deterioration. Replace the wires periodically, once a year if they are of the carbon, radio-protective type, or every two years if they are metallic.

Adjustment of Contact Points

The distributor contact points are in correct adjustment when they remain closed for a certain specified length of time relative to the rotation of the cam. The correct buildup of secondary voltage in the coil depends on the correct interval of opening and closing points; this interval can be set by setting a gap between the points at the "high point" when a lobe of the cam pushes the points apart to their fullest extent. However, a gap measurement can be deceiving on old points with surface irregularities which could make a feeler gauge ride peak-to-peak across deeper features which would give the effect of a wider gap than the gauge could sense.

A more accurate measurement of point adjustment is dwell angle. Dwell angle is defined as the angle of distributor cam rotation through which the contact points remain closed. This value is measured with a dwell meter, which is inexpensive and essential for accurate tune-up. Connected between the primary lead of the distributor and any good ground, with the engine running, the meter gives an exact reading of point dwell. The correct dwell angle for the Corvair distributor is 31 to 34° (corresponding to 0.019" gap).

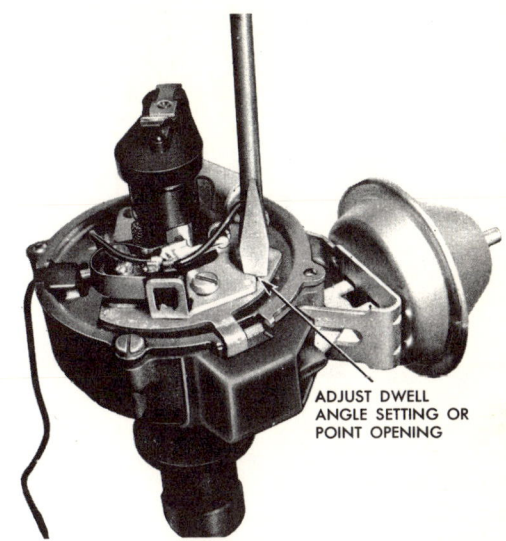

Point adjustment

Remove the distributor cap by unscrewing the retaining screws; adjust the points, as shown, by loosening the point attaching screw and inserting and twisting a screwdriver in the irregular slot in the breaker plate to move the points in or out from the cam. Tighten the point attaching screw when adjustment is complete and check the dwell after the distributor cap has been replaced.

Point Alignment

Correct and incorrect point alignment is illustrated. Adjust the support of a used set of points if the point faces do not meet squarely as shown.

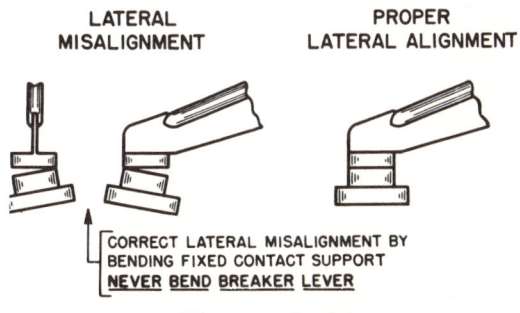

Alignment of points

Tune-Up Specifications

YEAR	MODEL AND DISPLACEMENT	SPARK PLUGS Type	Gap (In.)	DISTRIBUTOR Point Dwell (Deg.)	Point Gap (In.)	IGNITION TIMING (Deg.) ▲	CRANKING COMP. PRESSURE (Psi)	VALVES Tappet (Hot) Clearance (In.) Intake	Exhaust	Intake Opens (Deg.)	FUEL PUMP PRESSURE (Psi)	IDLE SPEED (Rpm) *
1960	140 Cu. In.	44FF	.035	31-36°	.019	4B	130#	■	■	43B	4-5	450-500☆
1961	145 Cu. In., T.A., M.T.	46FF	.035	33°	.019	4B	130#	■	■	43B	4-5	500☆
	145 Cu. In., T.A., A.T.	46FF	.035	33°	.019	13B	130#	■	■	43B	4-5	500☆
	145 Cu. In., Super T.A.	46FF	.035	33°	.019	13B	130#	■	■	54B	4-5	500☆
1962-63	145 Cu. In.; Turbo Air M.T.	46FF	.035	33°	.019	4B	130#	■	■	43B	4½	475
	145 Cu. In.; Turbo Air A.T.	46FF	.035	33°	.019	13B	130#	■	■	43B	4½	475
	145 Cu. In.; Monza A.T.	44FF	.035	33°	.019	13B	130#	■	■	43B	4½	475
	145 Cu. In.; Super Turbo Air	44FF	.035	33°	.019	13B	130#	■	■	54B	4½	475
	145 Cu. In.; Super Charged	44FF†	.035	33°	.019	24B	130#	■	■	54B	4½	800
1964	164 Cu. In.; Turbo Air M.T.	46FF	.035	33°	.019	2B	130#	■	■	44B	4½	500
	164 Cu. In.; Turbo Air A.T.	46FF	.035	33°	.019	10B	130#	■	■	44B	4½	500
	164 Cu. In.; Super Turbo Air	44FF	.030	33°	.019	12B	130#	■	■	54B	4½	600☆
	164 Cu. In.; Super Charged	44FF	.030	33°	.019	24B	130#	■	■	54B	4½	850☆☆
1965-67	164 Cu. In.; Turbo Air (95 HP)	46FF	.035	33°	.019	6B⊙	130#	■	■	44B	4½	500
	164 Cu. In.; Turbo Air (110 HP)	46FF	.035	33°	.019	14B⊙	130#	■	■	55B	4½	500
	164 Cu. In.; Turbo Air (140 HP)	44FF	.030	33°	.019	18B	130#	■	■	55B	4½	600

TUNE-UP AND TROUBLESHOOTING 13

	164 Cu. In.; Super Chg. (180 HP)	44FF	.030	33°	.019	24B	130#	■	82B	4½	850
1968-69	164 Cu. In.; Turbo Air (95 HP) M.T.	46FF ①	.035	33°	.019	6B	130#	■	26B	6	700
	164 Cu. In.; Turbo Air (95 HP) A.T.	46FF ①	.035	33°	.019	14B	130#	■	26B	6	600
	164 Cu. In.; Turbo Air (110 HP) M.T.	44FF	.030	33°	.019	4B	130#	■	37B	6	700
	164 Cu. In.; Turbo Air (110 HP) A.T.	44FF	.030	33°	.019	12B	130#	■	37B	6	600
	164 Cu. In.; Turbo Air (140 HP)	44FF	.030	33°	.019	4B	130#	■	70B	6	650●●

*— With manual transmission in N and automatic in D.
☆— 500 rpm with automatic in D.
☆☆— No automatic.
▲— With vacuum advance disconnected and plugged. NOTE: These settings are only approximate. Engine design, altitude, temperature, fuel octane rating and the condition of the individual engine are all factors which can influence timing. The limiting advance factor must, therefore, be the "knock point" of the individual engine.
■— 1 turn tighter than zero lash.
●— Powerglide—14 B.

●●— W/A.T., 140 HP—550 rpm.
◉— W/exh. emission—95 HP—TDC, 110 HP—4 B.
①— 1969—44FF.
B— Before top dead center.
#— Minimum.
†— 42FF for racing.
A.I.— Automatic transmission.
M.T.— Manual transmission.
T.A.— Turbo Air.
††— New points; used points = .016.

CAUTION

General adoption of anti-pollution laws has changed the design of almost all car engine production to effectively reduce crankcase emission and terminal exhaust products. It has been necessary to adopt stricter tune-up rules, especially timing and idle speed procedures. Both of these values are peculiar to the engine and to its application, rather than to the engine alone. With this in mind, car manufacturers supply idle speed data for the engine and application involved. This information is clearly displayed in the engine compartment of each vehicle.

TUNE-UP AND TROUBLESHOOTING

Contact Point Pitting

There are two kinds of electronic pitting (material transfer) which can occur in a set of contact points. One is a transfer of material from the negative to the positive side, indicating a condenser of too low capacity. The other is a transfer from positive to negative which indicates a condenser of too high capacity.

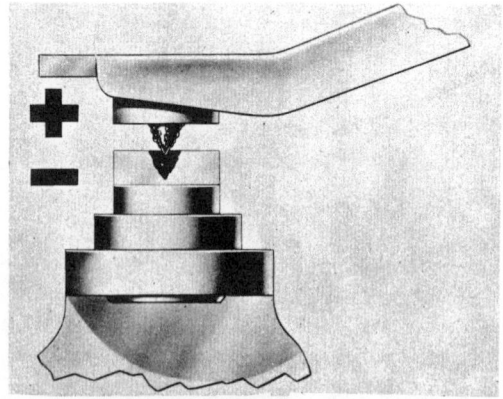

Material transfer—negative to positive point

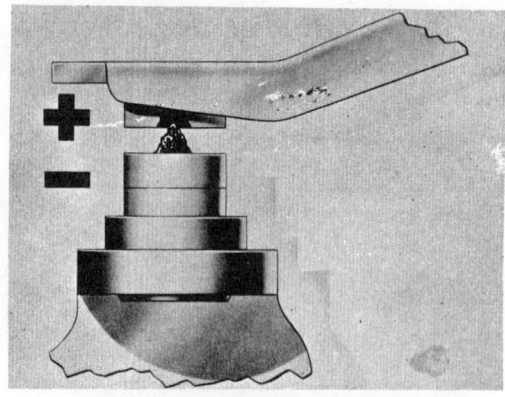

Material transfer—positive to negative point

Contact Point Replacement

The points and condenser should be replaced as part of a general engine tune-up, approximately once a year.

Unscrew the distributor cap and pull it up. Move it to one side to allow access to the points. Pull the rotor off and remove the dust shield (if so equipped). Unscrew the contact point attaching screw and pull the point lead from the quick-disconnect terminal. Remove the points and unscrew and remove the condenser.

Wipe out and inspect the breaker plate sur-

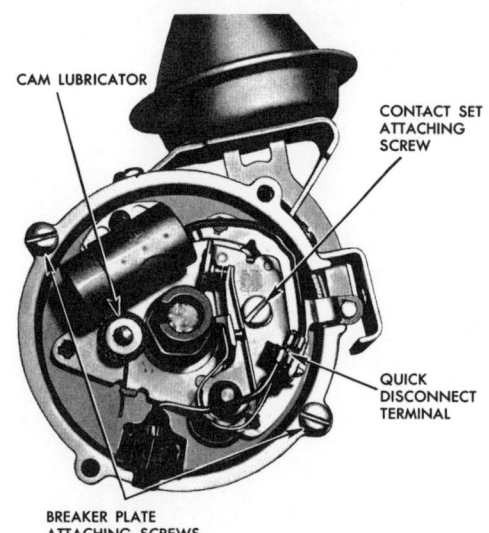

Breaker plate and attaching parts

face. Remove all traces of oil film or dust with a solvent moistened cloth or cotton swab.

While the points are out, inspect the advance unit by checking the breaker plate for free movement; grasp the plate and move it clockwise against spring pressure and let it snap back. This movement should be free and without drag.

Install the new points, screwing the attaching screw in finger tight. Install the new condenser and press the condenser and point leads into the quick-disconnect terminal.

Move the distributor cam so that any high point of the cam is directly under the rubbing block of the points. This can be done by "bumping" the engine with the starter. Insert a screw-driver in the irregular slot next to the point faces and twist the screwdriver to adjust the point opening to 0.019" using a feeler gauge between the points.

NOTE: The points should be checked with a dwell meter as described below.

Tighten the attaching screw when the points are gapped. Turn the cam lubricator 90° to expose a new surface to the cam (replace the lubricator if it is dry or worn). Replace the dust shield (if used), rotor, and distributor cap and screw the cap down firmly. Start the engine and check the dwell angle (31 to 34°). Check the engine timing (as described later) for any change caused by point replacement.

Removal and Disassembly of Distributor

If a timing check reveals that the advance units are not working properly, or if consistently

TUNE-UP AND TROUBLESHOOTING

poor point operation (such as fluctuating dwell) or noise indicates a fault, remove and disassemble the distributor.

Remove the distributor cap and disconnect the primary lead. Mark the relationship of the distributor to the engine to aid installation, then disconnect the vacuum (or pressure) line from the intake manifold, remove the clamp bolt at the crankcase, and pull the distributor from the engine.

Remove the rotor, contact points and condenser. Unscrew and remove the breaker plate assembly. Remove the advance (or retard) unit.

NOTE: The distributor is shown disassembled. It is unnecessary to disassemble past the breaker plate unless there is unusual wear of the shaft or gear.

Clean all parts thoroughly and check their condition. Move the mainshaft back and forth in the housing and check for serious wear which could influence contact point setting. Inspect the cam for roughness or damage. Check the control diaphragm by sucking (at the vacuum advance connection) or blowing (at the pressure retard connection), and observing the motion of the actuating arm. Inspect the distributor cap for cracks, burnt contacts, and carbon tracks on the underside between the contacts (which indicate short circuits).

Assembly and Installation of Distributor

Assemble the distributor, being sure the centrifugal advance weights are in their proper location. Do not stretch or distort the weight springs during installation. Install the advance diaphragm and breaker plate. Install the points and condenser and adjust the points to specifications. Install the rotor and cap.

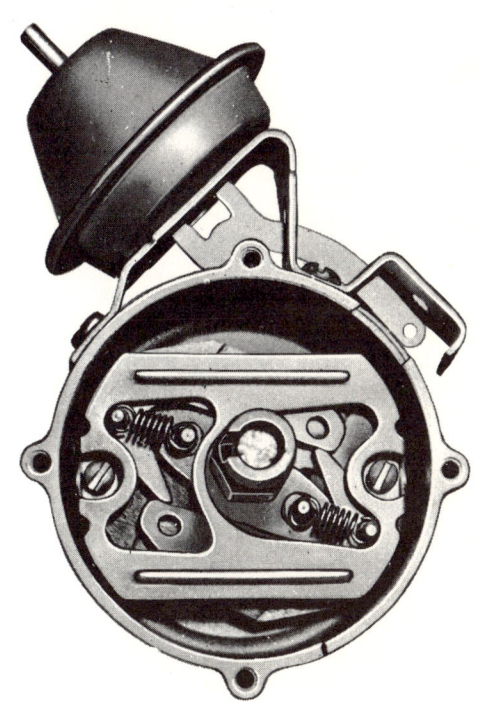

Weights, weight cover installed

1 Cap
2 Rotor
3 Dust shield
4 Contact point attaching screw
5 Contact points
6 Breaker plate screws
7 Condenser screw
8 Condenser
9 Breaker plate
10 Cam lubricator
11 Vacuum advance linkage boot
12 Vacuum control assembly
13 Housing
14 Weight cover screws
15 Weight cover
16 Weight springs
17 Advance wieghts
18 Cam assembly
19 Mainshaft assembly
20 Washer
21 Thrust washers
22 Roll pins
23 Drive gear

Distributor, exploded view

Install the distributor on the engine, aligning the reference marks made previously. Be sure the drive gear is fully in mesh with the camshaft gear in the crankcase. Tighten the clamp bolt and set the engine timing as follows.

Timing (Degrees BTDC)/Idle Speed (RPM)

Year	Trans.	80-85-95 HP	110 HP	140 HP (4-Carb)	180 HP (Turbo* Charged)
1960	Manual	4/500			
	Auto.	4/500			
1961	Manual	4/500	13/500		
	Auto.	4/500†			
1962	Manual	4/500	13/600		24/850
	Auto.	13/500†	13/500		
1963	Manual	4/500	13/500		24/850
	Auto.	13/500†	13/500		
1964	Manual	2/500	12/600		24/850
	Auto.	10/500	12/500†		
1965	Manual	4-8/500	12-16/650	16-20/650	24/850
	Auto.	12-16/*	12-16/650		
1966	Manual Std.	6/500	14/650	18/650	24/850
	Auto. Std.	14/500	14/500‡	18/650	
	Manual A.I.R.	9ATDC/500	1 ATDC/700	3/700	
	Auto A.I.R.	4ATDC/500	4/600	8/600	
1967	Manual Std.	6/500	14/650		
	Auto Std.	14/500	14/500‡		
	Manual A.I.R.	0/700	4/700		
	Auto A.I.R.	0/500	4/600		
1968	Manual	6/700	4/700	4/700	
	Auto	14/600	12/600	4/600	
1969	Manual	6/700	4/700	4/650	
	Auto	14/600	12/600	4/550	

†With transmission in Drive.
*Highest idle which will not cause vehicle to creep in drive.
‡With air-conditioning, 24° BTDC/500 RPM.

Ignition Timing Procedure

The distributor cam is in a fixed relationship to the engine, but the distributor body (containing the contact points) is movable around the axis of the cam, so that ignition timing can be changed by unclamping and rotating the distributor with or against the rotation of the cam (which rotates clockwise). Rotating the distributor clockwise will retard the timing, and rotating it counterclockwise will advance the timing.

Timing must be done with a strobe timing light, at the idle speed given in the chart. The timing mark will be found on the crankshaft pulley or harmonic balancer. On the harmonic

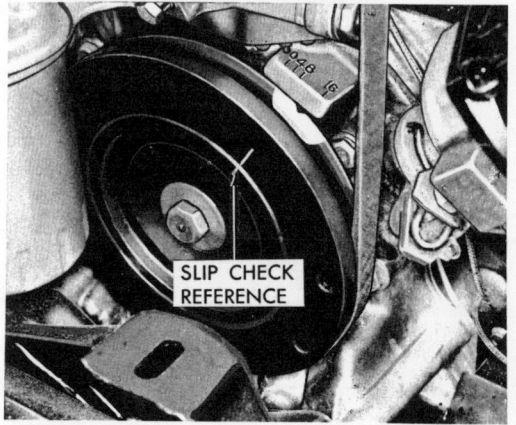

Harmonic balancer slip check reference mark

TUNE-UP AND TROUBLESHOOTING

Firing Order

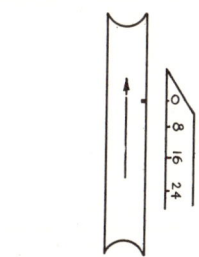

Timing marks—1966 140 and 180 H.P.; 1966-67 110 H.P., A.T., AC

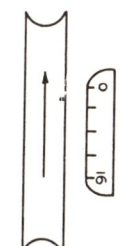

Timing marks—1965 95, 110, 140 H.P.; 1966 95, 110 H.P., and 1967-69 all

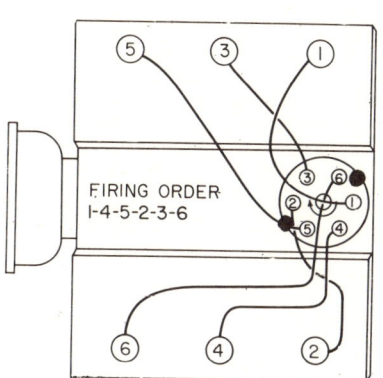

Firing order—1961-69

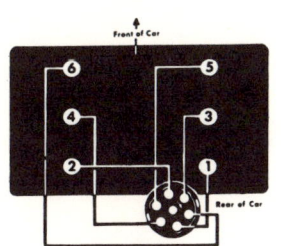

Firing order—1960

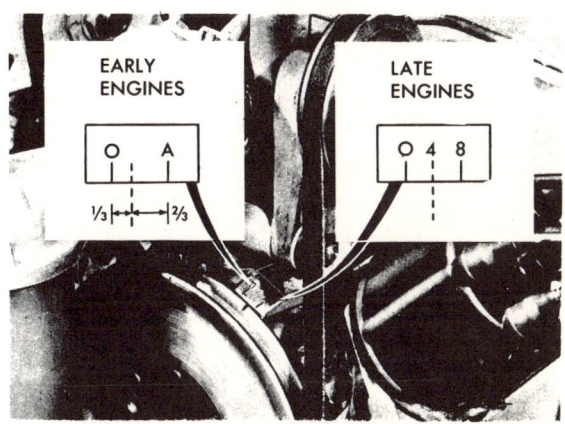

Timing marks—1960

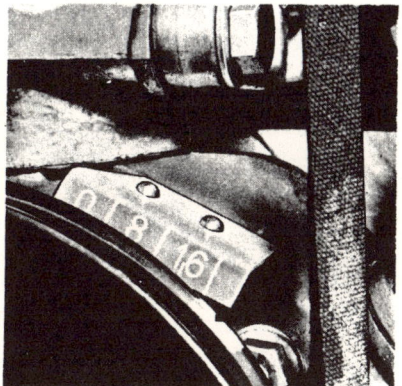

Timing marks—1962-65 turbo charged engines

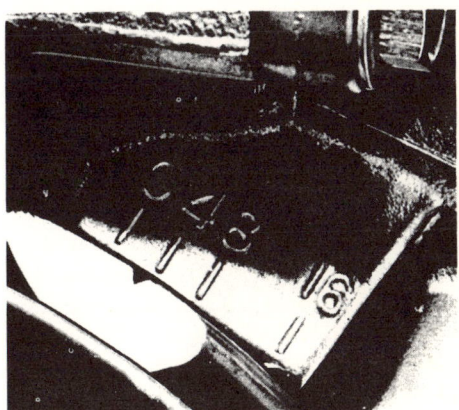

Timing marks—1961-64

Distributor Vacuum Advance
DISTRIBUTOR DEGREES ADVANCE @ INCHES HG VACUUM

Year and Type	80-85-95 HP	110 HP	140 HP	180 HP
1960	Start 4" Full 14.5-16" Max. 23°			
1961 Manual	Start 5-7" Full 14-16.25" Max. 23°	5-7" 14.5-17" 23°		
1961 Auto.	Start 6-8" Full 23° @ 15-17.25" Max. 23°	5-7" 14.5-17" 23°		
1962 Manual	Start 5-7" Full 23° @ 14-16.25" Max 11.5°	5-7" 23° @ 14-16.25" 11.5°		
1962 Auto.	Start 6-8" Full 23° @ 15-17.25" Max. 11.5°	6-8" 23° @ 15-17.25" 11.5°		
1963 Manual	Start 6" Full 23° @ 15" Max 11.5°	6" 23° @ 15" 11.5°		0° @ 1 psi -9° @ 2 psi
1963 Auto.	Start 7" Full 23° @ 15" Max. 11.5°	7" 23° @ 16" 11.5°		
1964 Manual	Start 6" Full 24° @ 14"	7" 24° @ 15"		0° @ 1 psi -6.5° @ 3.5 psi
1964 Auto.	Start 7" Full 24° @ 15"	7" 24° @ 15"		
1965 Manual	Start 6" Full 24° @ 14"	7" 24° @ 15"	6" 22° @ 14"	0° @ 2 psi 12° @ 4.5 psi
1965 Auto.	Start 7" Full 24° @ 15"	7" 24° @ 15"	6" 22° @ 14"	
1966 Manual	Start 6" Full 24° @ 14"	7" 24° @ 15"	6" 22° @ 14"	0° @ 2.25 psi -8° @ 3.62 psi
1966 Auto.	Start 7" Full 24° @ 15"	7" 24° @ 15"	6" 22° @ 14"	
1967 Manual	Start 7" Full 24° @ 15"	7" 24° @ 15"		
1967 Auto.	Start 7" Full 24° @ 15"	7" 24° @ 15"		
1968 Manual	Start 7" Full 24° @ 15"	7" 24° @ 15"	6" 22° @ 14"	
1968 Auto.	Start 7" Full 24° @ 15"	7" 24° @ 15"	6" 22° @ 14°	
1969 Manual	Start 7" Full 24° @ 16"	7" 24° @ 16"	7" 24° @ 16"	
1969 Auto.	Start 7" Full 24° @ 16"	7" 24° @ 16"	7" 24° @ 16"	

Distributor Centrifugal Advance
DISTRIBUTOR DEGREES @ DISTRIBUTOR RPM

Year and Type	80-85-95 HP	110 HP	140 HP	180 HP
1960	Start 0-2° @ 200 Int. 7-9° @ 1050 Max. 15-17° @ 1800			
1961 Manual	Start 0-2° @ 600 Int. 7-9° @ 1050 Max. 32° @ 3600	0-2° @ 700 6-8° @ 1375 24° @ 4800		
1961 Auto.	Start 0-2° @ 1400 Int. Max. 24° @ 3700	0-2° @ 700 6-8° @ 1375 24° @ 4800		
1962 Manual	Start 0-2° @ 600 Int. 7-9° @ 1050 Int. Max. 15-17° @ 1800	0-2° @ 425 2.25-4.25° @ 600 6-8° @ 1375 11-13° @ 2400		
1962 Auto.	Start 0-2° @ 800 Int. 5-7° @ 1270 Int. Max. 11-13° @ 1850	0-2° @ 925 3-5° @ 1300 6-8° @ 1675 9-11° @ 2050		
1963 Manual	Start 0-2° @ 600 Int. 6-10° @ 1350 Int. 15-19° @ 2200 Max. 32° @ 3600	0-2° @ 700 8-12° @ 1950 16-20° @ 3550 24° @ 4800		0-2° @ 3900 12° @ 4500
1963 Auto.	Start 0-2° @ 1400 Int. 4-8° @ 1975 Int. 13-17° @ 2850 Max. 24° @ 3700	0-2° @ 1600 2-6° @ 2100 20° @ 4100		
1964 Manual	Start 0° @ 700 Int. 4° @ 1200 Max. 28° @ 4200	0° @ 800 4° @ 1200 20° @ 4800		0° @ 3900 4° @ 1200 12° @ 4500
1964 Auto.	Start 0° @ 1700 Int. 4° @ 1200 Max. 24° @ 4200	0° @ 800 4° @ 1200 20° @ 4800		
1965 Manual	Start 0° @ 700 Int. 4° @ 1200 Max. 28° @ 4200	0° @ 800 4° @ 1200 20° @ 4800	0° @ 800 4° @ 1200 18° @ 4900	0° @ 4000 4° @ 1200 18° @ 4900
1965 Auto.	Start 0° @ 1700 Int. 4° @ 1200 Max. 24° @ 4200	0° @ 800 4° @ 1200 20° @ 4800	0° @ 800 4° @ 1200 18° @ 4900	
1966 Manual	Start 0° @ 700 Int. 4° @ 1200 Max. 28° @ 4200	0° @ 800 4° @ 1200 20° @ 4800	0° @ 800 18° @ 2800	0° @ 4000 18° @ 4900
1966 Auto.	Start 0° @ 1700 Int. Max. 20° @ 4200	0° @ 800 4° @ 1200 20° @ 4800	0° @ 800 18° @ 3200	
1967 Manual	Start 0° @ 700 Int. Max. 28° @ 4200	0° @ 800 4° @ 1200 20° @ 4800		
1967 Auto.	Start 0° @ 1700 Int. Max. 20° @ 4200	0° @ 800 4° @ 1200 20° @ 4800		
1967 A.I.R.* (all)	Start 0° @ 900 Int. 14.4° @ 1460 Max. 40° @ 4400	0° @ 900 14° @ 1425 26° @ 4400		
1968 Manual	Start 0° @ 900 Int. 14° @ 1425 Max. 28° @ 4200	0° @ 900 14° @ 1425 26° @ 4400	0° @ 900 20° @ 1420 32° @ 3000	
1968 Auto.	Start 0° @ 1700 Int. Max. 20° @ 4200	0° @ 800 4° @ 1200 20° @ 4800	0° @ 900 20° @ 1420 32° @ 3000	
1969 Manual	Start 0° @ 900 Int. 6° @ 1600 Max. 28° @ 4200	0° @ 900 14° @ 1425 26° @ 4400	0° @ 900 14° @ 1420 26° @ 3000	
1969 Auto.	Start 0° @ 1700 Int. 3° @ 2100 Max. 20° @ 4200	0° @ 800 4° @ 1200 20° @ 4800	0° @ 900 14° @ 1420 26° @ 3000	

*A.I.R. Air Injection Reactor.

balancer fitted to higher-powered Corvairs and all those equipped with automatic transmissions, a slip check mark is an indication of any slippage between the parts of the balancer, which should be remedied by replacement of the unit.

Brighten the timing mark on the pulley and on the reference tab with chalk. Connect the timing light and a tachometer and start the engine. On all vehicles (except those with turbochargers), disconnect and plug the vacuum advance line. Check the mark with the timing light while the engine is running. If not to specification, loosen the clamp bolt at the base of the distributor and turn the distributor until the mark moves to its proper position.

NOTE: On early-production 1960 cars, position the timing mark one-third of the way between the "O" and the "A" marks on the crankcase tab.

Distributor Specifications

Ignition timing operations normally are reliable, but if possible, a complete check of the distributor advance systems should be made periodically. Certain variables of distributor operation, such as vacuum advance operation, are hard to check on an installed distributor. A well-equipped service station or ignition service facility will have a distributor tester. If poor engine performance traceable to the distributor exists, a full check of the distributor should be made. Distributor specifications are given in the charts.

NOTE: Turbocharged vehicles operate under conditions of both negative and positive pressure in the intake manifold, so that a pressure-retard (rather than a vacuum advance) unit is fitted to the distributor.

Spark Plugs

At every tune-up remove the spark plugs and inspect them, then clean and regap them. Replace worn out plugs.

Removal of Spark Plugs

Pull off the spark plug wire caps at the cylinder shrouds and check them for cracks, burns, or excessive distortion. Remove the plugs with a suitable deep socket wrench on a ratchet handle.

NOTE: A special spark plug socket is available having a rubber insert and deep throat to protect the plug when removing and installing it. This tool is well worth the small investment and will prevent broken plug ceramics. A tool like that illustrated can be fabricated to ease

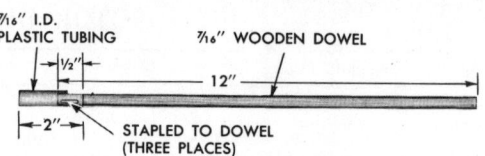

Spark plug holding tool

removal of plugs from the engine; be careful not to drop the plugs or gaskets into the engine shrouds.

Inspection of Spark Plugs

Much can be learned about engine condition from the spark plugs. The color of the ceramic around the center electrode is an excellent indicator of carburetor adjustment and ignition reliability.

Gap bridging (A)

May be traced to flying deposits in the combustion chamber. In some cases, fluffy deposits may accumulate on the plugs during intown driving and when the engine is suddenly put under high load; this material can melt and bridge the gap.

Scavenger deposits (B)

Fuel scavenger deposits shown may be white or yellow in color. They may appear to be harmful, but this is normal with certain brands of fuel. Note that accumulation on the ground electrode and shell areas may be unusually heavy, but the material is easily chipped off. Such plugs can be considered normal and can be cleaned using standard procedures.

Chipped insulator (C)

Usually results from bending the center electrode during gapping. Under certain conditions, severe detonation can also split insulator firing ends.

Preignition damage (D)

Caused by excessive temperatures, produces melting of the center electrode and, somewhat later, the ground electrode. Insulators will appear relatively clean of deposits. Check for correct plug heat range and overadvanced ignition timing.

Cold fouling (or carbon fouling) (E)

Dry, black appearance of one or two plugs in a set. Check for sticking valves or bad spark plug wires. Fouling of the entire set may be caused by a clogged air cleaner, a sticking exhaust manifold heat valve, or a faulty choke.

TUNE-UP AND TROUBLESHOOTING

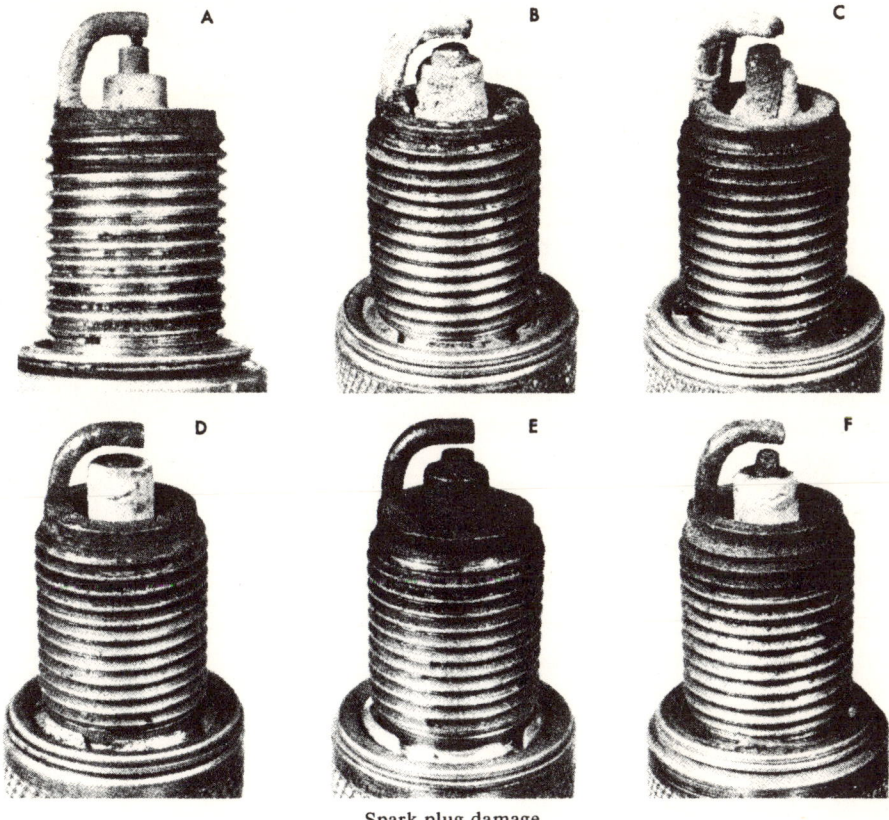

Spark plug damage

Overheating (F)

Dead white or gray insulator which appears "blistered." Electrode gap wear rate will be considerably in excess of .001"/1,000 miles. This may suggest that a cooler heat range should be used; however, overadvanced ignition timing, detonation and cooling system malfunctions can also overheat spark plugs.

Inspect the plugs for common defects, such as cracks in the ceramic, fouling, and incorrect gap. If the upper ceramic is very dirty, check for spark tracks which could point to a short-circuited plug.

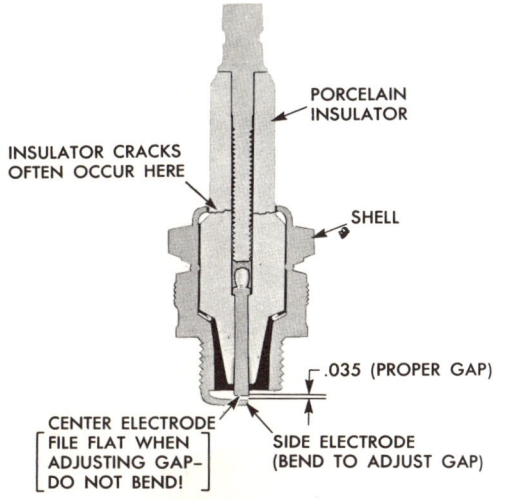

Spark plug detail

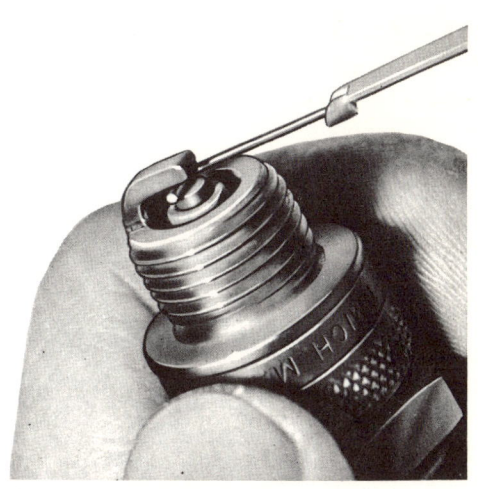

Setting spark plug gap

After inspection, wire-brush all serviceable plugs clean and regap them with a round gauge.

Install the plugs, making sure the gaskets are in place. Torque plugs to 20-25 ft. lbs. and replace the spark plug wires in their proper order.

NOTE: Be sure the plugs are of the right type (14 mm., ½-inch reach) and heat value, AC 46FF for 80 to 95 hp. models and AC 44FF for 110 hp. and higher, or their equivalent. The heat value of a plug refers to the design temperature at which it will run as a result of the length and thickness of its inner ceramic insulation. Too cold a plug will not burn itself clean; too hot a plug will erode quickly. Both extremes can cause detonation and possible engine damage.

Valve Lash Adjustment

Remove the rear wheels and support the vehicle securely on jackstands. Unbolt and remove the valve rocker covers and clean them in solvent. Discard the gaskets.

The rocker arms are now exposed and can be adjusted with a wrench from the wheel-well side.

NOTE: To contain the oil which will flow and spray around the valve area, make shields from a junk rocker cover cut in half lengthwise; bolt the halves in place on the lower side of each bank to catch the oil and contain any oil spray while making the valve adjustment.

Start the engine, and adjust valve lash as follows: loosen the rocker nut until the valve begins to click. Gradually tighten the nut until the clicking stops. Tighten the nut an additional turn (1¼ turns on turbocharged engines) in ¼ turn increments, waiting 10 seconds after each step to prevent piston to valve interference.

NOTE: When adjusting valve lash on the cylinder head adjacent to the muffler(s), a mechanic's stethoscope or a length of rubber hose placed near the valve being adjusted will aid in determining valve sounds.

TUNE-UP AND TROUBLESHOOTING

Troubleshooting

The following section aids the rapid diagnosis and solution of engine problems. A systematic format is used to diagnose problems ranging from engine starting difficulties to the need for overhaul. It is assumed that the reader is equipped with, or has access to basic tools and test equipment, and that he is familiar with the basic mechanics of the internal combustion engine.

The Troubleshooting Section is divided into two subsections. The first, General Diagnosis, determines the area in which the trouble may be located. This then refers the reader to the second section, Specific Diagnosis, where the problem is systematically evaluated.

I. GENERAL DIAGNOSIS

ENGINE WON'T START

Problem: Symptom	Begin Diagnosis at Section II, Number (below)
Starter doesn't turn	1.1, 2.1
Starter turns, engine doesn't	2.1
Starter turns engine very slowly	1.1, 2.4
Starter turns engine quickly	3.1, 4.1, 6.1
Engine fires intermittently	4.1
Engine fires consistently	5.1, 6.1

ENGINE RUNS POORLY

Problem: Symptom	Begin Diagnosis at Section II, Number (below)
Hard starting	3.1, 4.1, 5.1, 8.1
Rough idle	4.1, 5.1, 8.1
Stalling	3.1, 4.1, 5.1, 8.1
Engine dies at high speeds	4.1, 5.1
Hesitation (on acceleration from a standing stop)	5.1, 8.1
Poor pickup	4.1, 5.1, 8.1
Lack of power	3.1, 4.1, 5.1, 8.1
Backfire through the carburetor	4.1, 8.1, 9.1
Backfire through the exhaust	4.1, 8.1, 9.1
Blue exhaust gases	6.1, 7.1
Black exhaust gases	5.1
Running on (after the ignition is turned off)	3.1, 8.1
Susceptible to moisture	4.1
Engine misfires under load	4.1, 7.1, 9.1
Engine misfires at speed	4.1
Engine misfires at idle	3.1, 4.1, 5.1, 7.1

ENGINE NOISES[1]

Problem: Symptom	Probable Cause
Metallic grind while starting	Starter drive not engaging (see 2.1).
Constant grind or rumble*	Starter drive not releasing, worn main bearings.
Constant knock	Worn connecting rod bearings.
Knock under load	Fuel octane too low, worn connecting rod bearings.
Metallic tap (intermittent)*	Collapsed or sticky valve lifter (see 9.1).
Metallic tap (constant)*	Valve or valve lifter (see section 9), excessive end play in a rotating shaft.
Scrape*	Fan belt contacting a stationary surface.
Tick while starting	Starter brushes
Constant tick*	Generator brushes, shredded fan belt
Squeal*	Improperly tensioned fan belt.
Whistle*	Vacuum leak (see section 7).
Wheeze	Loose or cracked spark plug.

[1] It is extremely difficult to describe vehicle noises. While the above are intended as general descriptions of engine noises, those marked with a star (*) may possibly originate elsewhere in the vehicle. To aid diagnosis, the following list considers other potential sources of the above starred items.
Metallic grind:
 Throwout bearing
 Transmission gears, bearings, synchronizers
 Differential bearings, gears
 Something contacting brake drum or disc
Metallic tap:
 U-joints
 Fan to shroud contact
Scrape:
 Brake shoe or pad dragging
 Tire to body contact
 Suspension contact to undercarriage or exhaust system

Tick:
 Transmission gears
 Differential gears
 Radio (lack of supression)
 Vibration of body panels
 Windshield wiper motor and transmission
 Heater motor and blower
Squeal:
 Brakes
 Tires (improper inflation, excessive wear, uneven wear)
 Front end alignment (most commonly due to improperly set toe-in)
Hiss or whistle:
 Wind leaks (body and window)
 Heater motor and blower
Roar:
 Front wheel bearings
 Wind leaks (body and window)

II. SPECIFIC DIAGNOSIS

This section is arranged so that following each test, instructions are given to proceed to another test until the problem is solved.

INDEX

Section	Topic
1*	Battery
2*	Cranking System
3*	Primary Electrical System
4*	Secondary Electrical System
5*	Fuel System
6*	Engine Compression
7**	Engine Vacuum
8**	Secondary Electrical System
9**	Valve Train
10**	Exhaust System
11**	Cooling System
12**	Engine Lubrication

* - The engine need not be running.
** - The engine must be running.

SAMPLE

The following Sample Section indicates by arrows how the Specific Diagnosis Section should be used. After checking for spark in the "Test and Procedure" column, results are analyzed in the "Results and Indications" column, and the reader proceeds to the numbered section in the "Proceed To" column. Example: If the spark is "good in some cases" you would proceed to Section 4.3 (Check the Distributor Cap and Rotor).

SAMPLE SECTION

	Test and Procedure	Results and Indications	Proceed to
X.X	Check for spark: Hold each spark plug wire approximately ¼" from ground with gloves or a heavy, dry rag; observe the spark while cranking the engine:	If no spark is evident: If spark is good in some cases: If spark is good in all cases:	4.2 4.3 4.6

	Test and Procedure	Results and Indications	Proceed to
1.1	Check battery visually for case condition (cracks, corrosion) and water level:	If the case is cracked, replace battery. If the case is intact, remove corrosion with a baking soda and water solution and fill with water. (*Caution*: do not get solution into the battery)	1.4 1.2
1.2	Check battery cable connections: Insert a screwdriver blade between the battery terminal and cable connector; Turn the bright headlights on, and observe them as the screwdriver is gently twisted to ensure good metal to metal contact:	If the lights brighten, remove and clean the connector and post; coat the post with petroleum jelly, reattach and tighten the connector. If no improvement is noted:	1.4 1.3
1.3	Check the state of charge of the battery using an individual cell tester or hydrometer: 	SPECIFIC GRAVITY READING	CHARGED CONDITION
---	---
1.260-1.280	Fully Charged
1.230-1.250	Three Quarter Charged
1.200-1.220	One Half Charged
1.170-1.190	One Quarter Charged
1.140-1.160	Just About Flat
1.110-1.130	All The Way Down		If indicated charge the battery. If no obvious reason exists for the lack of charge (i.e. battery age, prolonged storage) check the charging system.	1.4

TUNE-UP AND TROUBLESHOOTING

II - SPECIFIC DIAGNOSIS—continued

Test and Procedure	Results and Indications	Proceed to
1.4 Check the battery cables visually for cracking, bad connection to ground, or bad connection to the starter solenoid:	If necessary, tighten connections or replace cables.	2.1

The Following Tests, Section 2 Through 6 Inclusive, Are Performed With the Coil High Tension Lead Removed, to Prevent Starting.

Test and Procedure	Results and Indications	Proceed to
2.1 Check the starter motor and solenoid: Connect a jumper from the battery post of the solenoid (or relay) to the ignition post of the solenoid (or relay):	If the starter turns the engine well:	2.2
	If the starter buzzes, or turns the engine very slowly:	2.4
	If no response, replace the solenoid.	3.1
	If the starter turns, but the engine doesn't, check to ensure that the flywheel ring gear is intact; if the gear is good, replace the starter drive.	3.1
2.2 Check the neutral safety switch (where applicable); bypass the switch with a jumper: Note: This applies to all ignition and starter override switches.	If the starter turns, adjust or replace the switch.	3.1
	If the starter doesn't turn:	2.3
2.3 Check the ignition switch "start" position: Connect a voltmeter or a 12V test lamp between the starter post of the solenoid (or relay) and ground: turn the ignition switch to the "start" position, and jiggle the key:	If the lamp doesn't light when the key is turned, check the ignition switch for loose connections, cracked insulation, or broken wires. Repair if necessary.	3.1
	If the lamp flickers when the key is jiggled, replace the ignition switch.	3.2
2.4 Remove and bench test the starter according to specifications; see Chapter Five:	If the starter is not working properly, repair or replace as needed.	
	If the starter is operating properly:	2.5
2.5 Determine whether the engine can turn freely: Remove the spark plugs. Attempt to turn the engine by hand (18" flex drive and socket on crankshaft pulley nut or bolt):	If the engine will turn freely only with the spark plugs out, check valve timing	9.2
	If the engine will not turn freely, and it is known that the clutch and transmission are free, the engine must be removed and disassembled for further evaluation.	Chap. Three

TUNE-UP AND TROUBLESHOOTING

The Following Tests, Sections 2 Through 6 Inclusive, Are Performed With the Coil High Tension Lead Removed, to Prevent Starting.

II - SPECIFIC DIAGNOSIS—*continued*

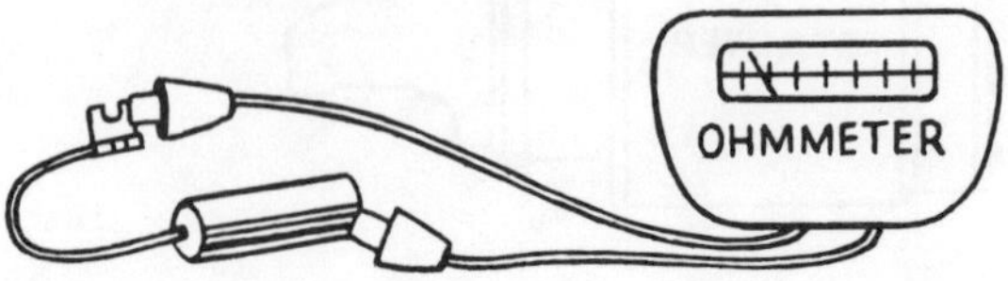

Test and Procedure	Results and Indications	Proceed to
3.1 Check the ignition switch "on" position: Connect a jumper wire from the distributor side of the coil to ground, and a voltmeter from the switch side of the coil to ground; turn the ignition switch on and jiggle the key:	If the meter reading is steady:	3.2
	If the meter reading fluctuates when the key is jiggled, replace the ignition switch.	3.2
	If no meter reading, check for loose connections. If none are found, remove the ignition switch and check for continuity. If faulty, replace; if good check the ballast resistor or resistance wire and replace if shorted or open.	3.2

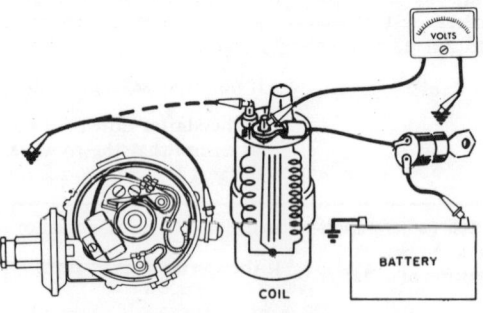

3.2 Check the breaker points; visually inspect the breaker points for pitting or excessive wear. (Note: Gray coloring of the point contact surfaces is normal.) Set point gap to specifications. *Caution:* Distributor cam lubrication is important to the proper operation of the breaker points. Follow manufacturer's recommendations for lubrication and never over lubricate.	If pitted or worn, replace the breaker points and condenser, and adjust the gap and dwell to specifications.	3.4
	If intact, adjust the gap and dwell to specifications.	3.4
	If the dwell meter shows little or no reading:	3.3

EXCESSIVE METAL TRANSFER OR PITTING   BURNED

3.3 Check the condenser for short; connect an ohmmeter from the condenser body to the pigtail lead:	If any reading other than infinite resistance is noted, replace the condenser.	3.4

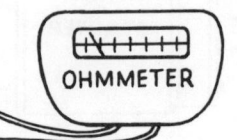

3.4 Check the coil primary circuit resistance; connect an ohmmeter across the coil primary terminals, and read the resistance on the low scale. Coils requiring external ballast resistors should read approximately 1.0 ohm; coils not requiring external ballast resistors should read approximately 4.0 ohms.	If the coil reading is not near the correct figure, replace the coil.	4.1

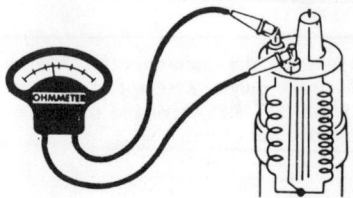

TUNE-UP AND TROUBLESHOOTING

The Following Tests, Sections 2 Through 6 Inclusive, Are Performed With the Coil High Tension Lead Removed, to Prevent Starting.

II - SPECIFIC DIAGNOSIS—*continued*

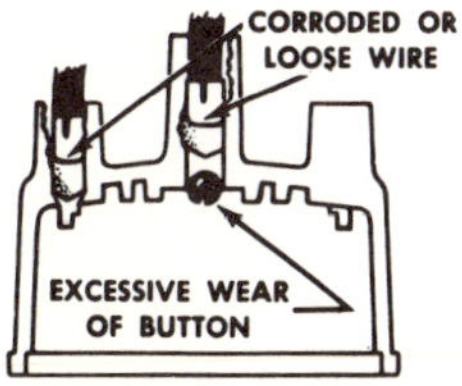

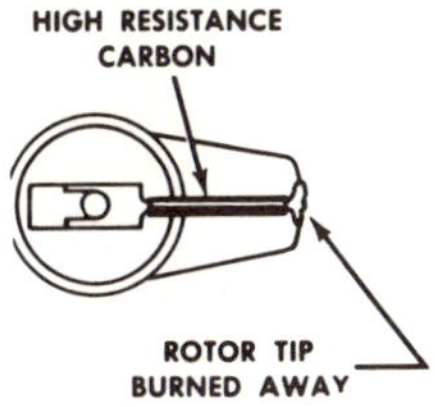

Test and Procedure	Results and Indications	Proceed to
4.1 Check for spark: Hold each spark plug wire approximately ¼″ from ground with gloves or a heavy, dry rag; observe the spark while cranking the engine:	If no spark is evident:	4.2
	If spark is good in some cases:	4.3
	If spark is good in all cases:	4.6
4.2 Check for spark at the coil high tension lead: Remove the coil high tension lead from the distributor cap and hold it ¼″ from ground with gloves or a heavy dry rag; crank the engine and observe the spark:	If the spark is good:	4.6
	If the spark is weak or non-existent, replace the coil high tension lead with an identical one, clean and tighten all connections and retest. If no improvement is noted, the coil must be tested per 3.4 and 4.4.	4.4
4.3 Check the distributor cap and rotor; visually inspect the cap and rotor for burned contacts, cracks, carbon tracks, or moisture:	If moisture is present, dry and retest per 4.1.	
	If burned contacts, cracks or carbon tracks are noted, replace the defective part(s) and retest per 4.1.	
	If the rotor and cap appear to be intact, thoroughly clean the distributor cap tower sockets and spark plug wire ends. Retest each lead per 4.1:	
	If the spark is good in all cases:	4.6
	If the spark is not good in all cases:	4.5
4.4 Check the coil secondary resistance: Connect an ohmmeter between the distributor side of the coil and the coil tower. Read the result on the high scale of the ohmmeter. A satisfactory coil will show between 4K and 10K.	If the resistance is extremely high (i.e. 40K), replace the coil, and retest per 4.1.	4.1
4.5 Check the spark plug wires: Remove the spark plug wires one by one, and test the resistance across the wire with an ohmmeter. The resistance of steel or copper core wire is very low, while the resistance of carbon or silicon suppression wire is approximately 4,000 ohms per foot.	Replace any wires with cracked or broken insulation. Also replace any wires with excessive resistance (over 8,000 ohms per foot for suppression wire).	4.6
4.6 Check the spark plugs; see Fig. 38 to 45.		

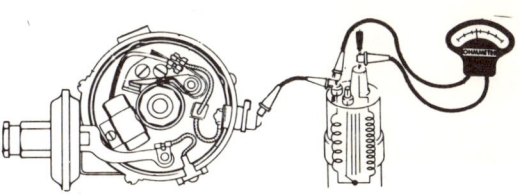

The Following Tests, Sections 2 Through 6 Inclusive, Are Performed With the Coil High Tension Lead Removed, to Prevent Starting.

II - SPECIFIC DIAGNOSIS—*continued*

Trouble	Cause	Remedy	Proceed to
Erosion of the electrodes, light brown deposits on the insulator.	Normal wear. Normal wear is indicated by approx. .001" wear per 1,000 miles driving.	Replace the spark plugs.	4.6

Carbon fouling (black, dry, fluffy deposits).	If present in one or two plugs only:
	    Faulty high tension leads.
	
	    Burnt or sticking valve.
	
	If present on most or all plugs:
	
	Overly rich fuel mixture, improper choke or heat riser, restricted air cleaner.
		
		Check high tension leads.
		
		Check valve train.
		
		Clean and recondition the spark plugs in either case.
		
		Check the fuel system.
			
			4.5
			
			9.1
			
			5.1

Oil fouling (wet, black deposits).	Worn engine components. (*Note*: Oil fouling may occur in new or recently rebuilt engines until broken in.)	Check engine vacuum and compression.	6.1
Lead fouling (Dark gray, black, tan or yellow deposits which may appear to be glazed or cinder-like.)	Fuel combustion by-products.	Recondition the spark plugs. If the problem recurs a heat range change is in order.	
Gap bridging (Deposits lodged between electrodes.)	Incomplete combustion or transfer of deposits from the combustion chamber.	Recondition or replace spark plugs.	

TUNE-UP AND TROUBLESHOOTING 29

The Following Tests, Sections 2 Through 6 Inclusive, Are Performed With the Coil High Tension Lead Removed, to Prevent Starting.

II - SPECIFIC DIAGNOSIS—continued

Trouble	Cause	Remedy	Proceed to
Overheating (Extremely white insulator with small black spots, and burnt electrodes.)	Ignition timing advanced too far.	Adjust timing to specifications.	4.6, 8.2
	Overly lean fuel mixture.	Check fuel system.	5.1
	Spark plugs not seated properly.	Clean spark plug seats.	
Fused spot deposits on the insulator.	Blow-by from the combustion chamber.	Recondition or replace spark plugs.	
Pre-ignition (Melted or severely burned, blistered insulators, or metallic deposits on the insulator.)	Incorrect spark plug heat range.	Replace with plug of proper heat range.	
	Ignition timing advanced too far.	Adjust timing to specifications.	4.6, 8.2
	Spark plugs not being cooled efficiently.	Check cooling system.	11.1
	Mixture too lean.	Check fuel system.	5.1
	Burned valve causing poor compression.	Check compression.	6.1
	Spark plugs not seated properly.	Clean spark plug seats.	
	Fuel grade too low.	Use higher octane rating fuel.	

Test and procedure	Results and Indications	Proceed to
4.7 Check static engine timing: Locate top dead center of the number 1 cylinder compression stroke (the timing mark may be used as a guide, but ensure that the cylinder is on its compression stroke): Adjust the distributor so that the rotor points toward the number 1 tower in the cap, and that the points are just opening.		4.8
4.8 Check coil polarity: Connect a voltmeter negative lead to the coil secondary lead, and the positive lead to ground (this procedure is for negative ground cars; reverse for positive ground). Crank the engine momentarily: 	If the voltmeter reads up-scale, the polarity is correct.	4.9
	If the voltmeter reads down-scale, the polarity is incorrect, and the coil leads must be reversed.	4.9

TUNE-UP AND TROUBLESHOOTING

The Following Tests, Sections 2 Through 6 Inclusive, Are Performed With the Coil High Tension Lead Removed, to Prevent Starting.

II - SPECIFIC DIAGNOSIS—*continued*

Test and Procedure	Results and Indications	Proceed to
4.9 Check to ensure that the spark plug wires are not causing crossfiring by induction: See that no two spark plug leads are very close to one another and parallel. Try to avoid crossing wires over one another.		5.1
5.1 Check to determine that the air cleaner is functioning properly; use an air filter tester, or hold it up to the light and try to see light through the filter material:	If the filter is functioning: If the filter is not functioning, clean or replace per specifications.	5.2 5.2
5.2 Determine whether a flooding condition exists; flooding may most easily be identified by a strong gasoline odor, and presence of excessive liquid in the bore(s) of the carburetor(s):	If flooding is not present: If flooding is present, permit engine to dry (a few minutes), and restart. If the flooding doesn't recur: If flooding recurs persistently:	5.3 5.3 5.5
5.3 Determine that fuel is reaching the carburetor: Detach the fuel line at the carburetor inlet; hold this line over a cup while cranking the engine:	If fuel flows smoothly: If fuel doesn't flow (be sure that there is fuel in the tank) or flows erratically:	5.6 5.4
5.4 Check the fuel pump and fuel lines: Remove the fuel line from the input side of the fuel pump; hold finger over the input hole, crank the engine (with electric pump, turn the ignition on), and feel for vacuum: *Note*: A no start condition could also be the result of a ruptured vacuum booster pump diaphragm (where applicable). This is caused by the vacuum from the pump drawing oil through the ruptured diaphragm, and pumping it to the intake manifold; thus, oil fouling of the spark plugs may result.	If vacuum is present, blow out the fuel line to the gas tank with low pressure compressed air, until bubbling is heard from the filler neck. Also blow out the line from the pump to the carburetor (both ends disconnected). If no vacuum is present, repair or replace the fuel pump.	5.5 5.5
5.5 Check the needle and seat; tap the carburetor in the area of the needle and seat:	If the flooding stops, a suitable gasoline additive will often alleviate the problem. If flooding continues, the fuel pump should be checked for excessive pressure at the carburetor (according to specifications). If the pressure is normal, the needle and seat must be removed and checked, and/or the float level adjusted.	5.6 5.6
5.6 Determine whether the accelerator pump is working; observe the operation of the accelerator pump by looking into the carburetor while operating the throttle:	If accelerator pump operates normally: If the accelerator pump is not operating the carburetor must be removed and reconditioned. Prior to removal:	5.7 5.7
5.7 Determine whether carburetor main fuel system is operating: Spray any good commercial starting bomb into carburetor while attempting to start engine; engine should start and run for a few seconds:	If the engine starts and dies quickly: If the engine doesn't start:	5.8 6.1

TUNE-UP AND TROUBLESHOOTING 31

The Following Tests, Sections 2 Through 6 Inclusive, Are Performed With the Coil High Tension Lead Removed, to Prevent Starting.

II - SPECIFIC DIAGNOSIS—*continued*

Test and Procedure	Results and Indications	Proceed to
5.8 Uncommon fuel system malfunctions: See below.	If the problem is solved:	6.1
	If the problem remains, remove and recondition the carburetor.	

Condition	Indication	Test	Usual Weather Conditions	Remedy
Vapor lock	Car will not restart shortly after running	Pour cool water over the components of the fuel system one by one, until the engine restarts.	Hot to very hot.	Once the location of the problem is established, correct as follows: Carburetor: Install spacer plate between carburetor and manifold. Check exhaust manifold heat control valve (10.1). Fuel lines: Move from the source of heat or replace with neoprene. Fuel pump: Install a vapor lock preventing device in the fuel line.
Carburetor icing	Car will not idle, stalls at low speeds.	Visually inspect the throttle plate area for frost.	High humidity, around 32° F.	Ensure that the exhaust manifold heat control valve is functioning (10.1), and that the intake manifold heat riser is not blocked.
Water in the fuel	Car sputters while running, may not start.	Pump a small amount of fuel into a glass container. Inspect the fuel for water droplets, a settled layer of water.	High humidity, extreme temp. change.	For droplets, use one or two cans of commercial gas dryer. For a layer of water, the tank must be drained, and the fuel lines blown out with compressed air.

Test and Procedure	Results and Indications	Proceed to
6.1 Check engine compression: Remove all spark plugs; insert the compression gauge into a spark plug hole, and crank the engine approximately four revolutions:	The readings are within specifications on all cylinders:	7.1
	The gauge reading is low on all cylinders:	6.2
	The gauge reading is low on one or two cylinders:	6.2

TUNE-UP AND TROUBLESHOOTING

The Following Tests, Sections 2 Through 6 Inclusive, Are Performed With the Coil High Tension Lead Removed, to Prevent Starting.

II - SPECIFIC DIAGNOSIS—*continued*

Test and Procedure	Results and Indications	Proceed to
6.2 Check engine compression (wet): Squirt approx. 30 cc. of 30 weight engine oil into the offending cylinders; test per 6.1.	If the readings improve, worn or cracked rings or broken pistons are indicated:	Chapter Three
	If the readings do not improve, burned or carboned valves or worn timing gear are indicated. *Note*: A worn timing gear is often indicated by difficult cranking.	9.1
7.1 Perform a vacuum check of the engine: Attach a vacuum gauge to the intake manifold below the carburetor, and observe the action of the needle.	See below	See below

Type of Reading	Probable Cause	Proceed to
Steady, from 17-21 in. Hg. (normal)		8.1
Low and steady.	Ignition or valve timing, low compression.	6.1
Very low.	Vacuum leak.	7.2
Needle fluctuates as engine speed increases.	Ignition miss, cylinder head gasket, leaking valve spring.	6.1
Gradual drop in reading at idle.	Excessive back pressure in the exhaust system.	10.1
Intermittent fluctuation.	Ignition miss, sticking valve.	8.3, 9.1
Drifting needle.	Improper idle mixture adjustment, or minor intake leak. Adjust the carburetor and retest. If the condition persists:	7.2

TUNE-UP AND TROUBLESHOOTING   33

II - SPECIFIC DIAGNOSIS—continued

Test and Procedure	Results and Indications	Proceed to
7.2 Check for intake manifold vacuum leaks: Attach a vacuum gauge per 7.1, and squirt a small amount of oil around the intake manifold gaskets, carburetor gaskets, and vacuum ports; observe the action of the vacuum gauge:	If the reading increases, replace the offending gasket or seal. If the reading remains low:	8.1 7.3
7.3 Test all vacuum hoses and vacuum accessories (windshield wipers, power assist brakes, etc.) per 7.2. Also check the carburetor body (throttle shafts, dashpots, automatic choke mechanism) for vacuum leaks:	If the reading improves, replace the offending part(s). If the reading remains low:	8.1 6.1
8.1 Check the breaker point dwell: Connect a dwell meter to the distributor side of the coil and ground; observe the meter reading:	If necessary adjust the point gap. *Note*: The larger the gap, the smaller the dwell, the smaller the gap the larger the dwell.	8.2

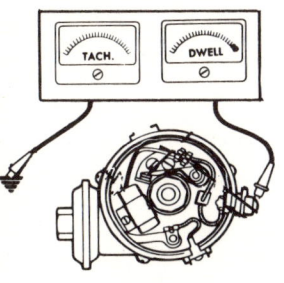 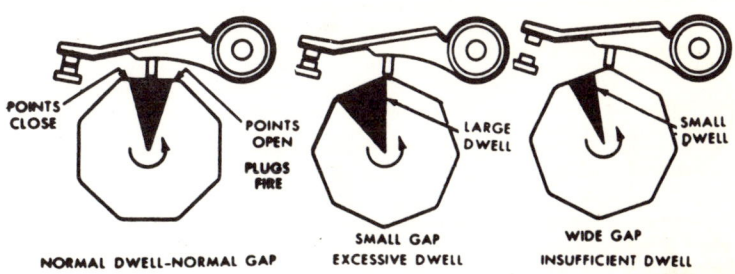

| 8.2 Check dynamic engine timing: Connect a timing light (per manufacturer's recommendation) and disconnect and plug the vacuum advance if specified; start the engine and observe the timing marks at the specified engine rpm: | If the timing is not correct, adjust to specifications by turning the distributor. | 8.3 |

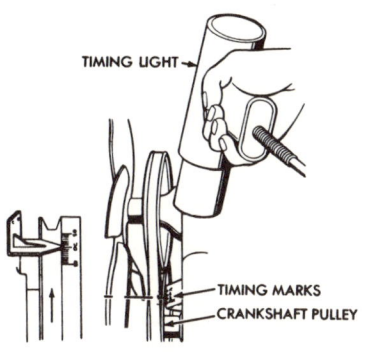

| 8.3 Check the distributor advance mechanism: Determine the type of advance mechanism utilized. If a compound system (mechanical-vacuum) is used, disconnect all but the mechanical (or vacuum, if vacuum only) and observe the timing mark as engine speed is increased from idle. If the mark moves smoothly, it may be assumed that the basic advance system is functioning properly. To test the secondary advance system (vacuum), alternately crimp and release the distributor vacuum line, and observe the timing mark for movement; If movement is noted, the system is operating: | If the systems are functioning:

If the systems are not operating properly, remove the distributor and test on a distributor tester. | 8.4

8.4 |

II - SPECIFIC DIAGNOSIS—continued

Test and Procedure	Results and Indications	Proceed to
8.4 Locate an ignition miss (where applicable): With the engine running, remove each plug wire, one by one, until one is found that doesn't cause the engine to roughen and slow down:	When the missing cylinder is identified:	4.1
9.1 Evaluate the valve train: Remove the valve cover and ensure that the valves are adjusted to specifications. Attach a timing light in the standard manner (to the specified cylinder) and observe the valves of that cylinder. Continue to attach the timing light to each cylinder and observe the valves until the problem or problems are located. A mechanic's stethoscope is also helpful in diagnosing engine noises originating from the valve train. The probe of the stethoscope is placed on or close to each rocker and push rod until the noise is isolated:	See below	See below

Indication	Probable Cause	Remedy	Proceed to
Erratic, irregular motion of the valve system.*	Sticking valve.	Recondition or replace valve guide and valve stem.	Chapter Three
Metallic tap through the stethoscope, you can push rocker arm (pushrod side) down by hand.	Collapsed or sticking hydraulic lifter.	Repair or replace the lifter. (See Chapter Three for method)	10.1
Eccentric motion of the push rod at the rocker arm.*	Bent push rod.	Replace the push rod.	10.1
Valve bounces as it closes.*	Weak valve spring or damper.	Remove and compare valve spring to specifications. Replace where necessary.	10.1

* - These items are indicated by use of the strobe light.

Test and Procedure	Results and Indications	Proceed to
9.2 Check the valve timing: The valve timing may be accurately checked by removing the engine front cover, and aligning the timing marks per specifications (see Chapter Three). An alternate method is the use of a degree wheel mounted on the crankshaft, compared to the intake valve opening (per specifications):	Any inaccuracies in valve timing should be corrected, and their causes (worn timing gear, excessive end play) eliminated.	10.1
10.1 Determine that there are no exhaust restrictions: Visually inspect the exhaust system for kinks or bends; any severely affected portion of the system should be replaced. Also note that gases are flowing freely from the tailpipe (place a hand immediately behind the tailpipe end and feel the flow of gases) indicating no restriction in the muffler or resonator:	Replace any portion of the system that will cause excessive back pressure in the exhaust system.	

TUNE-UP AND TROUBLESHOOTING

II - SPECIFIC DIAGNOSIS—*continued*

Test and Procedure	Results and Indications	Proceed to
11.1 Inspect the blower belt for tightness and wear: Visually inspect the blower belt for cracks and fraying. Tighten so that the longest span of the blower belt has approximately ½" play at its midpoint:	Replace and/or tighten the blower belt where necessary.	
12.1 Check the oil pressure gauge or warning light: If the gauge shows low pressure or the light is on, stop the engine and remove the oil pressure sender; install an accurate oil pressure gauge and run the engine momentarily: Note: If excessive oil consumption, knock and/or rumble or other signs of severe engine wear exist, proceed to Chapter Three.	If pressure builds normally, replace the sender and/or gauge.	
	If the pressure remains constantly low:	12.2
	If the pressure surges low to high:	12.3
12.2 Check the oil viscosity: Visually inspect the engine oil to determine that the viscosity is adequate (note that the oil is not watery or overly thin); if any indication of low viscosity is present, replace the oil and oil filter.	If the oil is normal:	12.3
	If after replacing the oil the pressure becomes normal.	
	If after replacing the oil the pressure remains low:	12.3
12.3 Check the oil pressure relief valve and spring: Inspect the valve to insure that it is not stuck; in all cases, remove and thoroughly clean the valve and spring:	If the pressure improves:	
	If no improvement is noted:	12.4

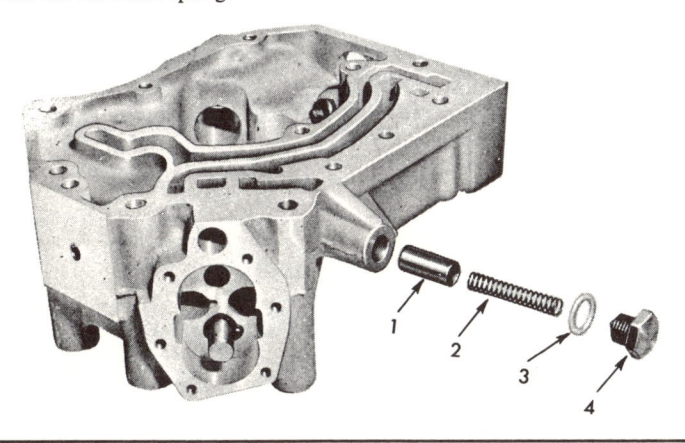

1 Valve
2 Spring
3 Nylon gasket
4 Plug

II - SPECIFIC DIAGNOSIS—continued

Test and Procedure	Results and Indications	Proceed to
12.4 Check to ensure that the oil pump is not cavitating (pumping air): Check that the crankcase is neither over nor underfull, and that the pickup screen in the sump is clear and free of sludge; fill or drain the crankcase to the proper capacity, and clean the pickup screen in a suitable solvent if necessary:	If no improvement is noted:	Chapter Three

CAMSHAFT DRIVEN GEAR

PARTING LINE

PICK-UP SCREEN

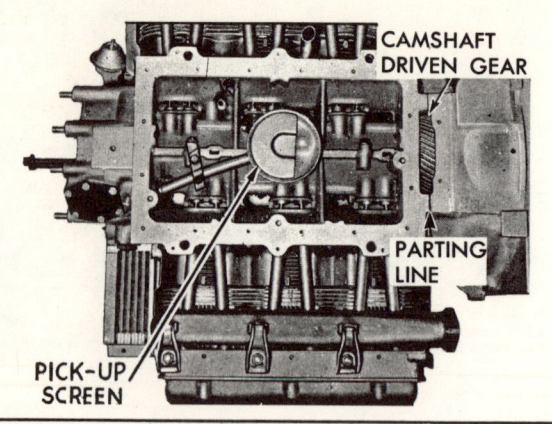

12.5 Completely drain the crankcase and remove the oil filter; following this, refill the crankcase with the proper weight oil and install a new oil filter.

3 • Engine

General

Adjusting, removing, and rebuilding the Corvair engine is a different, though not necessarily more difficult task than the equivalent job in another vehicle. Once the Corvair engine has been removed from the vehicle, it is a vastly more simple and manageable engine to disassemble than conventional, cast-iron, inline engines.

Many jobs on the Corvair engine can be performed either with the engine in place or with it dropped down very slightly to improve clearance. Whenever possible, of course, it is desirable to avoid removing the engine.

Before starting a full overhaul on a Corvair engine, check the following:

1. Note the proper location of all ducts, shrouds, and heating units, including the thermostats, baffles, etc. The exploded view shows the sheet metal arrangement for later production vehicles.

2. You should have a supply of routine replacement parts, such as pushrod tube O-rings, exhaust tube gaskets, oil cooler seals, oil pump gaskets, valve stem seals, rocker cover gaskets, etc.

NOTE: Parts such as gaskets and seals should be replaced as a matter of course. Use of old parts is false economy and can result in leaks and costly engine damage.

3. Have a variety of tools, including socket wrenches and extensions, torque wrenches in high (ft. lbs.) and low (in. lbs.) ranges, a suitable gear puller, a piston ring compressor, a valve spring compressor, and a dial indicator.

Engine Removal

Remove the spare tire; if desired, remove the engine compartment cover to allow the use of a hoist. On air conditioned vehicles, shift the compressor to one side but *do not disconnect any lines. The refrigerant is extremely dangerous.*

Remove the air cleaner assembly and disconnect the fuel lines from the tank to the fuel pump and to the carburetors. Remove the carburetors (or the turbocharger, if used), being careful to protect the linkages from damage when removing them.

NOTE: After removing the carburetors, clean and overhaul them as soon as possible, before dirt and gasoline varnish can harden in the jets and air passages.

Disconnect the mufflers at the front of each cylinder bank and remove the exhaust system from the vehicle.

Remove the blower belt and unbolt and remove the generator or alternator. Disconnect and remove the distributor as directed in Chapter Two. Disconnect the battery ground cable to prevent short circuits. Remove the upper engine shroud.

Disconnect the sender wires to the cylinder

37

General Engine Specifications

YEAR	CU. IN. DISPLACEMENT	CARBURETOR	DEVELOPED HORSEPOWER @ RPM	DEVELOPED TORQUE @ RPM (FT. LBS.)	A.M.A. HORSEPOWER	BORE AND STROKE (IN.)	COMPRESSION RATIO	VALVE LIFTER TYPE	NORMAL OIL PRESSURE (PSI)
1960	140 Std.	2-1-BBL.	80 @ 4400	125 @ 2400	27.3	3.375 x 2.600	8.0-1	Hyd.	35
1961	145 Turbo Air	2-1-BBL.	80 @ 4400	128 @ 2300	28.4	3.4375 x 2.600	8.0-1	Hyd.	35
	145 Super T.A.	2-1-BBL.	98 @ 4600	132 @ 2800	28.4	3.4375 x 2.600	8.0-1	Hyd.	35
1962-63	145 Turbo Air	2-1-BBL.	80 @ 4400	128 @ 2300	28.4	3.438 x 2.600	8.0-1	Hyd.	35
	145 Monza P.G.	2-1-BBL.	84 @ 4400	130 @ 2300	28.4	3.438 x 2.600	9.0-1	Hyd.	35
	145 Super T.A.	2-1-BBL.	102 @ 4400	134 @ 2900	28.4	3.438 x 2.600	9.0-1	Hyd.	35
	145 Super Chg.	1-1-BBL.	150 @ 4400	210 @ 3300	28.4	3.438 x 2.600	8.0-1	Hyd.	35
1964	164 Turbo Air	2-1-BBL.	95 @ 3600	154 @ 2400	28.4	3.438 x 2.937	8.25-1	Hyd.	35
	164 Super T.A.	2-1-BBL.	110 @ 4400	160 @ 2800	28.4	3.438 x 2.937	9.25-1	Hyd.	35
	164 Super Chg.	1-1-BBL.	150 @ 4000	232 @ 3200	28.4	3.438 x 2.937	8.25-1	Hyd.	35
1965-67	164 Turbo Air	2-1-BBL.	95 @ 3600	154 @ 2400	28.4	3.438 x 2.937	8.25-1	Hyd.	35
	164 Turbo Air	2-1-BBL.	110 @ 4400	160 @ 2800	28.4	3.438 x 2.937	9.0-1	Hyd.	35
	164 Turbo Air	4-1-BBL.	140 @ 5200	160 @ 3600	28.4	3.438 x 2.937	9.0-1	Hyd.	35
	164 Super Chg.	1-1-BBL.	180 @ 4000	265 @ 3200	28.4	3.438 x 2.937	8.0-1	Hyd.	35
1968-69	164 Turbo Air	2-1-BBL.	95 @ 3600	154 @ 2400	28.4	3.438 x 2.937	8.25-1	Hyd.	30
	164 Turbo Air	2-1-BBL.	110 @ 4400	160 @ 2800	28.4	3.438 x 2.937	9.25-1	Hyd.	30
	164 Turbo Air	4-1-BBL.	140 @ 5200	160 @ 3600	28.4	3.438 x 2.937	9.25-1	Hyd.	30

ENGINE

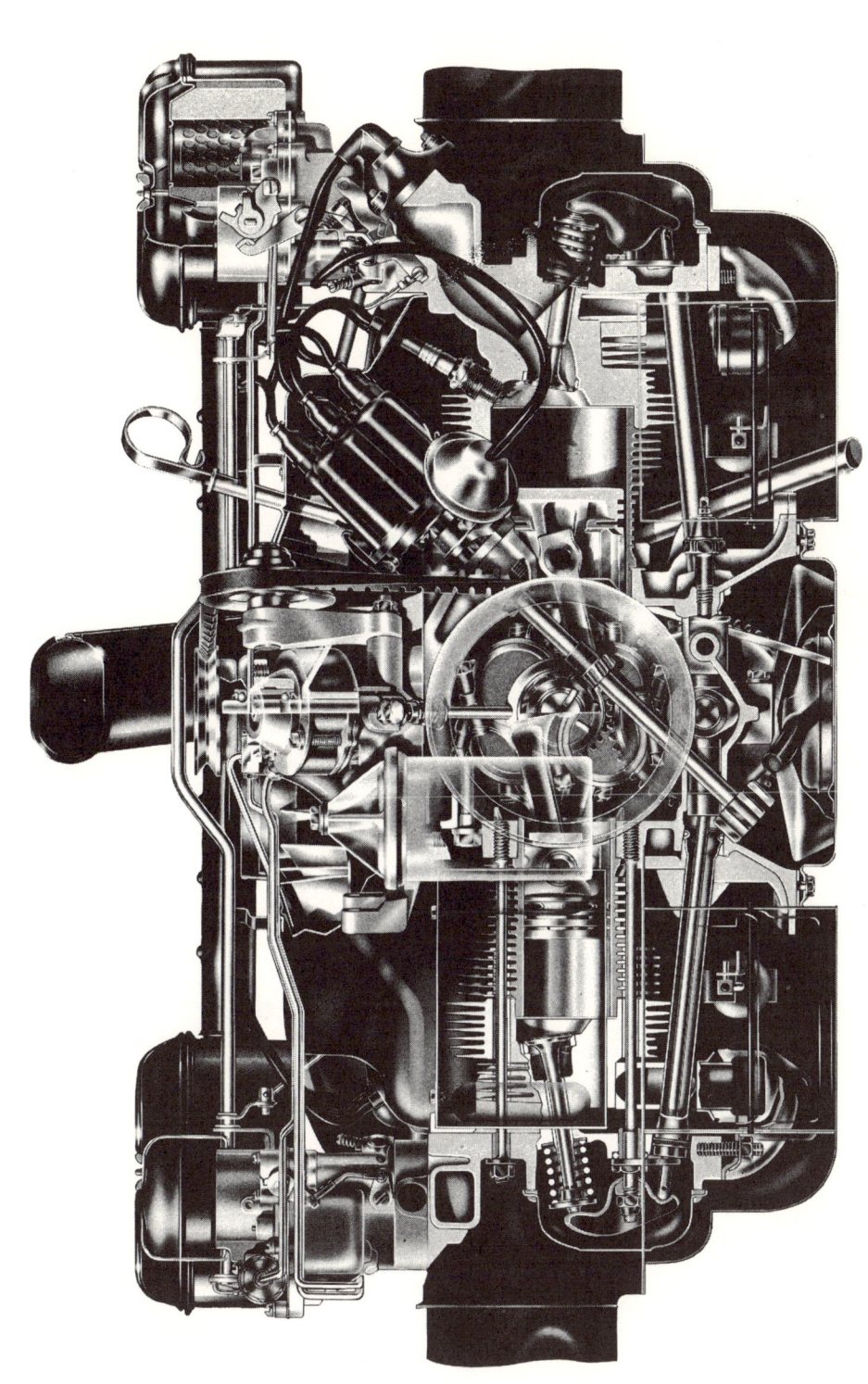

Engine cross-section across crankshaft

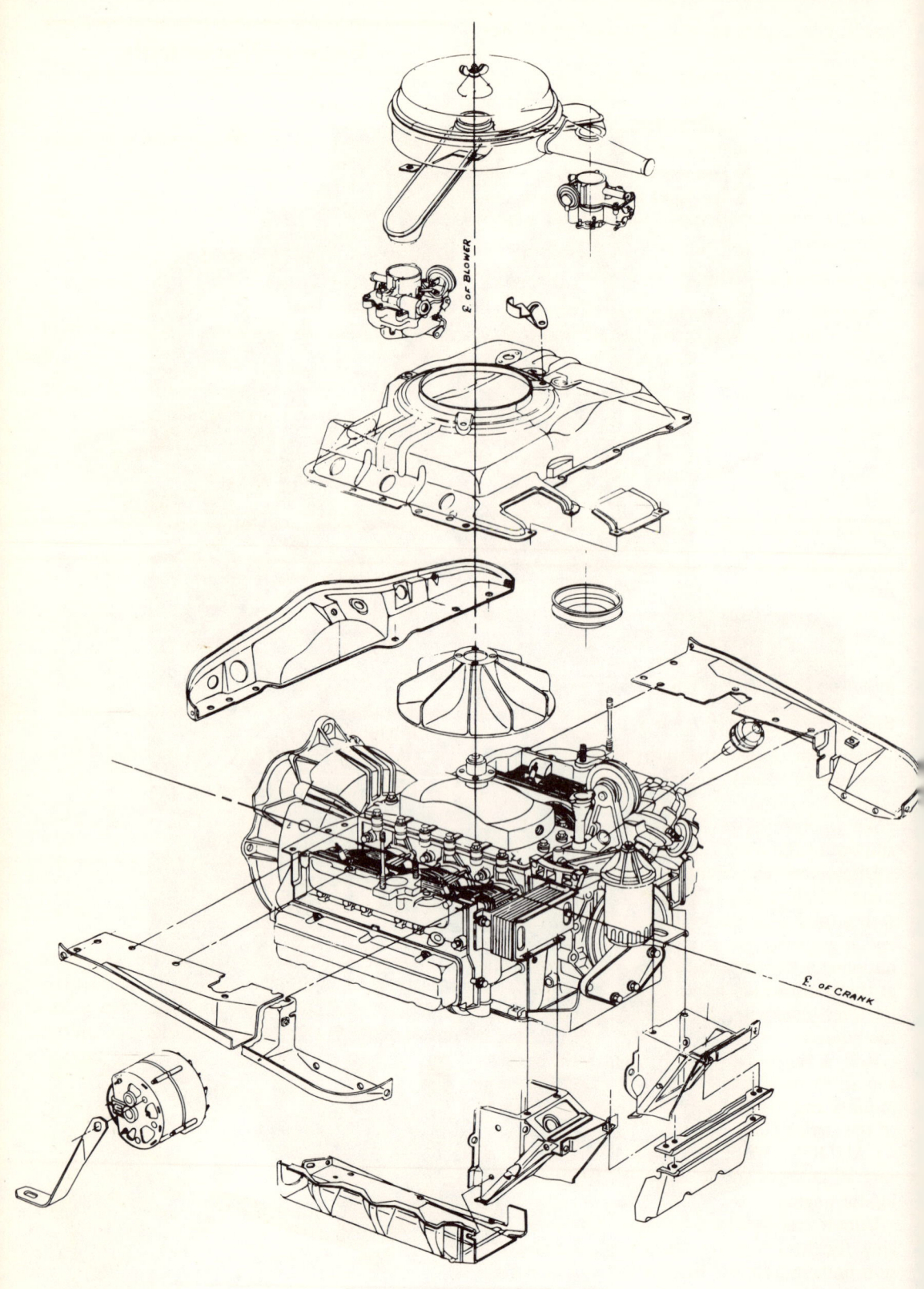

Engine sheet metal—exploded view

ENGINE

heads, if so equipped, and to the oil pump. Remove the dipstick.

Remove the rear grille and the rear center shield to permit access to the rear engine mount. Remove the oil cooler.

On 1965 or later vehicles, drop the strut rods from each side of the transaxle; slack off the adjusting cams at the outer ends, or brace the wheels outward while unbolting the rods at the inner ends.

Engine Removal—Without Transaxle

Support the differential carrier with a floor jack to take the weight of the gear train and unbolt the rear engine mount. Loosen the front mount and lower the rear end of the drive train until the flywheel housing can be removed and slid down and away from the differential carrier.

NOTE: Jack up the vehicle at the rear as high as safely possible and install sturdy jackstands. This method of engine removal is easier with an automatic transmission because a torque converter will be easier to align with the engine than a clutch input shaft. When using this method on an automatic transmission unit, be careful to secure the torque converter to the differential carrier as soon as the engine is pulled away, or it may fall off.

Engine Removal—With Transaxle

Drain the differential and the manual transmisssion (if used). Disconnect each universal joint at the differential side, unbolting the inner yoke to free the joint. Drop the shafts down and out of the way.

Disconnect the transmission; on a manual transmission, disconnect the clutch pull rod and spring (and disconnect the backup switch wiring, if present). On an automatic transmission, disconnect the shift cable by removing the bolt at the transmission housing, rotating the throttle lever clockwise, and pulling the cable from the housing.

Roll a floor jack squarely under the engine and drive train. Disconnect the front and rear mounts and lower the engine and transaxle out of the engine compartment.

CAUTION: Work slowly and carefully. Make sure all linkages are disconnected before lowering the engine.

Unbolt and remove the transaxle from the engine flywheel housing. On a manual transmission unit, unbolt and remove the clutch assembly (see Chapter Six). Unbolt and remove the flywheel. On an automatic transmission unit, remove the flex plate.

Engine Disassembly

Crankcase Cover

Unbolt and remove the crankcase cover after pulling off the blower impeller.

NOTE: This cover, like other parts of the Corvair engine, is made of cast aluminum and can be scratched or marred easily. Handle it carefully and do not rest it or drop it on its mating flange; any damage to the flange will cause oil leaks later.

Remove the crankcase vent and gaskets when the cover is off.

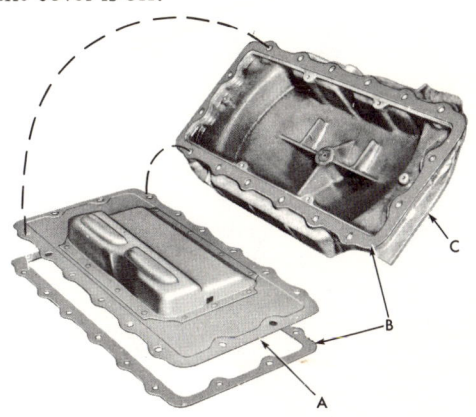

A Crankcase vent
B Gaskets
C Crankcase cover

Crankcase cover and vent assembly

Oil Filter Adapter Removal

Unbolt and remove the oil filter and generator-alternator adapter.

Crankshaft Pulley (or Harmonic Balancer) Removal

Remove the retaining bolt on the crankshaft pulley (standard power, manual transmission units) or harmonic balancer (high power engines and all automatic transmission units),

Removing crankshaft pulley

using a puller similar to that illustrated. Do not thread the puller bolts farther than 1/4" into the pulley, or the rear housing behind it may be damaged.

Cylinder Head Removal

Remove the rocker covers and wash or soak them in solvent. Remove the nuts securing each rocker arm to the cylinder head and remove each arm with its spherical bearing. Pull out each pushrod and wash it in solvent.

Unscrew and remove the rocker arm studs on which the rocker arms were mounted, using a deep wrench socket (be careful not to mar the rocker nut threads at the ends of the stud). Remove each stud and each pushrod guide from each cylinder bank. Remove and discard the rubber seal from each rocker stud hole in the cylinder heads.

Remove the pushrod tubes as follows: grasping the middle portion of each, pull it free from the crankcase at the inner end; remove the inner O-ring seal, then pull the tube the rest of the way out of the cylinder head, as illustrated.

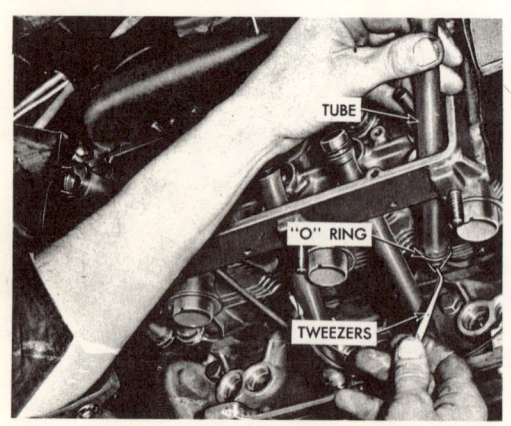

Removing pushrod oil drain tubes

Unscrew the cylinder head nuts at the edge of the intake manifold and pull the heads from the engine. Remove and discard the gaskets in each cylinder recess.

Valve Lifter Removal

Using a wire hook or strong magnet, pull out each lifter and mark each with its exact location (cylinder number, intake or exhaust), or place in a numbered rack. Clean the lifters as soon as possible in lacquer thinner.

Rear Housing Removal

Unbolt and remove the rear housing from the engine. Disassemble and clean the housing.

Cylinder Removal

Remove the sheet metal baffles from the cylinders. Invert the engine and remove the oil pan and gasket to expose the connecting rods. Turn the crank by hand or with a work bolt in the end of the crank to bring each connecting rod in turn around so that it can be reached with a ratchet socket wrench. Unbolt and remove each bearing cap, then immediately slip tubing or wrap tape around the exposed rod studs to prevent damage to the crank journal surfaces when the rods come out of the engine. As each journal is freed, pull the assembly (the cylinder, piston, and connecting rod) from the engine and install the bearing cap loosely to keep the parts together. Keep each cylinder assembly separate and mark the piston tops with the direction (up or down) in which they were installed.

Separating the Crankcase Halves

When handling the Corvair crankcase certain fundamental rules must be observed. The aluminum crankcase is lightweight and strong but is susceptible to scratches and dents from heavier, harder parts. The mating surfaces of the crankcase must be protected from damage; they must be kept in good condition or oil leaks will result. The crankshaft and camshaft bores must be protected or running clearances will be lost. The camshaft has *no replaceable bearing inserts* and runs in the metal of the crankcase itself. If the camshaft contact surfaces are marred or scratched, the entire crankcase will be ruined. Therefore, after the crankcase bolts have been removed, secure and brace one side of the crankcase, preferably so that one side slants upward at about 30°. It is permissible to rest the crankcase on its studs provided the strain is not enough to bend them.

With the crankcase assembly supported on a slant as described above, loosen and remove the eight cross-bolts holding the halves together and remove the bolt on the underside which holds the oil screen tube to the mating flange. Using a soft hammer as required, separate the crankcase halves and lift upward half carefully away, as illustrated.

It may be necessary to force the crankcase halves apart against the friction of the locating plugs, but do not use anything harder than a soft (rubber or plastic) hammer for this purpose.

NOTE: Be extremely careful that the camshaft stays in the lower half and does not bind or fall out of the crankcase.

ENGINE

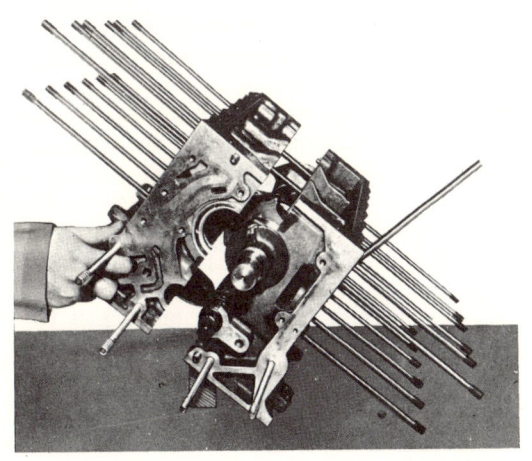

Removal and installation of crankcase sections

Carefully lift the camshaft out, turning while lifting to clear the timing gear and thrust washer. Put the camshaft in a safe place (do not lay it down on its cam lobes or journals on a hard surface).

Lift out the crankshaft, avoiding damage to the bearing inserts. Remove the bearing inserts from each crankcase half by rotating them along the curvature of their bores as shown.

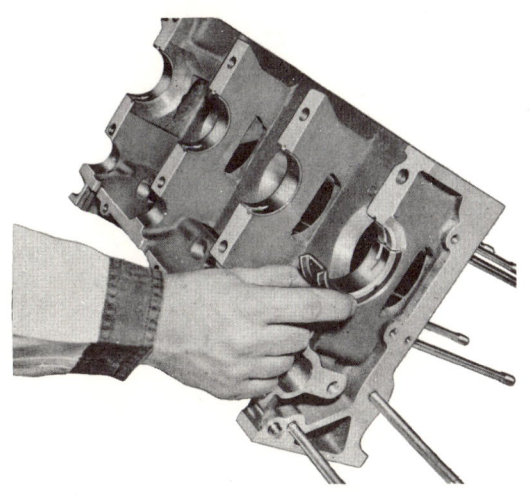

Removing and installing main bearings

Engine Inspection and Servicing

Main and Connecting Rod Bearings

The main and connecting rod bearings are of the common, replaceable-insert type. These "block" bearings are surprisingly frictionless under good lubrication conditions, but they are always subject to some wear and should be checked whether or not they were the original reason for disassembling the engine. The bearings and mating journals usually wear radially and not in an out-of-round pattern, but the journals should be checked for out-of-roundness just in case.

Journal Out-of-Roundness

Check the crankshaft main and crankpin journals for out-of-roundness using a micrometer or locking caliper (it is not necessary to measure the exact diameter, only the variation of the diameter). If any journal is out-of-round more than 0.001", the crankshaft should be reconditioned (ground undersize) or replaced. If any significant out-of-roundness is found, mark the point of the largest diameter on an adjacent part of the crank to aid in making the following check for bearing fit (running clearance).

Main Bearing Service

Clean the crankcase halves thoroughly and clean and install the bearing inserts in their proper places. Assemble the crankshaft and crankcase halves, slanting one half upwards as was done for disassembly. Lay the crankshaft carefully into the bearing inserts of the lower half, positioning any out-of-round "high point" marks on the crankshaft outward so that the gauging plastic ("Plastigage" is available from auto parts jobbers) will be positioned at that point.

NOTE: Inserting the gauge plastic at the "high point" on a journal ensures that the bearing clearance measured will be the lowest (tightest) value for the journal and that a too-tight bearing will not be chosen by mistake.

Lay a short piece of gauging plastic across (not around) each journal, lifting and adjusting the crank as necessary to be sure all high points are being measured.

Assemble the other crankcase half and torque

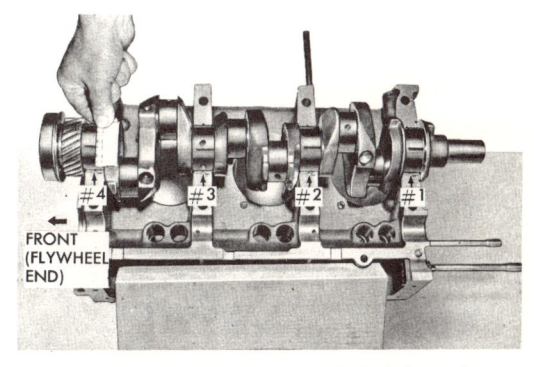

Measuring plastigage on crankshaft journals

the eight cross-bolts to 50-55 ft. lbs. Do not allow the crankshaft to turn, or it will smear the plastic around the journal and spoil the clearance reading.

Unbolt and remove one crankcase half and check the width of the flattened plastic with the graduated scale supplied with the plastic as shown. This scale converts the width of the compressed plastic to the thickness of compression (bearing clearance) in thousandths of an inch.

Bearing Selection

Main bearing clearance should be 0.0012-0.0027" on Nos. 1 and 2 bearings and 0.0007-0.0022" on Nos. 3 and 4. Bearings are available in standard, 0.001, 0.002, and (for No. 4 only) 0.003" undersizes, or in 0.010 and 0.020" undersizes (Nos. 1 through 4) for reconditioned crankshafts. See Main Bearing Chart. Both insert halves must be replaced at any one location.

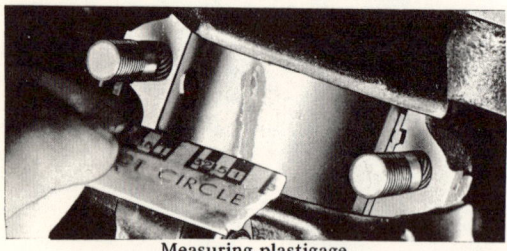

Measuring plastigage

Check the condition as well as the clearance of each bearing; if it has a uniform, dull but smooth finish, it is acceptable; if it is scored, scratched, or smeared to a bright finish in places, it should be replaced.

Connecting Rod Bearing Service

The connecting rod bearings are similar to the main bearings and are checked in the same way; the crankshaft need not be installed in the crankcase when the connecting rods are installed for checking.

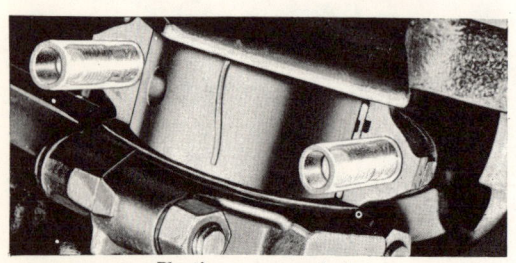

Plastigage on crankpin

Lay the gauging plastic across the crankpin journal and torque the bearing caps to 20-26 ft. lbs.

NOTE: Do not turn the crankshaft to obtain access to all six journals at once; this will smear the gauging plastic. Slip on tubing or tape to keep the rod studs from scarring the journals when installing and removing the rods.

Unbolt and remove the bearing caps and read the bearing clearance in the same manner as for main bearings, (as previously illustrated). This clearance should be 0.0007-0.0027". Select undersizes as necessary; 0.001 and 0.002" undersizes are available, or 0.010, 0.020, or 0.030" undersizes (U/S) for reconditioned crankshafts.

Replacement Main Bearings (in.)

Main Bearing Clearance	Replacement Bearing
0.0010	0.000 (Std)
0.0015	0.001 U/S
0.0020	0.001 U/S
0.0025	0.002 U/S
0.0030	0.002 U/S
0.0035	0.003 U/S (No. 4)
0.0040	0.003 U/S (No. 4)

Camshaft Bearing Service

Check camshaft journal clearance (three journals) at the same time as the main bearings are checked, by assembling the camshaft in the crankcase with gauging plastic.

NOTE: For the purposes of this check it is not necessary to index the timing marks on the camshaft gear.

Check out-of-roundness on all journals and check clearance with the crankcase bores; clearance for a used camshaft should be 0.002-0.004". Replace the cam if clearance is excessive. A new camshaft should have a 0.0015-0.0035" clearance with the crankcase.

Crankshaft

Check the main and crankpin journals as described above. As required, recondition journals by sending the crankshaft to a machine shop to be ground undersize and have matching bearings fitted.

NOTE: When having this work done it is usually advisable to have the crank balanced also. This procedure is inexpensive and insures safety and smoothness of operation.

ENGINE

Distributor Drive Gear

Under normal circumstances this gear need not be removed. Inspect it for chipped or broken teeth and replace it if is unserviceable (routine wear usually will not impair operation). Remove the gear, when necessary, using a puller as shown. Be careful not to damage the gear teeth while pulling gear from the shaft; a puller with locking jaws (shown in the figure) is the best type.

Install the gear with the fuel pump eccentric keyed into place, pressing the gear on with an arbor press.

NOTE: When using the press, support the crankshaft as close to the gear journal as possible so as not to distort the crankshaft by exerting high pressure over its entire length. Be sure the woodruff key, which positions the fuel pump eccentric and gear, is properly positioned.

Timing Gear

This gear need not be removed from the crankshaft unless excessively worn or damaged. Support the gear and press the crankshaft downward to remove the gear. Install the gear by pressing it back into place.

Camshaft

Inspect the running clearance of the cam with the crankcase bore as described above and replace it if the clearance if excessive.

Check the cam lobes for excessive wear or "tearing" of the lobe surfaces.

NOTE: Unusual damage to a cam lobe can point to trouble elsewhere in the engine; if a cam lobe is damaged, look for faults in the adjacent valve lifter, pushrods, rocker arms, etc.

Camshaft Gear

If the camshaft drive gear is damaged (chipped or broken teeth), remove it by supporting the camshaft on an arbor press and driving the shaft out of the gear.

Replace the gear by supporting the camshaft as close as possible to the gear journal (behind the front bearing journal) and pressing on the gear. Be sure the thrust washer is in place and that all surfaces are clean.

Cylinders, Pistons, and Connecting Rods

Each assembly of a cylinder, piston and rings, and connecting rod is serviced as an assembly; when replaced, a piston must be purchased complete with a cylinder mated to it, and vice versa. Be sure to mark all parts clearly with their cylinder number when it is necessary to separate them.

Cylinder, Piston, and Connecting Rod Dissassembly

Push the piston and connecting rod out through the bottom of each cylinder. Remove

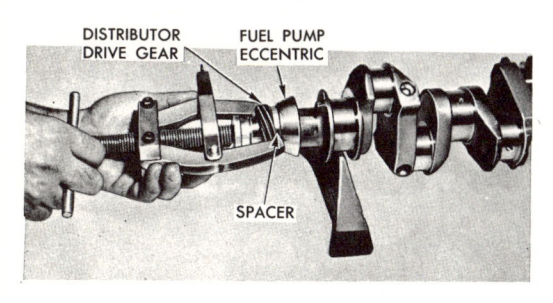

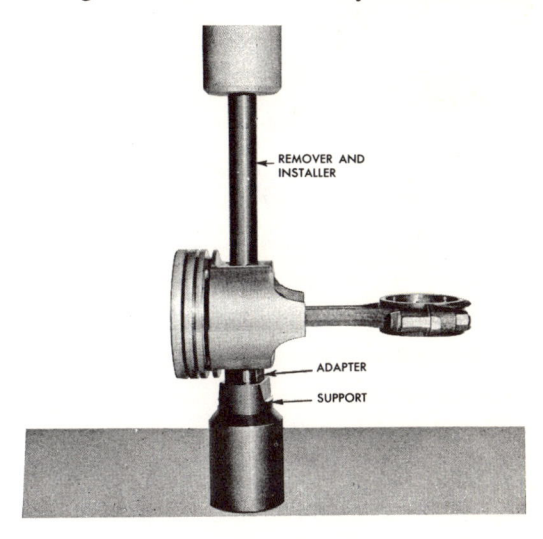

Removing distributor drive gear

Removing and installing piston pin

Crankshaft Bearing Journal Specifications

YEAR	MODEL	MAIN BEARING JOURNALS (IN.)			CONNECTING ROD BEARING JOURNALS (IN.)		
		Journal Diameter	Oil Clearance	Shaft End-Play Thrust On No.	Journal Diameter	Oil Clearance	End-Play
1960-69	All Engines	▲	■	.002–.006 1	1.799–1.800	.0007–.0027	.005–.010

▲—#1 & 2, 2.0978-2.0988; #3 & 4, 2.0983-2.0993 (1960—all four same as 1 and 2).
■—#1 & 2, .0012-.0027; #3 & 4, .0007-.0022.

the piston rings, uppermost first, by expanding them just enough to slip them out of their grooves and off the piston.

NOTE: Do not expand the rings any more than necessary or they will break. An aid to removal is a strip of shim stock inserted between the ends of a ring and the piston surface as soon as the ends are out of the groove, to give the ring ends a smooth surface to slide on and to prevent damage to the piston surface.

Press the wrist pins out of the pistons with an arbor press. It is permissible to heat the piston and rod assembly (in an oven, to approximately 300° F., *not* with a torch) if too much resistance is met.

Cylinder Inspection

Check each cylinder for damage, such as ring gouging or scuffed cylinder walls. Remove any ridge left by the piston rings with a ridge reamer. Measure the cylinder bore for diameter and out-of-roundness with an inside-outside micrometer. Out-of-roundness must not exceed 0.002"; taper (difference in diameter from the top to the bottom of the cylinder) must not exceed 0.005". Replace the cylinder (and piston) as required.

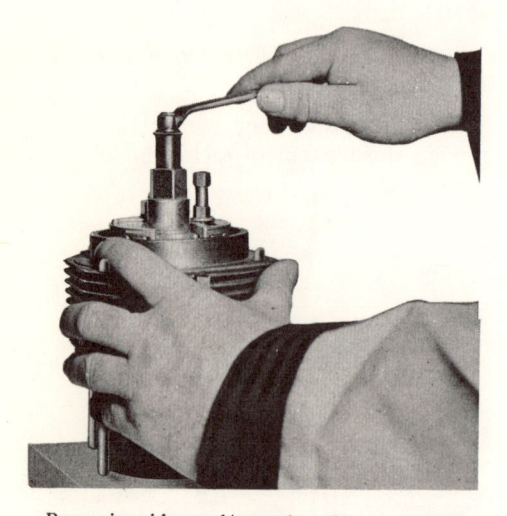

Piston Inspection

Check the pistons for marred or scuffed surfaces and replace them (with mating cylinders) as necessary.

Inspect the ring grooves for uneven wear on the ring contact surfaces; roll a compression ring around the grooves to detect blockage or distortion in the ring groove. Clean the grooves out with a standard groove cleaning tool, or a broken ring suitably ground, and probe all the oil supply ports in the oil control ring groove to be sure they are clear.

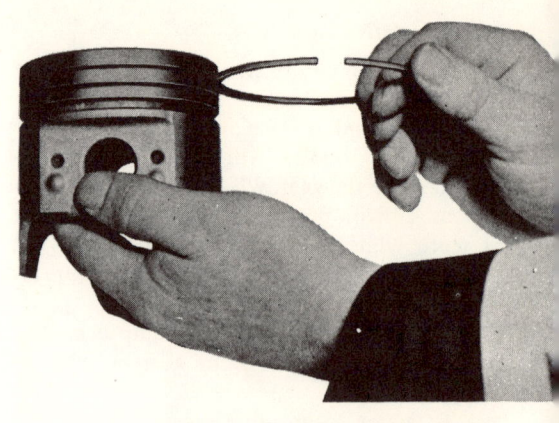

Check the wrist pin dimensions against the piston pin hole dimensions, using inside and outside micrometers; the pins should fit in the pistons with a 0.001" clearance (light press fit).

Piston Rings

Corvair pistons are fitted with two compression (solid) rings and one oil control (slotted) ring. They may be inspected to detect damage, but it is generally good practice to replace them. Check the compression rings in the cylinders in which they will be used as follows: install a piston (without rings) into the cylinder bore with the piston top about halfway up the bore. Slide a ring into the bore and against the top of the piston so that it is positioned squarely in the bore. Slide the piston downward from the ring and check the ring gap with a feeler gauge as shown.

This gap should be 0.013-0.025" for compression rings and 0.015-0.055" for oil control rings.

Ring Installation

Install the three-piece oil control ring carefully into its groove, using shim stock under the ring ends to aid installation. Position the spacer segment in the groove so that the anti-rotation tang locks in place. Install the center rail of the ring below the spacer and install the second rail above the spacer. Position the rail and spacer gaps as shown.

Install the compression rings in similar fashion, so that their "top" marks face toward the top of the piston. Position the gaps as previously shown.

ENGINE

Checking ring gap

Compression ring marking

Check the ring side clearance with a feeler gauge after installation, as illustrated. This clearance should be 0.0017-0.004" for compression rings and 0.0012-0.005" for oil control rings.

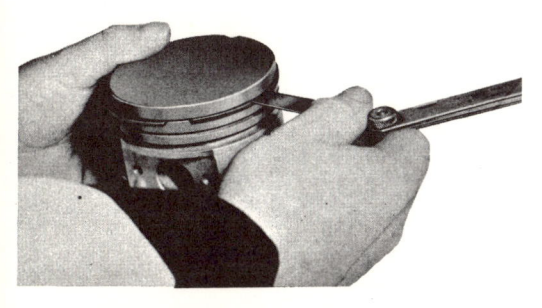

Measuring ring groove clearance

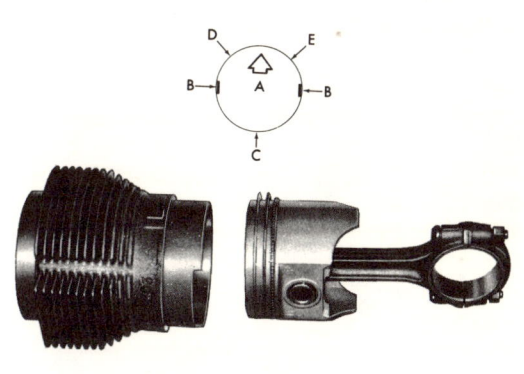

A Top of piston when installed
B Piston pin location
C Oil ring spacer gap
D Top oil ring rail gap, top compression ring gap
E Bottom oil ring gap, second compression ring gap

Piston rings installed

Cylinder Heads

The Corvair engine's cylinder heads are serviced according to the usual principles of maintaining cylinder sealing, valve condition, etc., with the exception that the cylinder sealing surfaces are recessed and therefore cannot be machined by the usual techniques of milling or grinding. The heads can be cleaned up by any good automotive machine shop having an inside milling cutter. Since the bulk of head repairs concern the valves, the procedures are given here for those who wish to do their own valve work.

Clean the heads thoroughly, including the spaces between the cooling fins. These fins should be free of surface grease as well as dirt, or else cooling will be affected.

Lightly clean the valve cover contact surfaces and the cylinder recesses of dirt, carbon, or gasket residue. Do not use any hard abrasive material; a fiber or plastic scraper would be best, light wire-brushing being confined to the combustion chamber recesses.

Remove the valves by compressing the valve springs, using a standard valve spring compressor as shown. Remove the retainers and spring caps when spring tension is released and remove the springs and any shim washers underneath. Invert the head and draw out each valve from its guide. Identify each valve by its cylinder number.

Clean the combustion chambers carefully with a wire brush to remove carbon. Do not brush the cylinder sealing surfaces or the valve seats any more than necessary.

Clean the valve guide bores with a *soft* (copper) brush, such as a rifle bore brush, to remove carbon buildup.

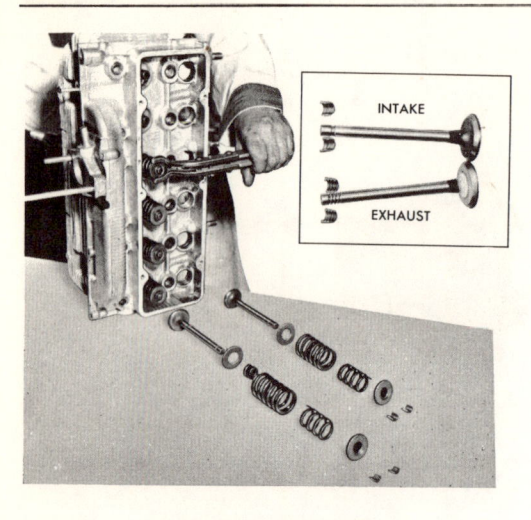

Compressing valve springs

Valves

Inspect all valves for condition and replace them (especially exhaust valves) if they show signs of burning which regrinding will not remove. A typically burned surface is black, porous, and partially eroded.

Check the valve stem clearance as shown. Install each valve in its guide and place a dial indicator against the stem at the outer side of the head. This clearance, with the valve moved off its seat about 1/16", must be as follows:

	Intake	Exhaust
New	0.001–0.0027"	0.0014–0.0029"
Used	0.001–0.004"	0.002–0.005"

A head assembly with too much valve stem clearance must be repaired by one of the following procedures.

1. "Knurling": This is a machining procedure which reduces the bore of the guide by forming grooves in it, pushing surrounding material inward to reduce the diameter. It is a service available at most auto machine shops.

2. Oversize Valves: Valves with oversize stems (0.003, 0.010, or 0.020") are available, and the guides must be reamed to accommodate them. This requires GM Tool J-5830 Hand Reamer Set, or equivalent.

3. Replacement Guides: On all Corvair engines except turbocharged models, the valve guides may be pressed out and replaced, then reamed to give the proper running clearance with the valve stem. Drive out the old guide from the outer side into the combustion chamber, then press in the replacement guide until the inner face of the guide (combustion chamber side) is approximately 1" from the surface of the valve seat. Ream the guide to accommodate the valve stem with the correct clearance.

NOTE: Guides with oversize outside diameters are also available for a head in which the guide bore is damaged. Ream this bore to 0.524–0.525" diameter and use a 0.010" oversize guide, or to 0.534–0.535" diameter and an 0.020" oversize guide. Ream the inner bore of the guide to achieve the proper stem clearance.

Grinding Valves

Recondition the valve seats by grinding the sealing surfaces of the valve face and cylinder

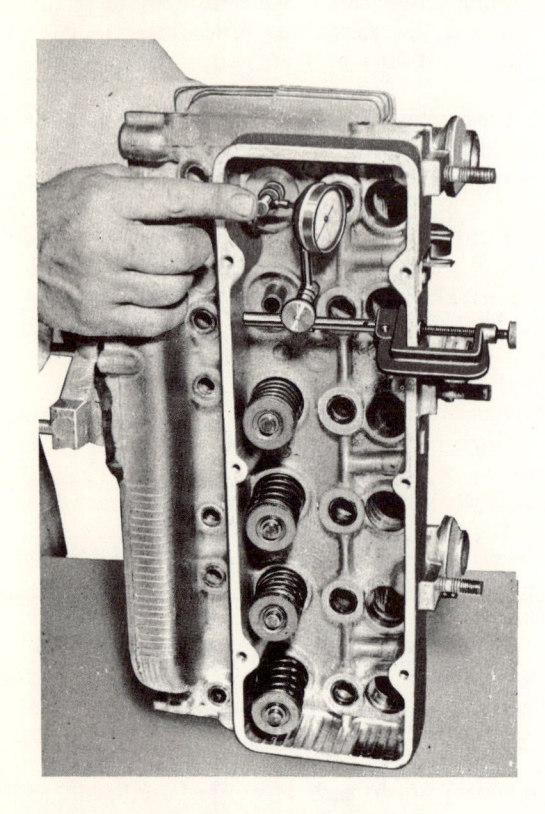

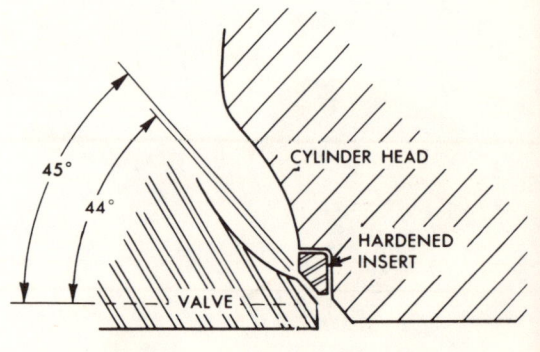

Measuring valve stem clearance

Relation of valve and seat angles

ENGINE

Valve Specifications

YEAR AND MODEL		SEAT ANGLE (DEG.)	FACE ANGLE (DEG.)	VALVE LIFT INTAKE (IN.)	VALVE LIFT EXHAUST (IN.)	VALVE SPRING PRESSURE (VALVE OPEN) LBS. @ IN.	VALVE SPRING INSTALLED HEIGHT (IN.)	STEM TO GUIDE CLEARANCE (IN.) INTAKE	STEM TO GUIDE CLEARANCE (IN.) EXHAUST	STEM DIAMETER (IN.) INTAKE	STEM DIAMETER (IN.) EXHAUST
1960	140 Cu. In.	45 in. 45 ex.	45 in. 44 ex.	.314	.344	144 @ 1.148	1.508	.0010-.0027	.0015-.0032	.3415-.3422	.3410-.3417①
1961	145 Turbo Air	45 in. 45 ex.	45 in. 44 ex.	.314	.344	144 @ 1.148	1.508	.0010-.0027	.0015-.0032	.3415-.3422	.3410-.3417①
	145 Super T.A.	45 in. 45 ex.	45 in. 44 ex.	.380	.380	165 @ 1.306	1.696	.0010-.0027	.0015-.0032	.3415-.3422	.3410-.3417①
1962-63	145 Turbo Air & Monza P.G.	45 in. 45 ex.	44 in. 44 ex.	.314	.314	144 @ 1.148	1.508	.0010-.0027	.0010-.0027	.3415-.3422	.3410-.3417①
	145 Super T.A. & Spyder T.C.	45 in. 45 ex.	45 in. 44 ex.	.378	.378	165 @ 1.306	1.696	.0010-.0027	.0010-.0027	.3415-.3422	.3410-.3417①
1964	164 Turbo Air & Super T.A.	45 in. 45 ex.	45 in. 44 ex.	.385	.385	175 @ 1.260	1.656 ±.030	.0010-.0027	.0014-.0029	.3414-.3422	.3407-.3418
	164 Spyder T.C.	45 in. 45 ex.	45 in. 44 ex.	.390	.390	175 @ 1.260	1.656 ±.030	.0010-.0027	.0014-.0029	.3414-.3422	.3407-.3418
1965	164 Turbo Air	45 in. 45 ex.	45 in. 44 ex.	.385	.385	175 @ 1.260	1.656 ±.030	.0010-.0027	.0014-.0029	.3414-.3422	.3407-.3418
	164 (110 & 140 H.P.)	45 in. 45 ex.	45 in. 44 ex.	.390	.390	175 @ 1.260	1.656 ±.030	.0010-.0027	.0014-.0029	.3414-.3422	.3407-.3418
	164 Spyder T.C.	45 in. 45 ex.	45 in. 44 ex.	.374	.374	175 @ 1.260	1.656 ±.030	.0010-.0027	.0014-.0029	.3414-.3422	.3407-.3418
1966-69	164 Turbo Air	46	45	.403	.403	175 @ 1.260	1.656 ±.030	.0010-.0028	.0014-.0029	.3414-.3422	.3407-.3418
	164 (110 & 140 H.P.)	46	45	.409	.409	175 @ 1.260	1.656 ±.030	.0010-.0028	.0014-.0029	.3414-.3422	.3407-.3418
	164 Spyder T.C.	46	45	.392	.392	175 @ 1.260	1.656 ±.030	.0010-.0028	.0014-.0029	.3414-.3422	.3407-.3418

① —Top; bottom = .3400-.3407.

head seat to their proper angle and circumferential smoothness. Use commonly available valve grinding tools to produce the angles shown. Runout (variation in the contour of the seat) must not exceed 0.002".

NOTE: Turbocharged engines should have a valve face angle of 45° rather than 44°. This gives additional cooling contact for the valve.

Do not grind valves so that the distance from the outer edge of the sealing face to the outer face of the valve is less than 1/32". If, with this limit, the valve cannot be made to "clean up" (produce a smooth, continuous, machined surface) it must be replaced.

Additional benefits can be gained by lapping the valves into the seats after grinding; using grinding compound and a common lapping spindle, spin the valve against its seat to mate the surfaces.

Valve Springs

The valve springs should be checked for tension with a standard tester, as illustrated. The valve springs should be 2.08" long in the free state and should register 78-86 lbs. at 1.660" compression, and 170-180 lbs. at 1.260". Springs out of specification more than 5 lbs. should be replaced.

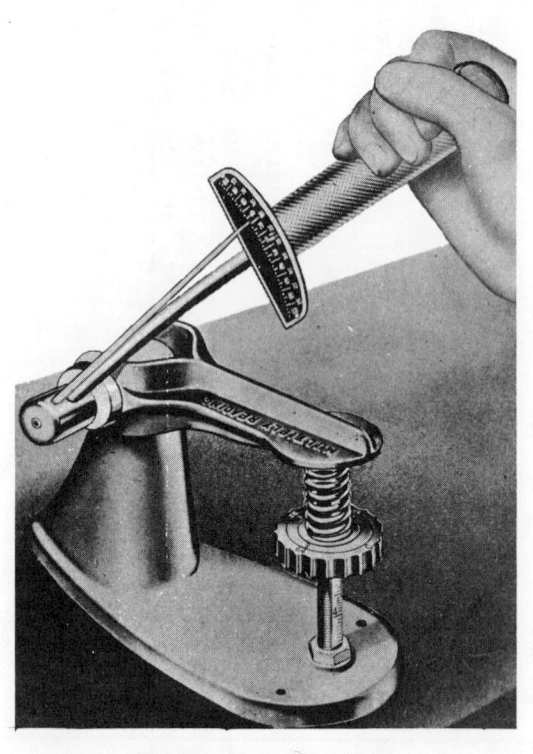

Checking valve spring tension

Check the installed height of the springs as follows: install the reconditioned valves in their guides and install the spring shim, cap, and

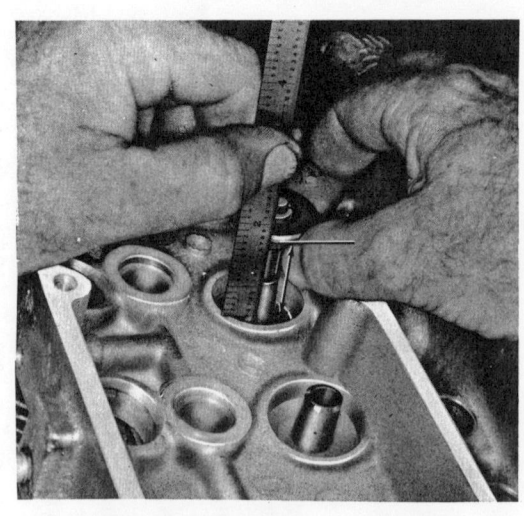

Measuring valve spring installed height

valve locks, without the spring. With the top of the cylinder head facing upward, pull up on the cap and check the distance from the shim to the cap as shown. The valve spring seat is recessed, so a thin or cut-away scale like that in the figure will be necessary. Select spring shims as necessary to produce a dimension of 1 21/32" ± 1/32". There are 0.030" shims available to correct spacing.

NOTE: Do not attempt to shim the springs below their specified height. The "float" resistance gained will be offset by accelerated wear to the camshaft lobes through increased friction.

Valve Lifters

The Corvair valve lifters are hydraulic, and consist of an internal, spring-loaded piston which is pressurized with crankcase oil to form an incompressible but self-adjusting lifting body. The different types are illustrated.

Clean the lifters thoroughly in solvent until they can be compressed freely. If they cannot be loosened up by cleaning, disassemble them and pull out the center plunger. Lift out the ball check valve with a screwdriver and remove the ball valve and spring from the plunger. Clean all parts and check for damage or signs of binding. Replace the entire lifter if damage is found. Check the inertia valve by shaking it after cleaning; if it can be heard to move, it is acceptable.

Assemble the lifters in reverse order of disas-

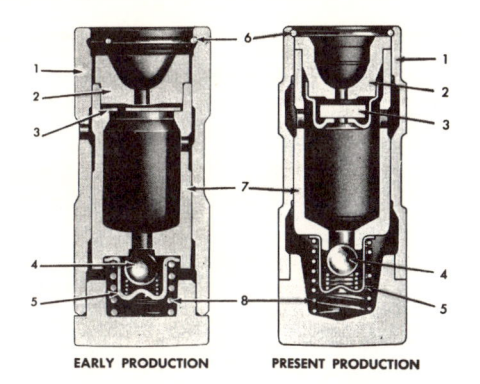

ENGINE

Hydraulic valve lifter

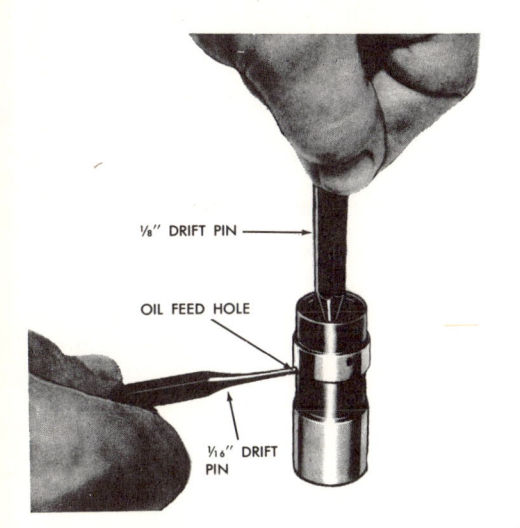

1. Lifter body
2. Pushrod seat
3. Inertia valve (present); metering valve (early)
4. Check ball
5. Ball retainer
6. Pushrod seat retainer
7. Plunger
8. Plunger spring

Assembling the hydraulic lifter

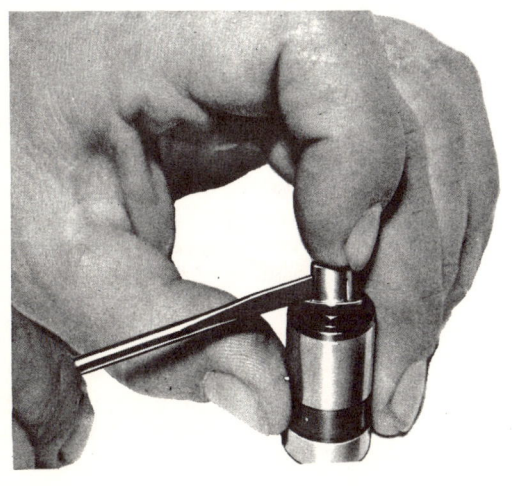

Removing ball check valve

sembly, inserting the check ball and spring in the plunger, followed by the retainer seated firmly in the plunger. Assemble the plunger and its spring in the lifter body, lining up the oil holes. Fill the lifter with oil, then insert a drift through the oil holes in the body and plunger as illustrated. Remove the drift holding down the plunger, then refill the lifter with oil. Install the pushrod seat and inertia valve assembly. Remove the second drift to release the plunger.

Rear Housing

The rear housing is an important subassembly of the Corvair engine because it contains the heart of the lubrication system. This unit should be cleaned as thoroughly as possible, first with probes and scrapers, then with solvent until all internal passages are clean and all flanges are free of foreign matter. Check the following component parts.

Oil Pump

Remove the oil pump by unbolting the cover and removing the gears. Clean all parts thoroughly and check for axial clearance: install the gears in their places and measure the distance between their top surface and the top of the pump boss, using feeler stock. The gears should protrude 0.0025-0.0045″ above the boss surface (to allow for gasket thickness). Obtain 0.001″ oversize (thickness) gears as necessary

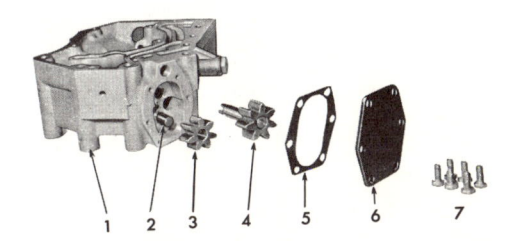

Oil pump, exploded view

1. Engine rear housing
2. Idler gear shaft
3. Idler gear
4. Drive gear and shaft
5. Gasket
6. Cover
7. Bolts

to obtain this limit. The gears should have 0.002-0.005″ clearance with the pump housing wall; gear backlash, measured with a dial indicator point against the point of one gear tooth, should be 0.002-0.008″.

Oil Pressure Regulator

The oil pressure regulator, should be carefully cleaned and checked, since it controls oil pressure within the engine and can cause oil system failure even when the pump itself is performing perfectly. Clean all parts well and check for damage.

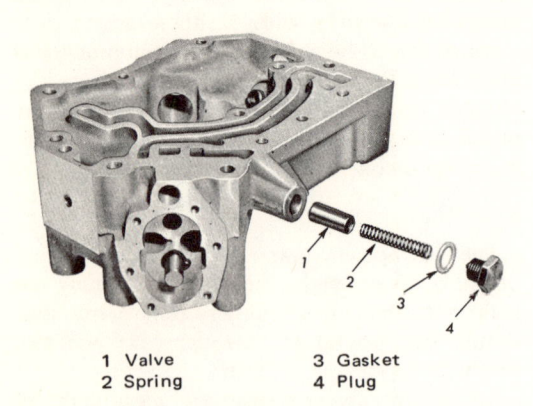

1 Valve
2 Spring
3 Gasket
4 Plug

Pressure regulator, exploded view

Rear Seal

Replace the rear seal as shown, removing the old one with a drift, cleaning the contact surface, then installing the new one with a soft drift and hammer. Be sure the new seal is coated with high-temperature grease.

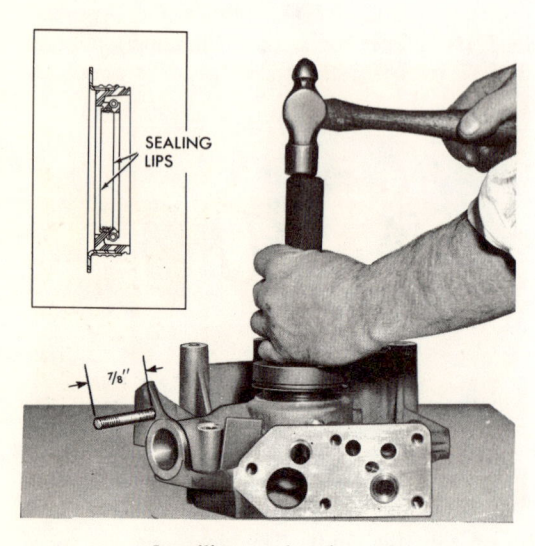

Installing rear housing seal

Oil Cooler By-Pass Valve

This valve routes oil around the oil cooler in the event the cooler core becomes too clogged to sustain oil flow. Remove this valve with a small tool, clean it carefully and replace it. If a large amount of dirt was found in the valve, check the oil cooler for contamination.

Engine Assembly

Install the main bearings in the crankcase halves, lightly coated with engine oil. Support one half of the crankcase as was done for disassembly.

NOTE: On certain 1962 and 1963 models, the front main bearing (No. 4) has only one flanged half, to be installed in the *right* crankcase half. See the illustration.

Front main bearing installation

Lay the crankshaft carefully in the supported crankcase half and install the camshaft below it, with the timing marks aligned as shown. Be sure that the thrust washer on the camshaft is in the proper groove.

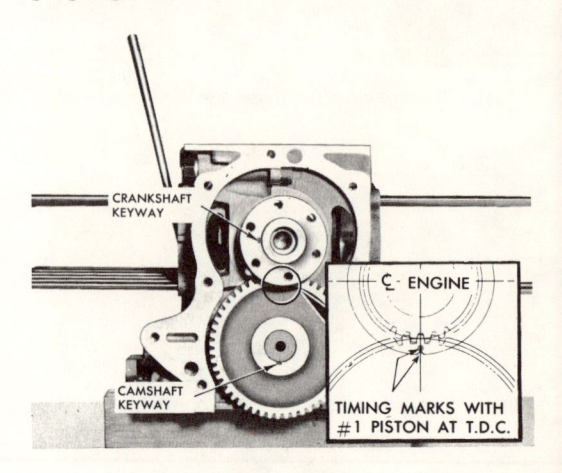

Timing marks

Install the left crankcase half and thread the eight cross-bolts in place fingertight. Install the ninth bolt through the oil screen bracket and torque all bolts to 50-55 ft. lbs. in the sequence shown.

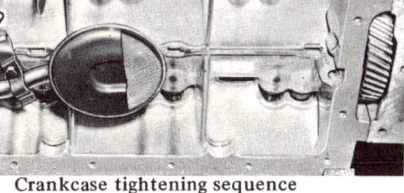

ENGINE

Crankcase tightening sequence

Check the crankshaft end play with a dial indicator as shown; when the crankshaft is pushed end-to-end this play should be 0.002-0.006". Camshaft end play, measured in the same fashion, should be 0.002-0.007". Play in excess of this indicates a worn crankcase or thrust washer.

Backlash of the timing gear, measured on a camshaft gear tooth with the point of a dial indicator, should be 0.002-0.004".

Install the flywheel housing with a new seal and torque the bolts to 20-30 ft. lbs.

Install the assembled rear housing with a new gasket and torque the bolts to 7-13 ft. lbs. Install the crankshaft pulley, aligning the keyway. Pull it into place with a work bolt threaded into the center of the shaft and tightened against the pulley.

NOTE: Do *not* try to drive the pulley on with a hammer; this will damage the bearings.

Bolt the oil cooler adapter in place and torque bolts to 7-13 ft. lbs.

Install each piston assembly in its cylinder by installing a piston ring compressor and tightening it to squeeze the rings flush with the piston surface. Insert the top of the piston into the cylinder and push it all the way out of the compressor and into the cylinder.

Install each cylinder assembly in its proper location, torquing the bearing caps to 20-26 ft. lbs.

Check the connecting rod side clearance with feeler stock, as shown. This side clearance

Checking crankshaft end play

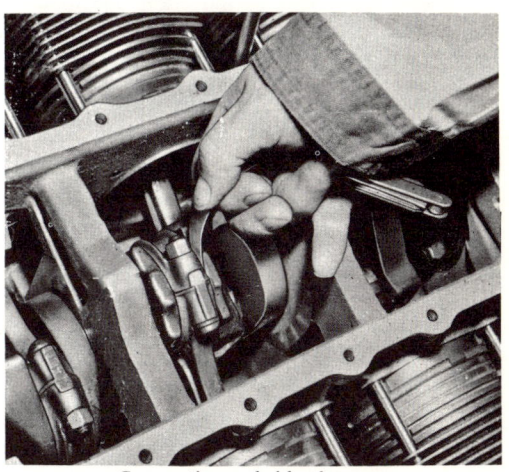

Connecting rod side clearance

Torque Specifications

YEAR	MODEL	CYLINDER HEAD BOLTS (FT. LBS.)	ROD BEARING BOLTS (FT. LBS.)	MAIN BEARING BOLTS (FT. LBS.)	CRANKSHAFT BALANCER BOLT (FT. LBS.)	FLYWHEEL TO CRANKSHAFT BOLTS (FT. LBS.)	MANIFOLD (FT. LBS.) Intake	MANIFOLD (FT. LBS.) Exhaust
1960-69	All	27-33	20-26	42-48	60-80	20-30 ①	None	12-27

①—All 1960-64 = 20-30 FT. LBS., same for 1965-69 Powerglide models.
  1965-69 Standard transmission models = 40-50 FT. LBS.

should be 0.005-0.010". Install the cylinder baffles under each cylinder.

Install each cylinder head, with new cylinder gaskets in each combustion chamber. Seat each head on its cylinder bank. Install the valve lifters, pushrod sockets facing outward, into the same crankcase bore from which they came. Install the pushrod tubes with new O-rings and tap them into place. Install the pushrod guides, then thread in the rocker studs (with the threads for the rocker arms), fingertight. Torque the cylinder head nuts and rocker arm studs to 32-38 ft. lbs. in the sequence shown.

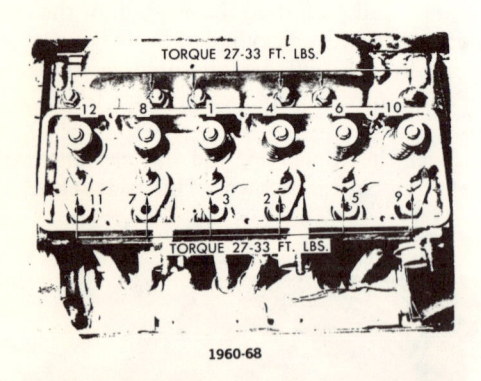

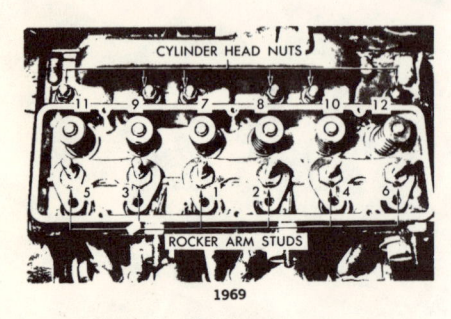

Install the pushrods, with their side oil hole on the outer end. "Feel" them in until they enter their sockets in the top of each lifter. Install the rocker arms over their studs and secure them loosely with their adjusting nuts (radiused surface inward), fingertight. Take up these adjusting nuts with a wrench until all free play is taken out of the rocker arm.

Valve Lash

Set the valve lash by this method:

1. With No. 1 cylinder on Top Dead Center (compression stroke), make the setting (see below) for the No. 1 intake, No. 1 exhaust, No. 3 intake, No. 5 exhaust, No. 4 exhaust, and No. 6 intake.

2. With the No. 2 cylinder (check for compression stroke) on T.D.C., set No. 3 exhaust, No. 5 intake, No. 2 intake and exhaust, No. 4 intake, and No. 6 exhaust.

Set the lifters with one additional clockwise turn beyond the point at which the free play of the rockers is taken up.

NOTE: Adjustment can also be made by bringing each cylinder in turn around to T.D.C. and adjusting the lifters for that cylinder alone. Check the operation of the lifters again after the engine is back in the vehicle and running (see "Valve Lash Adjustment" in Chapter Two).

Install the exhaust manifolds on the lower side of each cylinder head with a new gasket on each manifold pipe. Tap each manifold to seat it on the cylinder and clamp it in place securely.

Install the crankcase vent and cover on the top side of the crankcase, using *new* gaskets. Torque the attaching bolts evenly to 7-13 ft. lbs. Install the blower impeller on its bearing and install the upper engine shroud.

Replace the lower sheet metal shrouds and baffles; check the thermostatic damper adjustment by pulling the actuating rod to its full length and matching the link's position with the mating hole in the door, and adjust as necessary to line up the linkage.

Move the engine to TDC on the No. 1 cylinder with a wrench on the crankshaft pulley nut.

Manual Transmission Units: Bolt the flywheel housing on the back of the crankcase and torque the bolts to 20-30 ft. lbs. Bolt the flywheel on the crankshaft and torque the bolts to 40-50 ft. lbs. Install the clutch assembly as directed in Chapter Six, and assemble the engine to the transaxle.

Automatic Transmission Units: Bolt the flywheel housing on the back of the crankcase and torque the bolts to 20-30 ft. lbs. Bolt the

ENGINE

flex plate on the crankshaft and torque the bolts to 20-30 ft. lbs. Assemble the engine to the transaxle and bolt the flex plate to the torque converter through the ports in the flywheel housing.

NOTE: When rejoining the engine to the transaxle (on the ground or on the vehicle), be sure that the torque converter (automatic transmission) is correctly splined onto its shafts, or that the clutch shaft (manual transmission) is seated in the transmission and is entering the clutch disk correctly.

Lift the engine (or the engine and its transaxle) into the engine compartment and secure the mounts.

Connect the throttle and transmission linkages and connect the exhaust system. Install the distributor with the rotor pointing toward the No. 1 tower in the cap, and the points about to open.

4 • Fuel System

General

The Corvair uses one of three carburetion systems: dual single-throat carburetors, quadruple single-throat carburetors, or turbocharging with a single-throat, side-draft carburetor.

Almost annual changes and improvements were made in the carburetor systems and in the carburetors themselves. From 1960 to 1964, dual Rochester model H carburetors were used. In 1960 and 1961 the choke was located in the air cleaner assembly. Later models featured an automatic choke in the carburetor actuated by a bimetallic thermostatic coil on the cylinder head.

From 1962 to 1967, turbocharging was available, with a Carter YH carburetor installed upstream of an exhaust-driven supercharger.

From 1965 to 1969, dual Rochester HV carburetors with automatic chokes were standard, with an optional four-carburetor system consisting of a Rochester HV and a secondary Rochester H on each cylinder bank. The 1965 and 1966 units feature an additional power enrichment circuit in the main system.

NOTE: Perform carburetor adjustments only after other adjustments have been made, such as ignition timing, spark plug gap, contact point dwell, etc. As a general rule, check out the ignition before making any carburetor adjustments. When setting the idle speed for any engine, refer to the timing chart in Chapter Two.

Fuel Filter

Check the standard bronze fuel filter element in the fuel inlet and clean it in solvent. Replace it if it becomes too contaminated.

Throttle Control

Check the scope of the throttle linkage from the pedal to the cross-shaft periodically. The throttle plates in the carburetors should be wide open when the accelerator pedal is still 1″ (manual transmission) or 1½″ (automatic) from the floor. Adjust the swivel on the cross-shaft if necessary.

Carburetors

Since the Rochester H and HV carburetors are essentially the same, the removal and repair procedures are given here for the HV and the differences will be obvious from the exploded diagrams of the H and HV carburetors.

Carburetor Synchronization

Initial Adjustments

With engine off, perform the following adjustments, in sequence, with both throttle rods disconnected at the carburetor cross-shaft levers.

FUEL SYSTEM

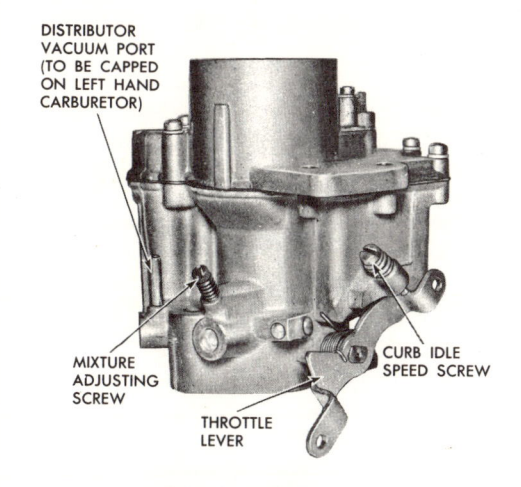

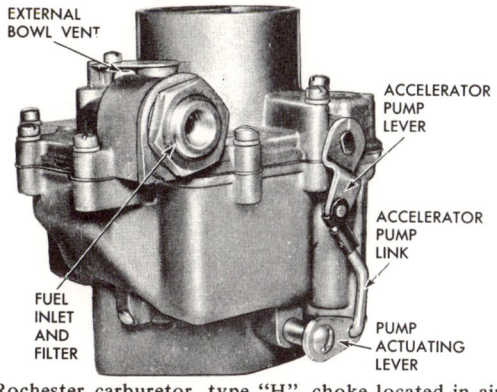

Rochester carburetor, type "H", choke located in air cleaner

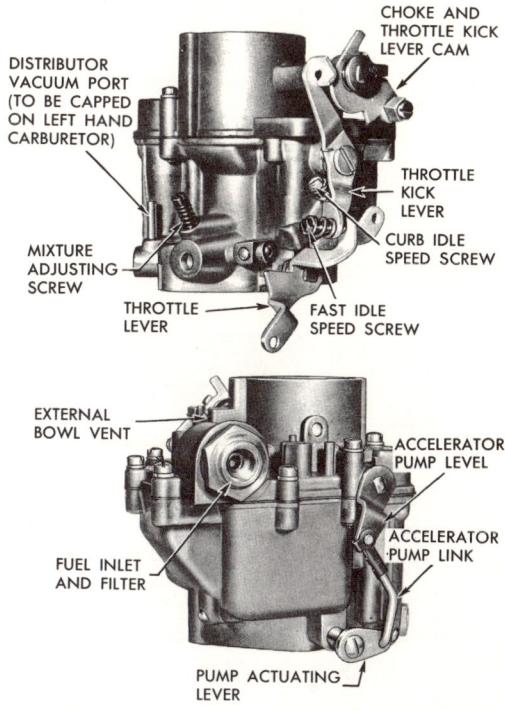

Rochester carburetor, type "H", choke located in carburetor

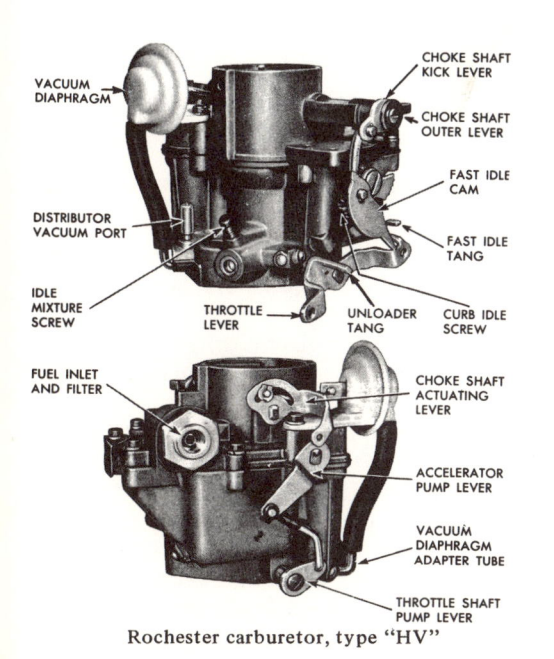

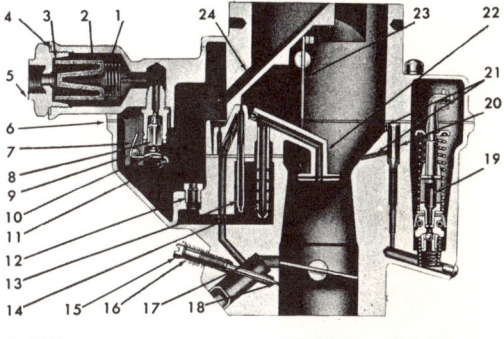

Rochester carburetor, type "HV"

1. Filter spring
2. Filter
3. Filter gasket
4. Inlet nut gasket
5. Inlet nut
6. Float seal gasket
7. Float drop adjusting tang
8. Float needle
9. Float hinge pin
10. Float level adjusting tang
11. Float hanger arm
12. Main metering jet
13. Idle tube
14. Main well tube
15. Idle mixture adjusting screw
16. Idle mixture adjusting spring
17. Secondary idle port
18. Primary idle port
19. Accelerator pump
20. Pump discharge valve
21. Pump discharge ports
22. Venturi cluster
23. Choke valve
24. Bowl internal vent

Rochester carburetor, schematic cross-section, typical

NOTE: Adjustments must be made on each carburetor.

a. Back the curb idle speed and fast idle speed adjustment screws away from carburetor throttle shaft lever.

b. Curb Idle Speed: Place a .003″ feeler gauge between the curb idle speed screw and the carburetor throttle shaft lever. Turn the screw until it just contacts the gauge, then remove the gauge and turn the screw 1½ more turns to set the throttle valve.

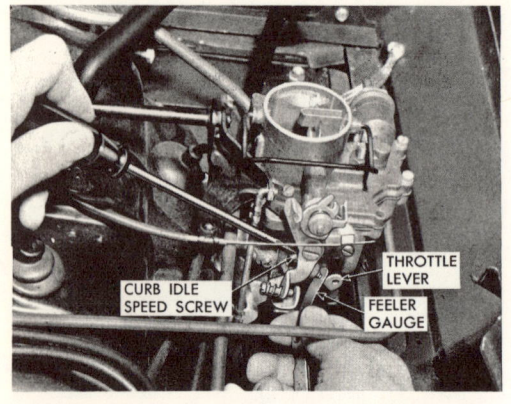

Curb idle speed screw adjustment

c. Fast Idle—1960-1961 (choke fully open): Place a feeler gauge (.010″ on automatic and .030″ on synchromesh transmission) between fast idle speed screw and pad (tang) on throttle lever and adjust the screw until it contacts (or holds) the gauge. From 1962 on there is no fast idle screw.

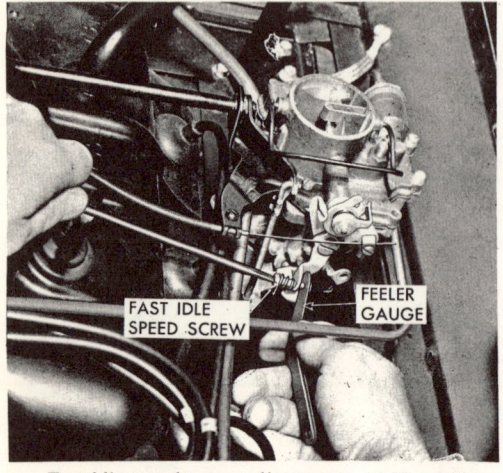

Fast idle speed screw adjustment—1960-1961

d. Turn the idle mixture screw lightly to its seat and back out 1½ turns.

CAUTION: Do not turn idle mixture screws

tighly against seats or damage to needle seat will result.

Throttle Rod Connections

a. Right Carburetor: Connect throttle rod to carburetor cross-shaft lever using retainer clip.

b. Left Carburetor: Rotate carburetor cross-shaft (with accelerator rod) to ensure positive closing of the right carburetor throttle valve. Adjust throttle rod length with the swivel until rod freely enters hole on carburetor cross-shaft lever. Secure rod with retainer clip.

NOTE: (1962-on) It may be necessary to hold the choke valve open so fast idle cam is clear of throttle lever.

NOTE: The carburetors are now mechanically matched. Any further curb idle speed screw adjustment or idle mixture must be duplicated on both carburetors.

Preliminary Curb Idle Speed and Mixture Adjustment

a. Start engine and allow to reach operating temperature.

b. Check timing.

c. Connect vacuum gauge to adapter on vacuum balance tube. Remove transmission vacuum line (automatic transmission) or cap (synchromesh) from balance tube adapter.

d. Connect tachometer to engine.

e. Adjust curb idle speed (duplicate adjustment on both carburetors) to attain approximately 500 rpm (automatic transmission in drive and synchromesh in neutral, hand brake applied). Adjust idle mixture screws on both carburetors to obtain peak steady vacuum at given idle speed.

f. Remove vacuum gauge and close adapter as required for given transmission model.

Carburetor Balance—Vacuum Check

NOTE: Ordinarily carburetors are satisfactorily synchronized at this point, and this procedure is merely a vacuum test comparing the two banks.

a. Remove choke diaphragm hose from each carburetor base adapter and connect vacuum gauge to the adapter. (Best results can be obtained using 2 equally calibrated gauges.)

CAUTION: Do not turn tubing in carburetor body.

NOTE: One gauge can be used by constructing a "T" line to both carburetors from the gauge. Pinch hose closed between gauge and one carburetor and read vacuum of opposite carburetor.

FUEL SYSTEM

b. Operate engine at idle speed. Check vacuum at each carburetor and note difference. If difference is one inch or less, the carburetors are satisfactorily synchronized. If difference is more than one inch, adjust left carburetor throttle rod one turn (up to increase left carburetor vacuum and down to decrease) and recheck vacuum readings. Make the adjustment by disconnecting rod at cross-shaft and rotating it in the swivel.

Hose setup for attaching vacuum gauge. And turnbuckle, for positioning throttle linkage

NOTE: It is preferable to have higher reading on right carburetor (spark advance side).

CAUTION: When making linkage adjustments, move the cross-shaft by grasping accelerator rod only. Do not open throttle by grasping other portions of linkage as this might upset geometry and synchronization.

c. Remove gauge/or gauges and replace choke diaphragm hoses.

Final Curb Idle Speed and Mixture Adjustment Check

NOTE: Always make final idle speed mixture adjustment with air cleaners installed.

a. Replace air cleaners.
b. Reconnect vacuum gauge to vacuum balance tube adapter.
c. Read vacuum at idle speed. If necessary, adjust curb idle speed and mixture screws to highest steady vacuum reading between 14-18 inches.

CAUTION: Any necessary adjustment must be duplicated at each carburetor. Do not turn idle mixture screws tightly against stop or damage to needle seat will result.

Recheck Fast Idle Setting—1960-1961

This setting depends upon final curb idle 500 rpm setting.

Fast Idle Cam Clearance—1962-On

NOTE: This adjustment must be made after curb idle speed has been set on the car.
Stop engine.
With throttle lever on second highest step of fast idle cam, bend tang to obtain .078" clearance between idle speed screw and throttle lever.
Start engine and recheck speed as above.

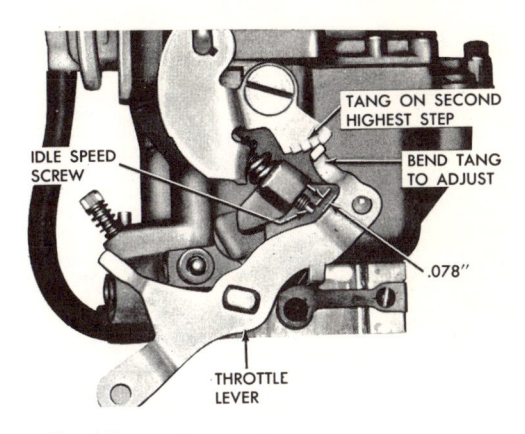

Fast idle speed tang adjustment—1962 and on

Choke Adjustment—1960-1961

1. With the slide ¼" from the rear of the mounting bracket and choke knob on dashboard out approximately 1/8", tighten the slide screw onto main choke cable wire.
2. Assemble cable and housing assemblies loose at both carburetor mounting brackets. Extend cable housing approximately ¼" beyond mounting bracket clamp and tighten clamp at each carburetor.
3. With slide approximately ¼" from rear of mounting bracket slot, tighten swivel at each choke lever and throttle kick cam when choke valve is fully open. Cut the cable wire so about ¼" extends past the swivel. Do not bend cable wire.
CAUTION: Hold swivel with a wrench, when tightening screw, to avoid kinking the choke cable wire.
4. Pull choke knob to check for proper operation.
a. Choke valve should just begin to move when pull knob is approximately 3/8" to 1/2" out.
NOTE: During the first 3/8" to 1/2" choke

FUEL SYSTEM

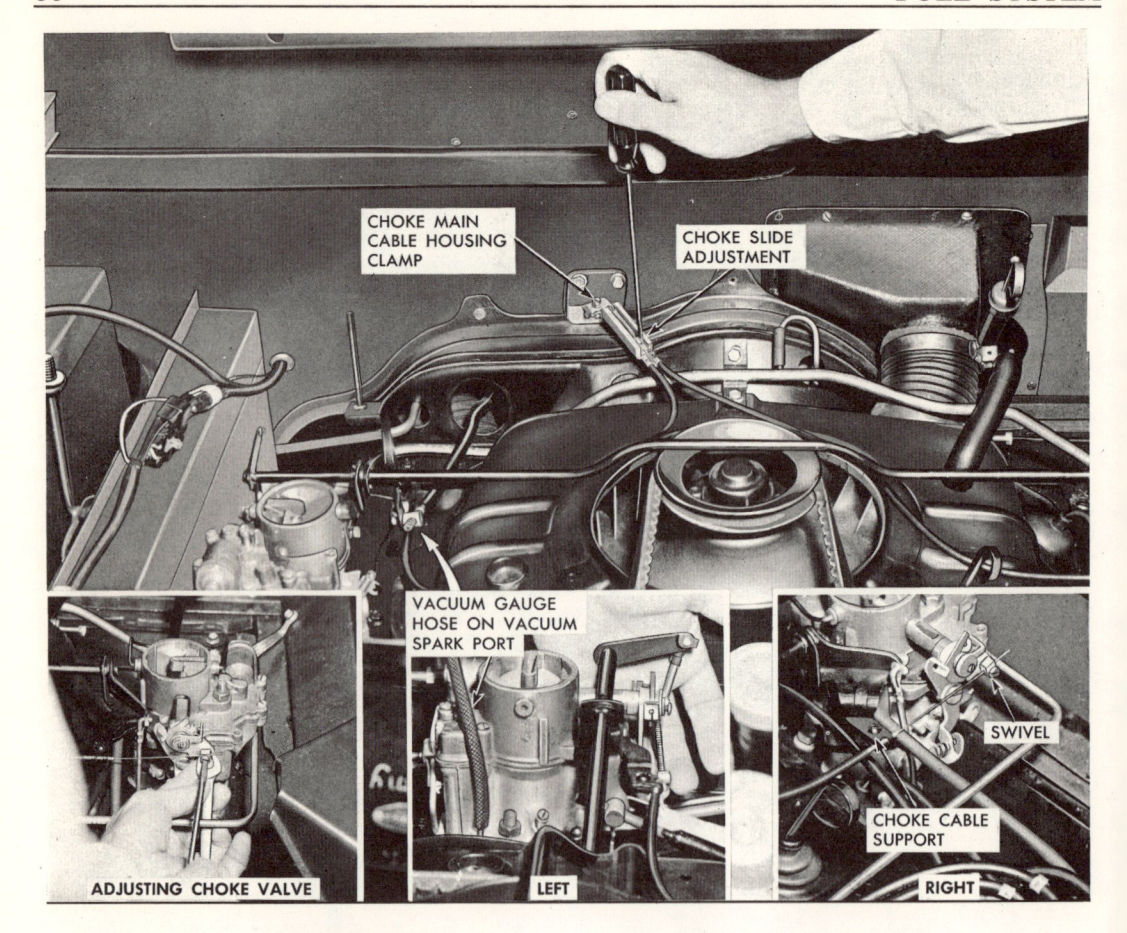

1. Inlet nut
2. Fuel filter gasket
3. Inlet nut gasket
4. Fuel filter element
5. Fuel filter spring
6. Accelerator pump lever and shaft
7. Bowl cover
8. Clip
9. Accelerator pump
10. Float pin
11. Bowl cover gasket
12. Needle seat gasket
13. Needle seat
14. Needle
15. Float assembly
16. Fast idle rod
17. Choke shaft lever screw
18. Choke shaft outer lever
19. Choke shaft kick lever
20. Vacuum diaphragm
21. Retainer screws
22. Choke valve
23. Choke shaft and lever assembly
24. Diaphragm link

Choke linkage

knob travel, the fast idle cam raises idle speed without moving the choke valve.

b. Pull knob full out and choke valve should be closed.

Automatic Choke Adjustment—1962-On

Perform adjustment with engine off.

1. Disconnect choke control rod at choke shaft lever.
2. Hold choke valve closed and, while holding the control rod up against the stop in the choke thermostat bracket, adjust the upper choke control rod until it freely enters the hole in the choke shaft lever.

CAUTION: To minimize the possibility of deforming the control rod while adjusting, always turn the vertical portion. Do not "crank" the rod using offset portion.

3. Start engine and warm up—check the choke position after warm up. Choke valve should be open and fast idle cam should clear the throttle lever.

Unloader Adjustment

Check unloader adjustment by holding the throttle valve in wide open position and insert a 0.250" (0.312" for 1964 and later Corvairs) wire gauge between the choke valve lower edge

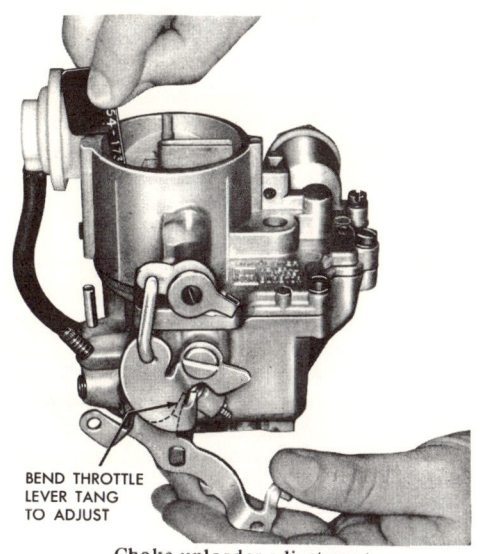

FUEL SYSTEM

Choke unloader adjustment

Carburetor Disassembly

When poor performance, malfunction, or visible contamination is evident, remove the carburetors and disassemble them for cleaning and inspection.

Unscrew and remove the mounting nuts at each carburetor flange, after removing the air cleaner and disconnecting the linkages and fuel lines.

CAUTION: Plug the fuel lines after removal and do not spill gas into the engine shrouds.

Remove the carburetors and disassemble them separately; disconnect the accelerator pump linkage and vacuum hose and unscrew and remove the bowl cover. Remove the floats carefully from the cover by moving the hinge pin to one side. Lift the float needle from its seat. The seat may be unscrewed and removed if desired.

and the wall of the air horn. To adjust, if necessary, bend tang on throttle lever.

NOTE: Unloader adjustment should be checked especially if it has been necessary to adjust the choke shaft outer lever tang during choke diaphragm link check.

Pump Rod Adjustment

1. Back off idle screw until throttle valve is completely closed.
2. Holding throttle valves closed, check to see that the scribe mark on the accelerator pump lever is aligned with the mark cast into the bowl cover.
3. The accelerator pump rod may be carefully bent, using a carburetor rod bending tool, to obtain the correct adjustment if necessary.
4. Synchronize and adjust carburetors.

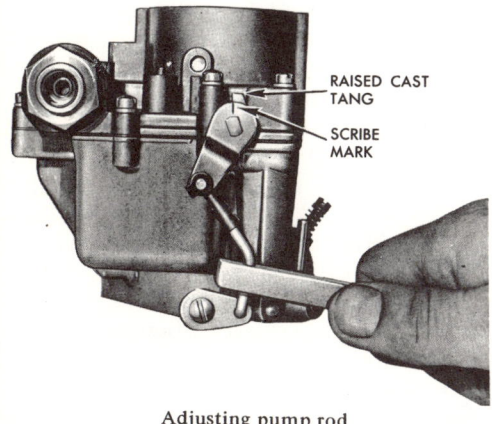

Float needle removal

Unscrew and remove the venturi cluster, being careful not to lose or damage the power enrichment needle underneath (1965-1966).

Remove the idle mixture needle and main metering jet. Pull out the pump discharge valve.

The Rochester H and HV carburetors are shown fully disassembled. The linkages usually may be left intact; do not disturb the throttle and choke valves unless they are obviously damaged or distorted.

Clean all parts in clean carburetor solvent and remove as much surface varnish and dirt as possible. Do not immerse the accelerator pump piston in solvent; it is leather and will be damaged by the solvent.

Wipe the float bowl clean and blow air through all jets and metering ports to be sure they are clear. Check the idle mixture needle for grooves or scars on its point.

Float Drop

Assemble the float valve and floats to the bowl cover and check the float drop as shown.

Adjusting pump rod

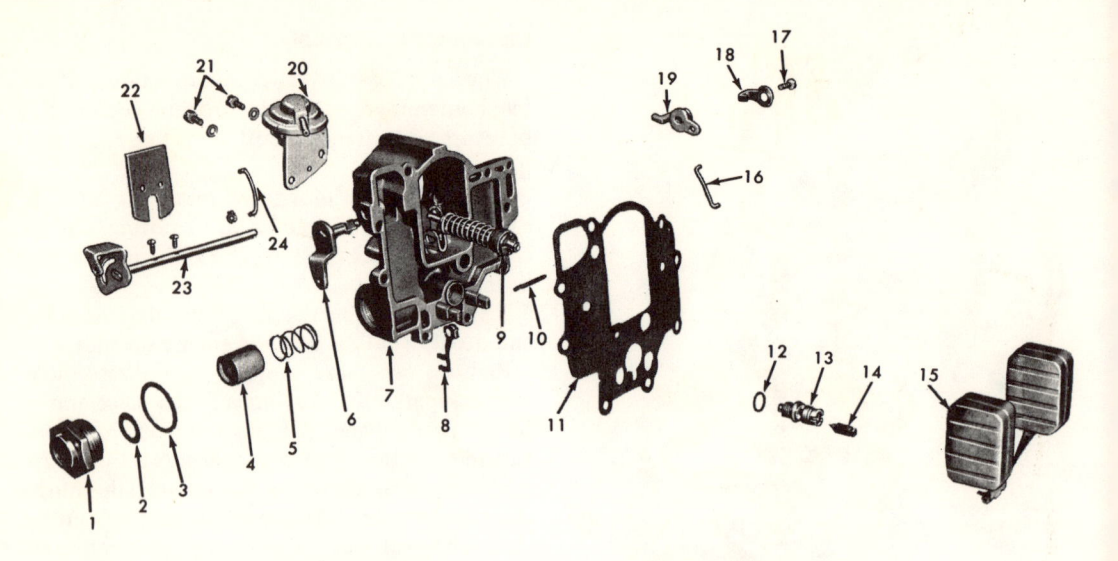

1 Inlet nut	13 Needle seat
2 Fuel filter gasket	14 Needle
3 Inlet nut gasket	15 Float assembly
4 Fuel filter element	16 Fast idle rod
5 Fuel filter spring	17 Choke shaft lever screw
6 Accelerator pump lever and shaft	18 Choke shaft outer lever
7 Clip	19 Choke shaft kick lever
8 Bowl cover	20 Vacuum diaphragm
9 Accelerator pump	21 Retainer screws
10 Float pin	22 Choke valve
11 Bowl cover gasket	23 Choke shaft and lever assembly
12 Needle seat gasket	24 Diaphragm link

Bowl cover, exploded view, typical

Bend the hinge tang to obtain the 1½″ (1 3/4″ in 1964 and earlier Corvairs) distance; invert the bowl cover (floats facing upward) and check that the floats "bottom" when they are parallel to the cover flange.

NOTE: An additional check for the floats and float valve can be made by blowing air into the fuel inlet with the cover right side up, then moving the floats up by hand. The flow of air should be cut off when the floats are parallel with the cover flange.

Assemble the carburetor, making sure that all jets and metering ports are clear; install the venturi cluster with a new or serviceable gasket. Install the pump discharge needle and the power enrichment needle.

Before installing the bowl cover on the float bowl, half fill the bowl with clean gasoline. Install the bowl cover and floats with a new or serviceable gasket, inserting the accelerator pump piston into its bore. When all linkages are connected, actuate the pump linkage and check for proper pump action: the pump should spray gasoline from the venturi cluster and there should be no leaks at any of the carburetor body or venturi mating flanges.

Install the idle mixture needle and adjust it 1½ turns out of its seat.

Connect the linkage and vacuum line between the carburetor body and the diaphragm of the choke.

Preset the fast idle screw clearance as directed in the section on synchronization. Hold the vacuum diaphragm arm against the diaphragm and check for a 0.180-0.195″ clearance between the choke valve and the wall of the carburetor throat. Adjust the diaphragm arm if necessary.

Check the vapor vent valve as shown, by moving the fast idle lever to its highest step; the vent should start to move at this point.

Install the carburetors on the engine and connect the linkages and fuel lines. Synchronize the carburetors as directed above.

NOTE: Be sure the carburetors are bolted tightly to the intake manifolds; minor air leaks at the attaching flanges will cause erratic fuel mixture during engine operation.

Rochester HV and H (Four-Carburetor Arrangement)

From 1965 on, the Corvair was offered with an optional four-carburetor arrangement. This

FUEL SYSTEM

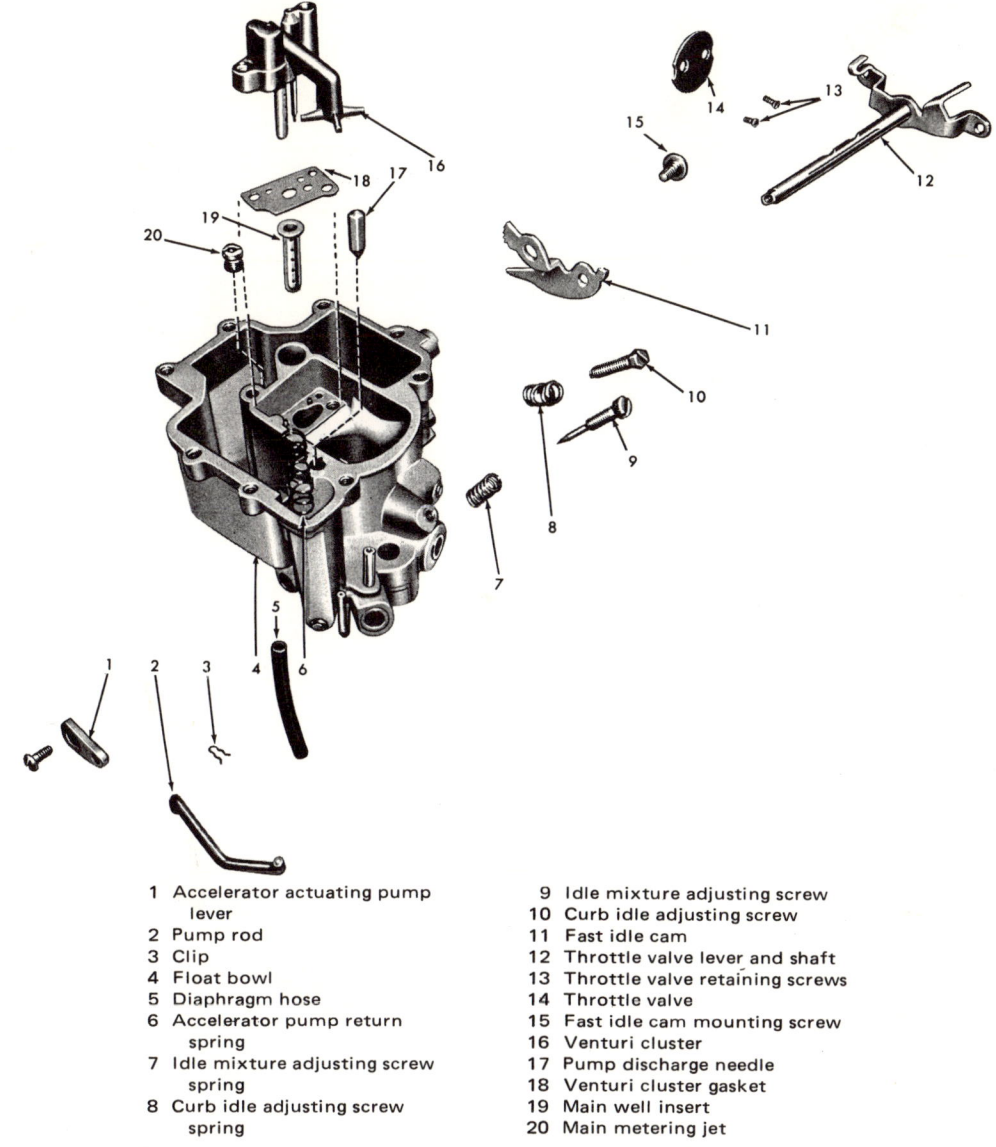

1. Accelerator actuating pump lever
2. Pump rod
3. Clip
4. Float bowl
5. Diaphragm hose
6. Accelerator pump return spring
7. Idle mixture adjusting screw spring
8. Curb idle adjusting screw spring
9. Idle mixture adjusting screw
10. Curb idle adjusting screw
11. Fast idle cam
12. Throttle valve lever and shaft
13. Throttle valve retaining screws
14. Throttle valve
15. Fast idle cam mounting screw
16. Venturi cluster
17. Pump discharge needle
18. Venturi cluster gasket
19. Main well insert
20. Main metering jet

Rochester carburetor, type "H", exploded view of body

arrangement consists of a primary Rochester HV and a secondary Rochester H carburetor on each cylinder bank. The secondary carburetor is on a mechanical linkage from the primary carburetor and operates at the advanced throttle position of the primary carburetor.

In mid-1965 a lockout linkage was added to the secondary carburetor to keep it from operating before the engine had warmed up; this linkage is actuated by the opening of the automatic choke valve on the primary carburetor, so that the secondary carburetor is free to operate when the choke is open.

Adjustment and Maintenance

The quadruple carburetors are surprisingly simple to maintain and synchronize, largely because of the simplicity of the secondary carburetor. This secondary carburetor on each cylinder bank has no slow or fast idle setting, no choke, and no extra power circuits. This carburetor is little more than an augmenting main metering system which operates at an advanced power level as signaled by the primary carburetor. It requires no adjustment except for the accelerator pump, float system, and lockout linkage.

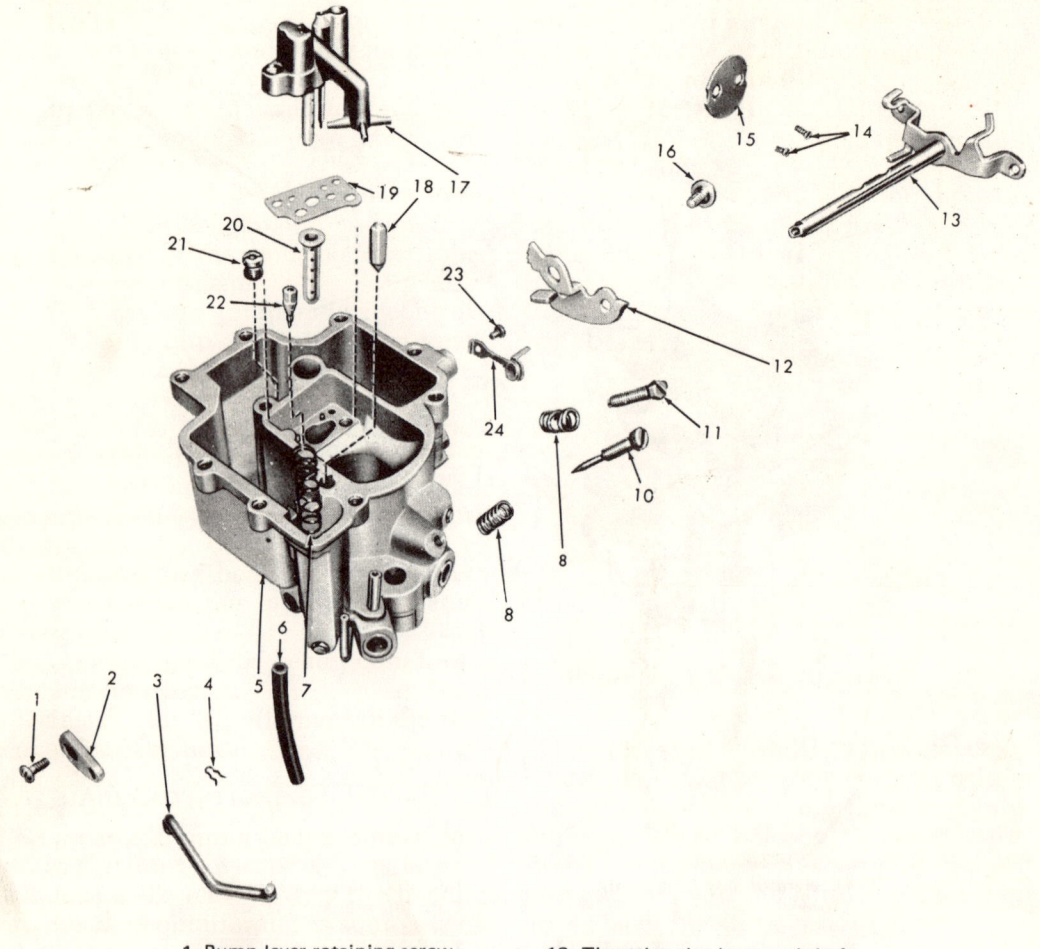

1 Pump lever retaining screw	13 Throttle valve lever and shaft
2 Accelerator actuating pump lever	14 Throttle valve retaining screws
3 Pump rod	15 Throttle valve
4 Clip	16 Fast idle cam mounting screw
5 Float bowl	17 Venturi cluster
6 Diaphragm hose	18 Pump discharge needle
7 Accelerator pump return spring	19 Venturi cluster gasket
8 Adjusting screw springs	20 Main well insert
10 Idle mixture adjusting screw	21 Main metering jet
11 Curb idle adjusting screw	22 Power enrichment needle
12 Fast idle cam	23 Vapor vent retaining screw
	24 Vapor vent valve

Rochester carburetor, type "HV", exploded view of body

Synchronization

Synchronize the primary carburetors as directed for the dual-arrangement Rochester HV. Disconnect the throttle rods from the cross-shaft to the secondary carburetors to prevent confusing engine response at higher engine speed, and synchronize the primary carburetors alone.

After the primary carburetors have been satisfactorily synchronized, check that the cold-engine lockout linkage (found on most four-carburetor installations) is correctly aligned. As shown, hold the primary's choke valve fully-open with the fingers, check for 0.160" between the lockout lever and the throttle lever on the secondary. Holding this dimension, adjust the *trip lever* by bending it until it just touches the primary's choke lever.

Adjust the secondary linkage by closing the primary carburetor's choke valve with the fingers (thus locking out the secondary throttles, if the lockout device is present). Pull the pri-

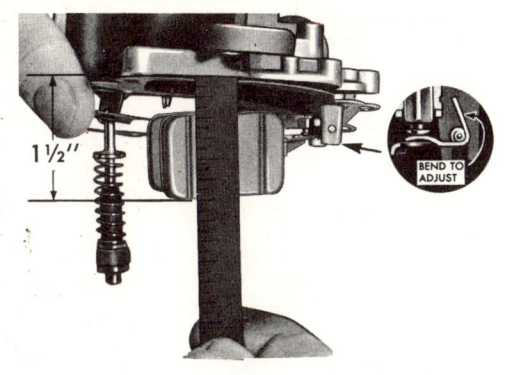

FUEL SYSTEM

Measuring float drop

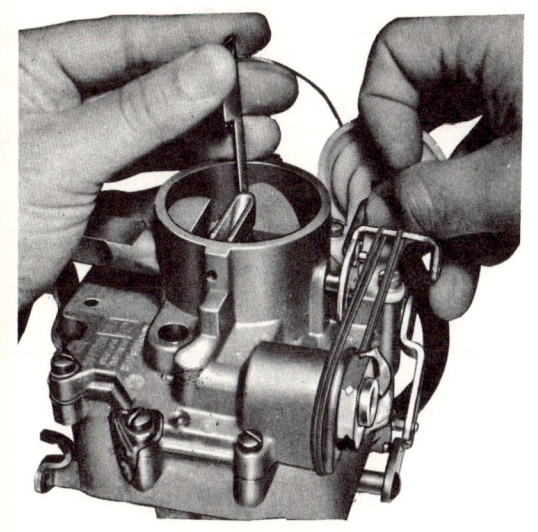

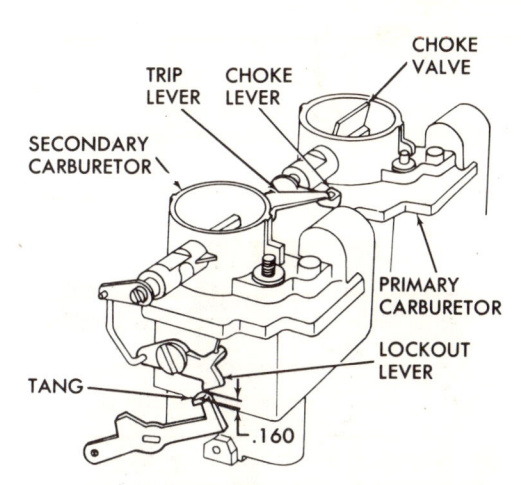

Checking alignment of cold-engine lockout linkage

Vacuum diaphragm adjustment

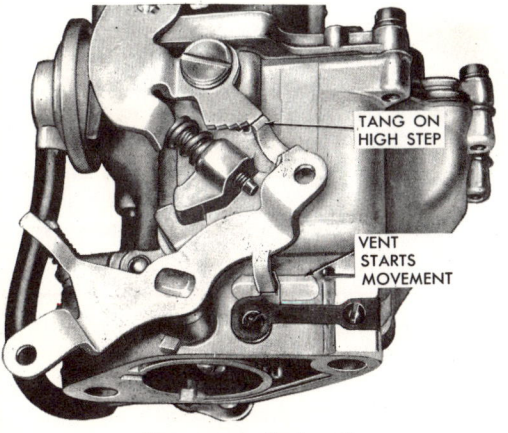

Vapor vent adjustment

mary throttle position to fully-open, then adjust the secondary carburetor actuating rod, compressing the spring, until it just enters its proper hole in the cross-shaft lever. From this setting, lengthen the rod 2-3 turns on the swivel and install the swivel in the cross-shaft lever.

NOTE: On units without the lockout device, adjust the secondary actuating rod so that at full secondary throttle position, it just enters its cross-shaft lever when the primary carburetor (connected to its cross-shaft lever) is at its full-throttle position.

Check the adjustment, first with the primary choke closed: close the primary choke valve and pull the cross-shaft to full throttle with the accelerator lever; the primary carburetor should be at full throttle but the secondary should be locked out (choke closed). Check again with the primary choke open: with the choke open (held open, if necessary), pull the linkage to full throttle; both primary and secondary carburetors should be wide open.

Rochester H (Secondary) Overhaul

The Rochester H secondary carburetor contains only an accelerator pump and a main power system as illustrated. This carburetor should be taken apart and checked whenever the primary carburetors are overhauled, or when poor high-speed performance indicates that the secondary system is not operating properly.

Disassembly

Unscrew the attaching nuts and remove each carburetor after the air cleaners and linkages have been disconnected.

Unscrew and remove the bowl cover and carefully remove the float assembly by moving the hinge pin to one side. Lift out the float needle and unscrew the seat.

Unscrew and remove the venturi cluster and

main metering jet. The Rochester H carburetor body is shown fully disassembled. It is unnecessary to remove the throttle valve or linkage parts unless they are obviously damaged or distorted.

Clean all parts in clean carburetor solvent, with the exception of the accelerator pump piston, which is leather and could be damaged by the solvent.

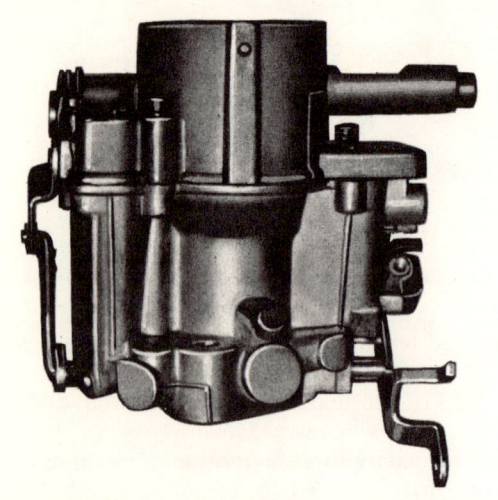

Wipe the float bowl clean and blow air through the jet and metering ports to make sure they are clear.

Assemble the float valve and floats as previously shown on the bowl cover and check for float drop in the Synchronization Section. Bend the hinge tang to obtain 1½" distance. Invert the cover, floats facing upward, and check that the floats "bottom" when they are parallel to the cover flange.

NOTE: An additional check for the float valve and floats can be made by blowing air into the fuel inlet with the cover right side up, then moving the floats up by hand. The flow of air should be cut off when the floats are parallel with the cover flange.

Assemble the carburetor body, making sure that the jet is clear and that the bowl cover and carburetor mating surfaces are in good condition. The carburetor body and venturi cluster gaskets should be in good condition (not hardened or distorted), or new. Half fill the float bowl with clean gasoline before installing the cover; when the cover is in place and the linkages are in place, actuate the pump and check to be sure that it sprays gasoline through the venturi cluster and that there is no leakage to the outside of the carburetor body or venturi

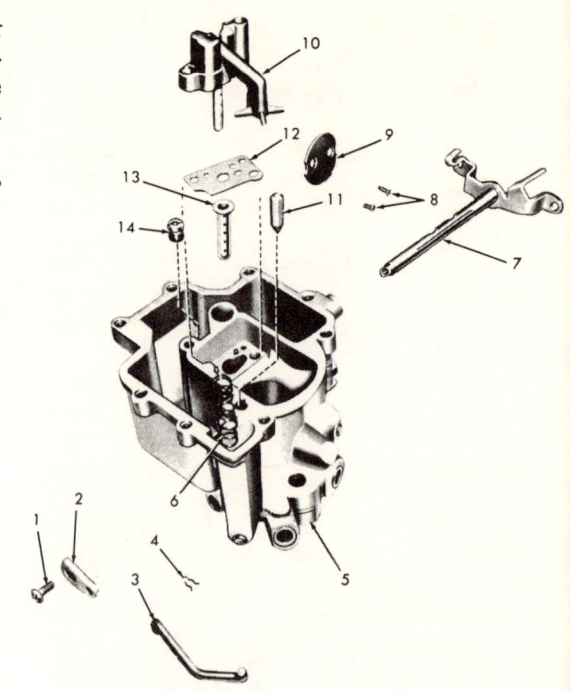

Rochester carburetor, type "H"—1965-1969

1. Pump lever retaining screw
2. Accelerator actuating pump lever
3. Pump rod
4. Clip
5. Float bowl
6. Accelerator pump return spring
7. Throttle valve lever and shaft
8. Throttle valve retaining screws
9. Throttle valve
10. Venturi cluster
11. Pump discharge needle
12. Venturi cluster gasket
13. Main well insert
14. Main metering jet

Rochester carburetor, type "H"—1965-1969, exploded view

cluster. Check the pump link rod as shown in the Synchronization Section, with the throttle valve fully closed; at this position the scribe mark on the lever should align with the raised casting portion on the upper carburetor body.

Install the carburetors on the engine and adjust them to the primary carburetors as described in this section.

NOTE: Be sure the carburetors are tightened securely to the intake manifolds; minor air leaks at this mating surface can cause erratic fuel mixture at high speed.

Turbocharged Corvair

Description

From 1962 to 1965 turbocharging was available on the Corvair. An exhaust-driven supercharger is mounted downstream of a side-draft

FUEL SYSTEM

carburetor, supplying pressurized fuel mixture to the cylinders at high speed.

Supercharging is the principle of supplying fuel mixture to the cylinders at a positive pressure, rather than at a vacuum as in "aspirated" engines. The Corvair unit is an exhaust turbocharger, a supercharger driven by exhaust gas pressure ducted against a turbine wheel; the compressor, linked directly to the turbine wheel, speeds up to match the needs of an accelerating engine because of the increased gas pressure generated.

The turbocharged Corvair is "aspirated" (suction-fed) at low speed and supercharged (pressure fed) at high speeds. The basic engine is of a lower compression ratio than the other Corvair engines because the supercharging principle moves more fuel mixture into the cylinders than could ever be sucked in by the pistons of a higher-compression engine. For this reason, the turbocharger must never be used with any engine other than the one for which it was designed, or cylinder detonation would certainly result.

Adjustment

The turbocharger system utilizes a single, side-draft carburetor, so that carburetor adjustments are simpler than in other Corvairs. Adjust the carburetor by the same principles as for other units, that is, set throttle position, mixture, and idle, as follows:

Remove the air cleaner. Disconnect the accelerator rod swivel from the cross-shaft and obtain Angle X of approximately 126 degrees as shown. Adjust the throttle rod as necessary to obtain this. Pull the accelerator rod all the way out and move the throttle (carburetor) linkage to the full-throttle position (against the stop on the carburetor flange), and adjust the rod swivel at this setting. Move the assembled linkage from idle to full-throttle several times to be sure that the full range can be reached without binding.

Adjust the idle screw so that the throttle is barely open with the throttle lever at its stop. Adjust the idle mixture screw 3/4 turn out from its seat.

Connect a tachometer and vacuum gauge (to the distributor "pressure retard" line fitting) and run the engine at idle (850 rpm) until it is fully warmed up. Be sure the automatic choke is fully open. Adjust the idle screw if necessary to obtain a steady 850 rpm idle, then thread the idle mixture screw out, then in until the highest vacuum is registered on the gauge.

On units equipped with a throttle return check valve (illustrated) adjust this valve while

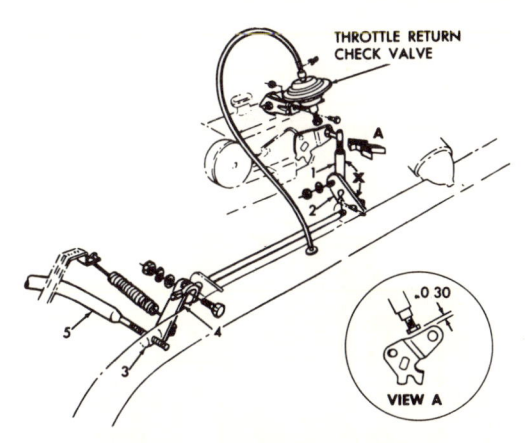

Throttle linkage—turbocharged Corvair

the engine is idling; measure the clearance shown in the figure and adjust it to 0.030" if necessary by slacking off the locknut and threading the shaft in or out.

Carter YH Carburetor Overhaul

Remove the air cleaner, choke heat tube, fuel line, and accelerator linkage. Unscrew the mounting nuts and remove the carburetor from the turbocharger flange.

NOTE: The entire carburetor and turbocharger assembly can be removed as a unit if rebuilding the turbocharger is also intended.

Remove the inlet screen and float bowl cover; remove the float pin to release the float and remove it with the float needle and seat. Remove the metering rod arm assembly and the entire pump housing group, as shown. Remove the choke linkage and choke housing cover; remove the throttle body and idle metering screw.

NOTE: The Carter YH carburetor is shown fully disassembled. Parts other than those described above may be removed if desired; the choke piston and throttle plate should not be disturbed unless they are damaged or distorted, or if the throttle plate shaft has excessive clearance with the throttle body.

Clean all parts in clean carburetor solvent and remove as much contamination as possible. Clean the accelerator pump and choke coil housing in gasoline only; they contain materials which could be damaged by solvent.

Inspect the choke piston by working it back and forth to check for free movement. Remove it only if absolutely necessary, by drilling out the welsh plug at the end of the cylinder. A new plug must be pressed in place after the piston has been replaced.

Check all jets and metering ports to be sure

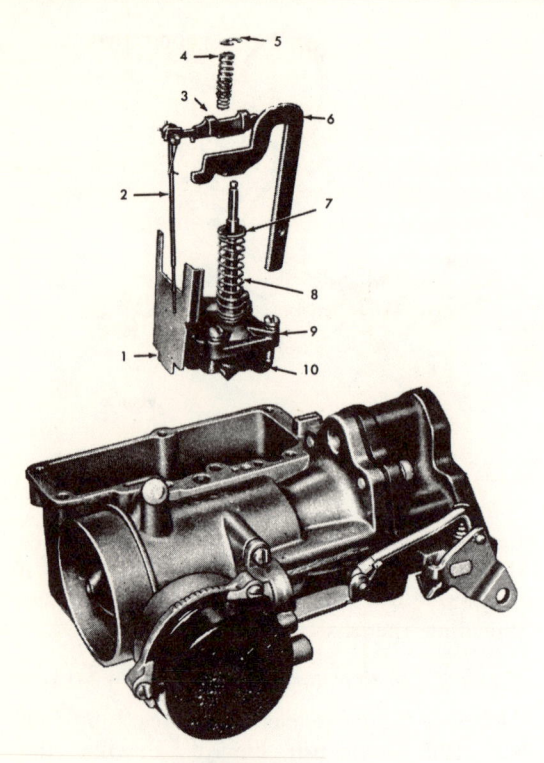

FUEL SYSTEM

valve and the bore of the throttle body (opposite the idle port) when the choke and throttle are closed and the fast idle link is on the high step of the cam. Adjust by bending the fast idle link.

Check the unloader adjustment with the throttle held wide open; at this setting, with the choke plate held gently in the closed direction, there should be 7/16" between the choke plate and the carburetor throat opposite the vent tube.

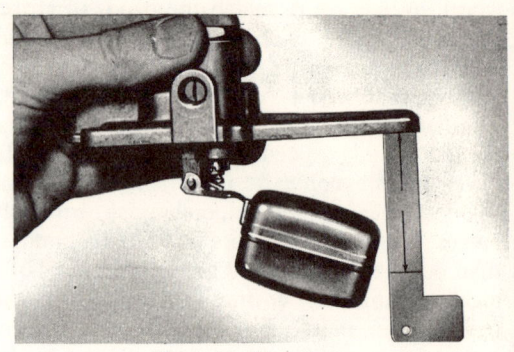

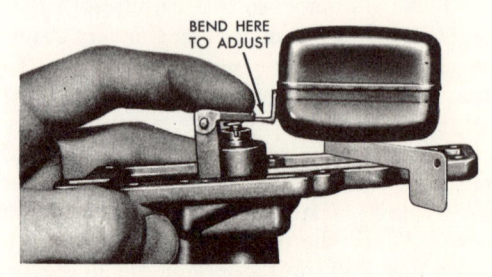

1 Splash shield
2 Metering rod
3 Metering rod arm
4 Upper springs
5 Upper spring seat
6 Pump link
7 Lower spring seat
8 Lower spring
9 Pump housing
10 Diaphragm assembly

Pump and metering rod assembly

Measuring float drop

Adjusting float level

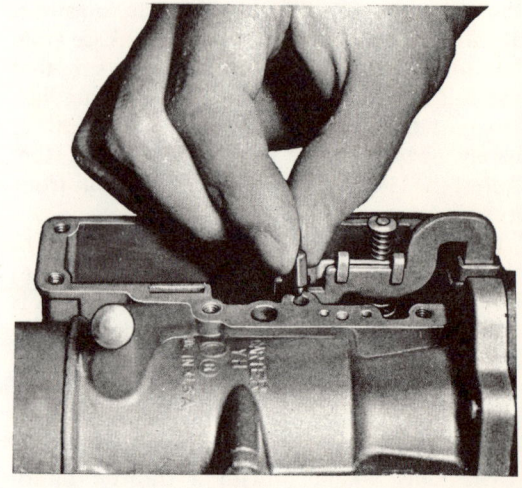

Installing pump discharge needle

they are clear. Inspect the needles and seats for smoothness.

Wipe the float bowl clean and check the float for leaks or dents. Install the float, with the needle and seat assembly, to the bowl cover. Check the float drop as shown; this drop dimension should be 2 3/8" (± 1/16"). To correct, bend the hinge end of the lever. Invert the bowl cover and check float level (5/8") as shown, using a scale or spacer to make the check. Blow air into the fuel inlet and move the float up and down to check the needle valve action.

Install the pump discharge needle; install the pump assembly and half fill the float bowl with clean gasoline. Install the bowl cover with a new or serviceable gasket. Install the throttle body and assemble the choke as shown. Assemble the fast idle linkage and choke link. The fast idle is correctly adjusted when a 0.030" gauge will just go between the throttle

FUEL SYSTEM

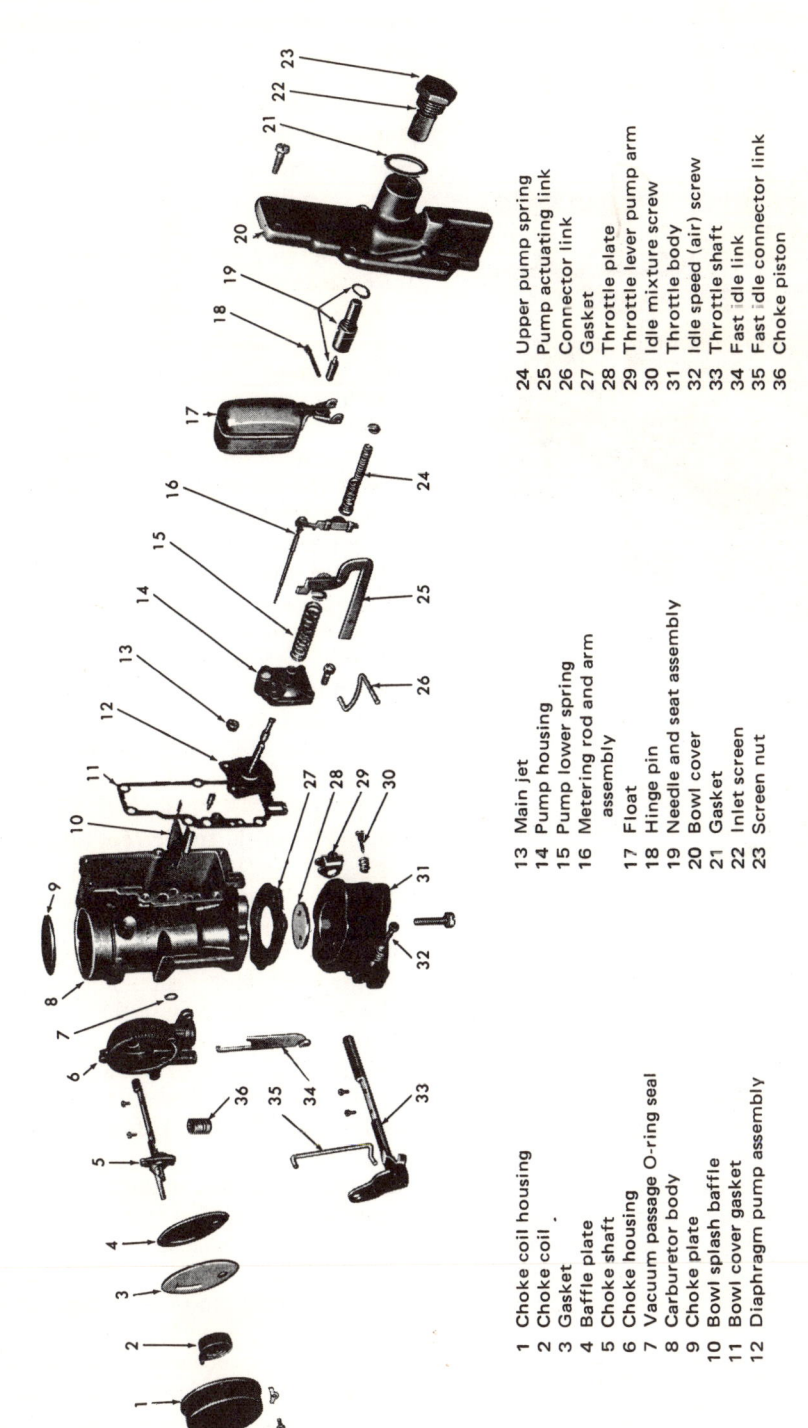

1 Choke coil housing
2 Choke coil
3 Gasket
4 Baffle plate
5 Choke shaft
6 Choke housing
7 Vacuum passage O-ring seal
8 Carburetor body
9 Choke plate
10 Bowl splash baffle
11 Bowl cover gasket
12 Diaphragm pump assembly
13 Main jet
14 Pump housing
15 Pump lower spring
16 Metering rod and arm assembly
17 Float
18 Hinge pin
19 Needle and seat assembly
20 Bowl cover
21 Gasket
22 Inlet screen
23 Screen nut
24 Upper pump spring
25 Pump actuating link
26 Connector link
27 Gasket
28 Throttle plate
29 Throttle lever pump arm
30 Idle mixture screw
31 Throttle body
32 Idle speed (air) screw
33 Throttle shaft
34 Fast idle link
35 Fast idle connector link
36 Choke piston

Carter carburetor, type "YH", exploded view

Install the choke baffle, gasket, and housing. Adjust the housing index marks according to specifications.

Install the idle mixture screw *gently* against its seat and back it out 3/4 turn.

Install the carburetor on the turbocharger and connect the choke heat tubes, fuel line, and air cleaner.

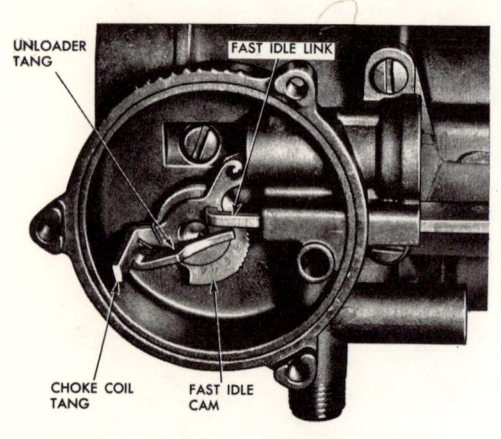

Choke housing and fast idle linkage

Adjust the linkage and idle as directed above.

Fuel Filter

The turbocharged engine uses a remote fuel filter, mounted on the air cleaner support bracket, in the fuel line which should be checked periodically and replaced when necessary.

Turbocharger

The Corvair turbocharger is a centrifugal-impeller air compressor driven by a turbine wheel. This unit is driven by exhaust gas pressure and must rotate very freely to respond to the engine's needs quickly and accurately. For this reason the rotating elements are balanced and lubricated with engine oil piped from the oil filter adapter on the engine.

The compressor impeller vanes are susceptible to foreign object damage, so make an extra effort to keep the air cleaner in good condition and to cover the turbocharger opening when the carburetor is removed.

While the turbocharger is in place on the engine, start the engine and listen for noise from the turbocharger at various engine speeds. Check for vibration or noise with a stethoscope or listening rod to pinpoint the location before removing the unit and overhauling it.

NOTE: The turbocharger's lubrication system can be checked before disassembly by starting the engine with the drain line disconnected at the turbocharger side and a hose connected from the outlet to a container to catch the oil. Oil flow from the drain should be approximately one quart per minute at idle.

Removal and Disassembly

Remove the air cleaner and carburetor and overhaul the carburetor as directed in this section. Disconnect the oil tubes to and from the turbocharger. Unclamp and remove the turbocharger leaving the turbine housing in place on the engine.

When the turbocharger is off the engine, inspect the turbine side for damage or contamination. If there are cracked or broken vanes or carbon contamination disassemble further and repair.

Check the rotor for free movement; the compressor and turbine wheels should rotate freely when the shield is compressed against the spring ring to release the turbine wheel.

Remove the compressor housing and check the condition of the compressor impeller. Check the turbine shaft end play with a dial indicator, resting the indicator point on the impeller nut. Rest the assembly squarely on the hub of the turbine wheel. Then push down on the housing and record the indicator reading. Release pressure on the housing and repeat the operation at least once to check the measurement. (The shield spring ring acts to return the wheel and shaft opposite the pressure on the housing; it is not necessary to hold the shield away from the turbine wheel.) The allowable end play is 0.005-0.008″. If end play is excessive, the supercharger should be rebuilt.

Check the radial play of the shaft by supporting the outer housing and moving the shaft from side to side. Measure the play at one point and at another 90° from it to get a representative reading; 0.022″ maximum radial play is acceptable.

If necessary, disassemble the turbocharger further by unscrewing the impeller nut *clockwise* (left-hand thread), as shown. Protect the hand from the turbine vanes with a cloth as shown; *do not* attempt to clamp the turbine in a vise, or the vanes will be damaged.

The impeller has a press fit with the turbine shaft and must be pressed out with an arbor press, using suitable supports and protectors for all parts. Do not allow the turbine wheel to be damaged when it drops free at the bottom side. Lift out the impeller wheel and any shims, and remove the shaft sleeve. Remove the turbine shield and spring ring from the turbine side.

FUEL SYSTEM

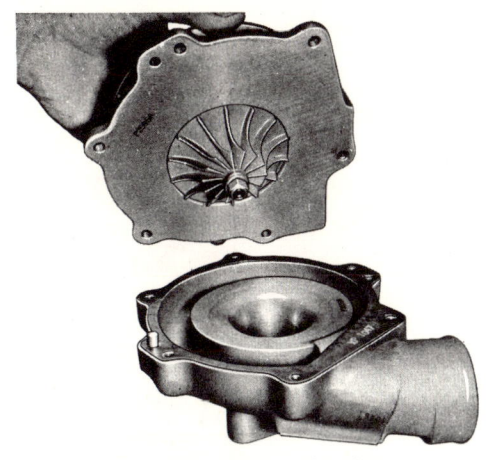

Removing compressor housing

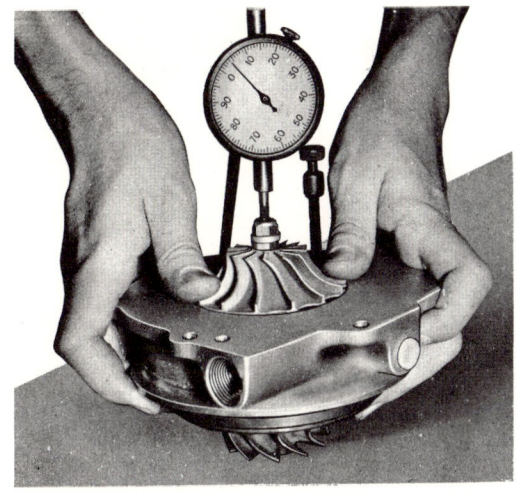

Gauging turbine shaft end play

The turbocharger is shown fully disassembled. If the housing shows signs of oil leakage (on the impeller or housing surfaces), or if the bearing or shaft seems worn or damaged, remove the oil seal retaining ring and pull out the seal. Remove the bearing retaining ring and push out the bearing and its shim.

Clean all parts thoroughly in solvent to remove carbon, oil sludge, and gasoline varnish. Inspect the compressor and turbine wheels for nicks or dents in the vanes. It is permissible to blend out small nicks in the vane surfaces with a fine-cut file or stone.

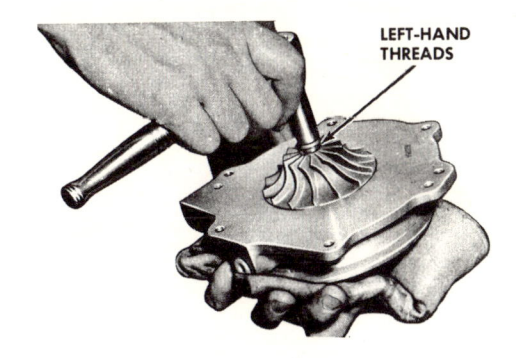

LEFT-HAND THREADS

Removing impeller nut

Check the turbine and compressor housings for signs of vane rubbing; repair light damage by smoothing it with fine emery cloth and check the shaft and bearings for condition and end play as described below.

Make the following clearance checks prior to assembling the turbocharger:

Install the bearing, mating ring, and shaft sleeve on the turbine shaft and measure the clearance between the bearing and the shaft while holding the mating ring against the shoulder. Make a note of this clearance.

Pull the bearing off the shaft and install the bearing and its shim in the bearing housing; secure it with its retaining ring. Position an indicator on the housing with the indicator point against the bearing and check the end play of the bearing by moving the bearing back and forth with the fingers.

Reduce the bearing-to-housing end play to 0.001-0.002" with selected shims; shims of 0.008, 0.009, 0.010, 0.011, 0.012, and 0.014" thickness are available. Measure the end play once more after correction to obtain a corrected value.

Compute the "total" end play of the shaft in the housing as the sum of the bearing-to-shaft clearance and the corrected bearing-to-housing end play. Make a note of this sum for use in the impeller clearance check described later.

Install the selected shim, bearing, and retaining ring in the housing, with the mating ring centered on top. Coat the O-ring seal with pe-

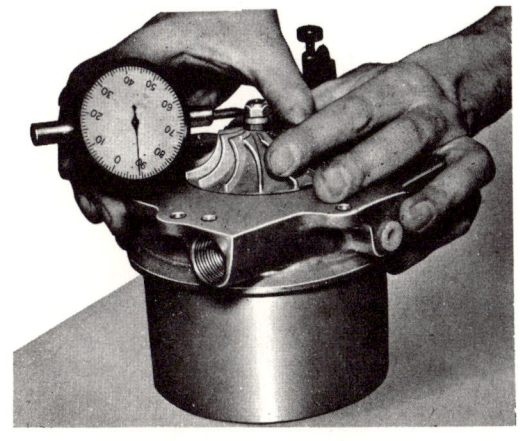

Gauging turbine shaft radial play

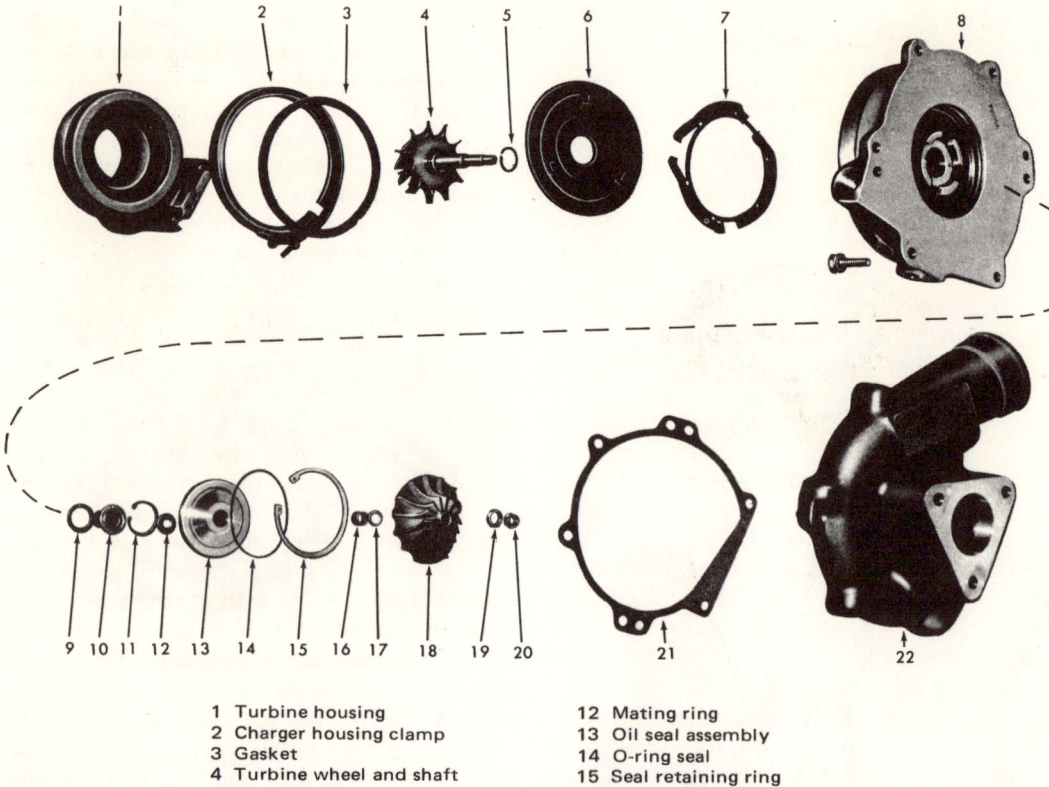

FUEL SYSTEM

Turbo-Supercharger, exploded view

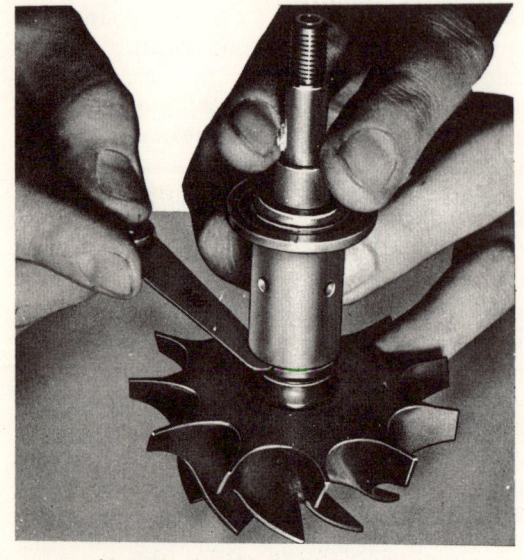

1 Turbine housing
2 Charger housing clamp
3 Gasket
4 Turbine wheel and shaft
5 Turbine shaft oil seal ring
6 Shield plate
7 Spring plate
8 Bearing housing
9 Bearing shim
10 Bearing
11 Bearing retaining ring
12 Mating ring
13 Oil seal assembly
14 O-ring seal
15 Seal retaining ring
16 Shaft sleeve
17 Impeller shim
18 Impeller
19 Impeller special washer
20 Impeller nut
21 Compressor housing gasket
22 Compressor housing

Measuring bearing to shaft end play

troleum jelly or silicone grease and install in the groove of seal assembly. Install the seal assembly in the housing and install the retaining ring over the seal.

Determine the impeller-to-housing clearance by installing the impeller in the compressor side of the bearing housing and installing the cover (with its gasket) with three equally spaced bolts torqued to 80 in. lbs. Install the turbine shaft from the turbine side, just far enough into the impeller bore to hold the impeller to the shaft. Move the impeller from one end of its cavity to the other by pushing and pulling on the turbine hub and measure this free movement with a dial indicator positioned on the turbine hub. Make a note of this free travel.

Obtain the necessary impeller clearance shim value by subtracting the "total" shaft end play measured previously from the free travel value. Correct this clearance by subtracting the

FUEL SYSTEM

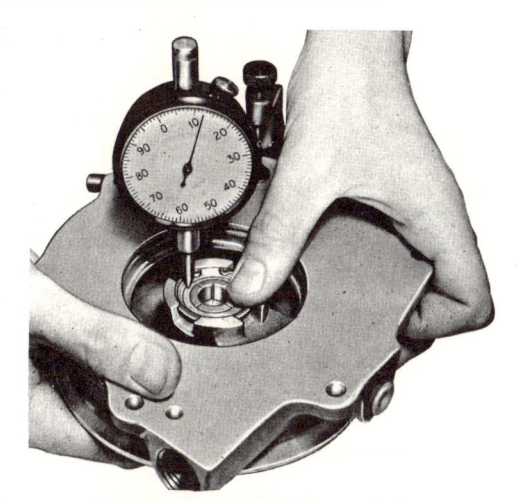

Gauging bearing to housing end play

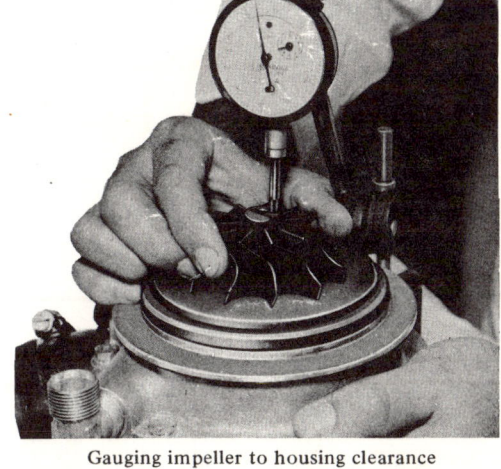

Gauging impeller to housing clearance

"design" clearance of the impeller, 0.015 to 0.020", to obtain the thickness required for the impeller shim. Shims of 0.010 and 0.015" thickness are available.

Unbolt and remove the compressor cover and remove the impeller and turbine shaft.

Assembly

Assemble the turbocharger as follows: Install the spring ring on the turbine side of the bearing housing and position the turbine shield with its lugs on the *flats* of the spring ring (not between the prongs). Clamp this housing group to keep it assembled.

Install the turbine shaft oil seal ring on the shaft and compress it with a knot or twist of copper wire. Lubricate the shaft lightly and install it in the bearing housing from the turbine side and pull the wire loose from the seal ring when the ring is safely engaged in the bearing.

Install the shaft sleeve and impeller shim (determine from the clearance check above) on the shaft at the compressor side of the housing. Set up the housing assembly on an arbor press with the turbine hub supported and press on the impeller hub (the impeller may be heated to 300°F. in an oven and installed without a press if desired). Secure the impeller with the special

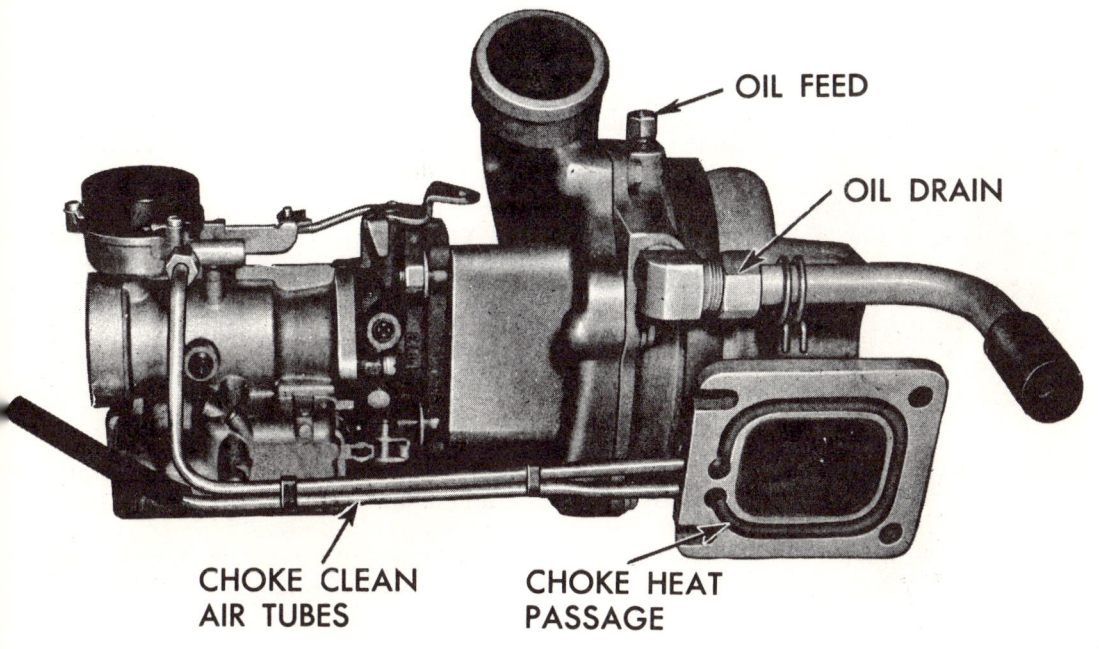

Carburetor fittings and passages

washer (radiused surface outward) and the locknut (left-hand thread). Torque the nut to 80 in. lbs.

Install the compressor cover and gasket and torque the bolts to 80 in. lbs. Pour oil into the oil inlet hole until it drains out the drain hole; install the carburetor, connecting the air tubes as shown.

Install the assembly on the turbine housing on the engine with its screw clamp.

Fuel Pump

The Corvair engine uses a diaphragm-type fuel pump, mechanically actuated by an eccentric collar on the crankshaft through a pushrod. The fuel pump operates continuously, maintaining a head of fuel pressure in the line between the pump and the carburetors, so that the fuel is fed to the float bowls of the carburetors when the carburetor float drops low enough to open the float valve. Engine misfiring or "cutting out" at high speed, or mysterious stalling, is traceable to the fuel pump.

Test the fuel pump by disconnecting the outlet line of the pump and leading it into a can or jar; pull the secondary wire out of the distributor cap so that the engine will not start, then crank the engine with the starter for several seconds.

NOTE: It is best to have an assistant crank the engine with the starter switch rather than to use a remote starting cable. On alternator-equipped vehicles (1965 and on), the ignition circuit will be damaged unless the primary wire from the distributor to the coil is disconnected and the ignition switch is turned ON.

The fuel pump should produce one pint of fuel in 40 seconds at cranking speed, in a strong, regular stream or pulse.

It is also possible to check fuel pressure, using a suitable pressure gauge attached to the outlet line: start the engine (all ignition leads must be reconnected) and run the engine on the residual fuel in the carburetor float bowls; at 500 to 1000 rpm the fuel pressure should be 4 to 5 lbs. at any point of the rpm. If the pressure varies significantly between 500 and 1000 rpm, or if it is too high or too low, remove the pump and overhaul it.

Removal and Disassembly

Disconnect the fuel lines to and from the pump, leaving the T-connector in place. Loosen the setscrew jam nut and back out the setscrew to release the pump housing. Pull the pump carefully from the accessory housing on the engine. Pull out the pushrod and the spring.

Remove as much surface dirt from the cover as possible and unbolt the cover; remove the cover, spring, and diaphragm and body assembly, then remove the lower body and pulsator diaphragm from the pulsator cover. The pump is shown fully disassembled. If desired, remove the valve disks from the lower body by cutting away the staked metal around them and pulling them out, noting their position (facing in or out) for future reference.

Clean all parts in solvent and inspect them for damage.

NOTE: The principal problems occurring in fuel pumps are diaphragm damage and contamination from fuel varnish and dirt. Pay particular attention to the cleanliness of all parts, especially the diaphragm.

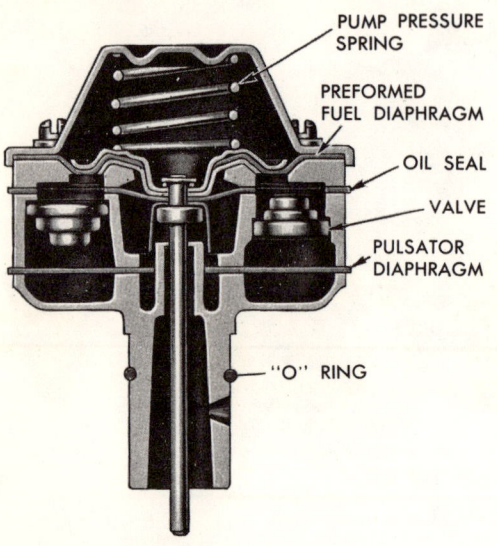

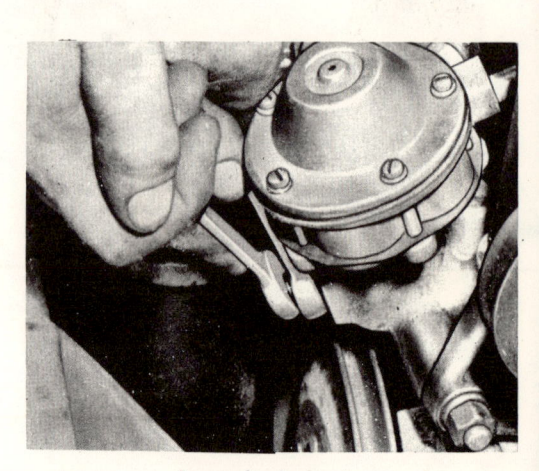

Fuel pump, cross-section

Loosening locknut

FUEL SYSTEM

Removing pushrod

Assemble the pump, being careful to assemble all parts in their correct order and place. If the valve disks were removed, they must be replaced facing in their proper directions and some of the surrounding body metal must be staked (forced inward with a small, sharp punch) to retain them. Shake the body assembly after, to make sure the valves are free to move.

Install the diaphragm, spring, and cover, and tighten the cover screws evenly. Install the connector in the pump outlet, if removed. Install the pushrod and return spring in the accessory cover on the engine and install the pump carefully in place. Rotate the pump while slowly tightening the setscrew, until the point of the screw is felt to align with the dimple in the pump body. Tighten the screw to 9-15 ft. lbs. and tighten the locknut to 9-15 ft. lbs. Connect the fuel lines to the carburetors and test the fuel pump.

Air Injection Reactor (A.I.R.)

The Air Injection Reactor System ("A.I.R.") was fitted on some vehicles from 1966 to 1969 to minimize exhaust gas contamination from unburnt fuel. With this system, air is injected into the exhaust manifold slightly downstream of the exhaust valves. At periods of high intake manifold vacuum (deceleration and idle), a mixture control valve (1966 and 1967) vents pressurized air into the intake manifold to lean out the mixture during this rich period, or a diverter valve (1968 and 1969) shuts off air to the exhaust port areas, to prevent backfiring. On all installations the pump remains basically the same. The illustrations below show the engine compartment arrangements for any model year. Check valves in the lines to each bank of cylinders prevent reverse flow of exhaust gases back to the air pump.

Checking System Operation

Check the drive belt tension and adjust if necessary to prevent slippage. Check for leaks in the tubes by dabbing a soap and water solution on suspicious areas and joints with the engine running; any bubbles are an indication of a leak.

Check Valves

Inspect the check valves by opening the connection for each one and blowing into it; the valve should allow air to be blown in but not sucked out.

Mixture Control Valves—1966 and 1967

Run the engine with the inlet tubes disconnected. Little or no suction should be felt at

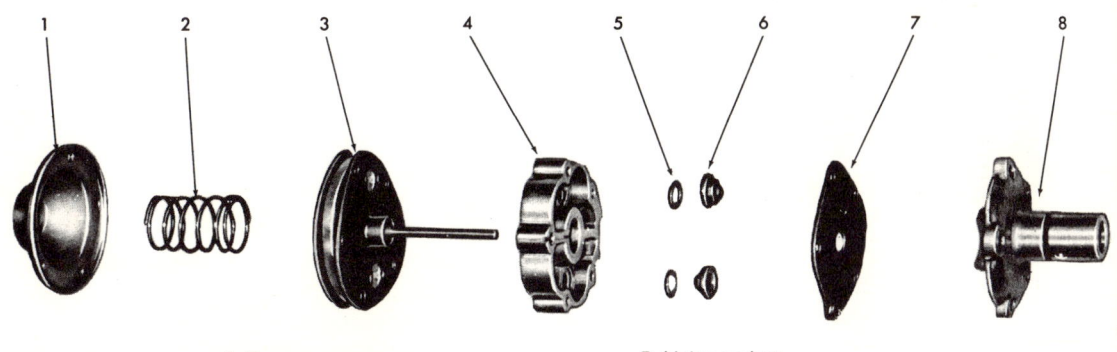

1 Cover
2 Spring
3 Diaphragm and body assembly
4 Lower body
5 Valve gasket
6 Valve
7 Pulsator diaphragm
8 Pulsator cover

Fuel pump, exploded view

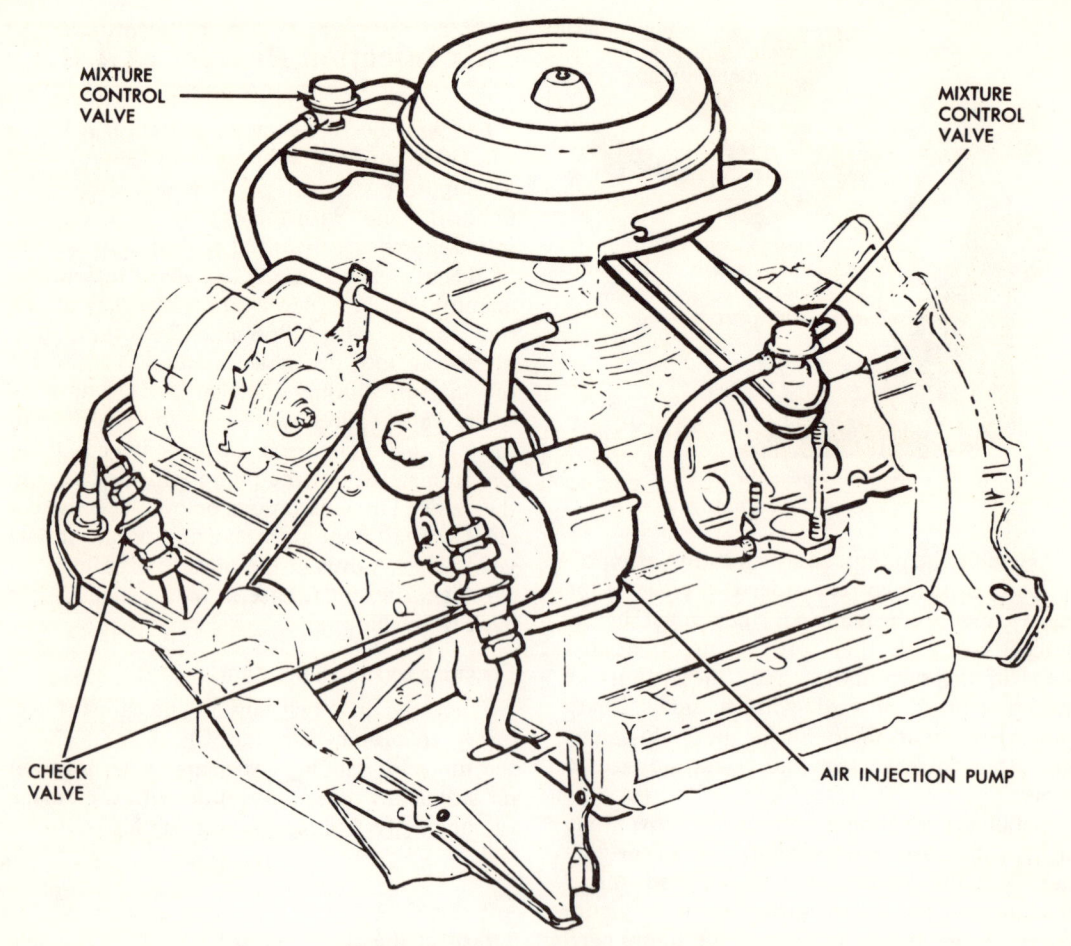

Air injection reactor system—1966-1967

the inlet of each valve. Accelerate the engine quickly once or twice and note valve action; the valve should actuate briefly upon throttle closing (high vacuum) and should close thereafter.

Diverter Valves—1968 and 1969

Disconnect the signal tubes and check for vacuum with the engine running. Disconnect the pump inlet-to-diverter valve tube; when the engine is speeded up and dropped back to idle, the valve should open and blast air for one second, then close.

Pressure Relief Valve

Check for sounds of air leaking from the valve with the engine running, indicating a leak. Disassemble and inspect the valve as directed below.

Injection Pump

Check the pump for satisfactory airflow while the engine is running at 1,500 rpm. Disconnect an air outlet hose and observe the air flow. If the air flow increases as the engine speed increases, without excessive noise or vibration, the pump is satisfactory.

Removal and Disassembly of the A.I.R. System

Remove the pressure relief valve tube and remove the valve as shown, by tapping it gently off with an adjustable wrench and a hammer. Remove the pressure setting plug and inspect it, snapping it carefully back into position if it is satisfactory. Tap the valve back on the tube as shown, using a deep socket as a drift.

Disconnect the inlet and outlet hoses at the pump and unbolt and pull off the drive pulley. Jack up the engine with a transmission jack to obtain clearance, then unbolt and remove the pump.

Spin the pump rotor to check for bad bearings or binding vanes before disassembling the unit. Unbolt and remove the cover assembly *straight upward*, tapping carefully. Unscrew the ring and bearing assembly and pull out the vane shoes and the vane assembly. The pump is

FUEL SYSTEM

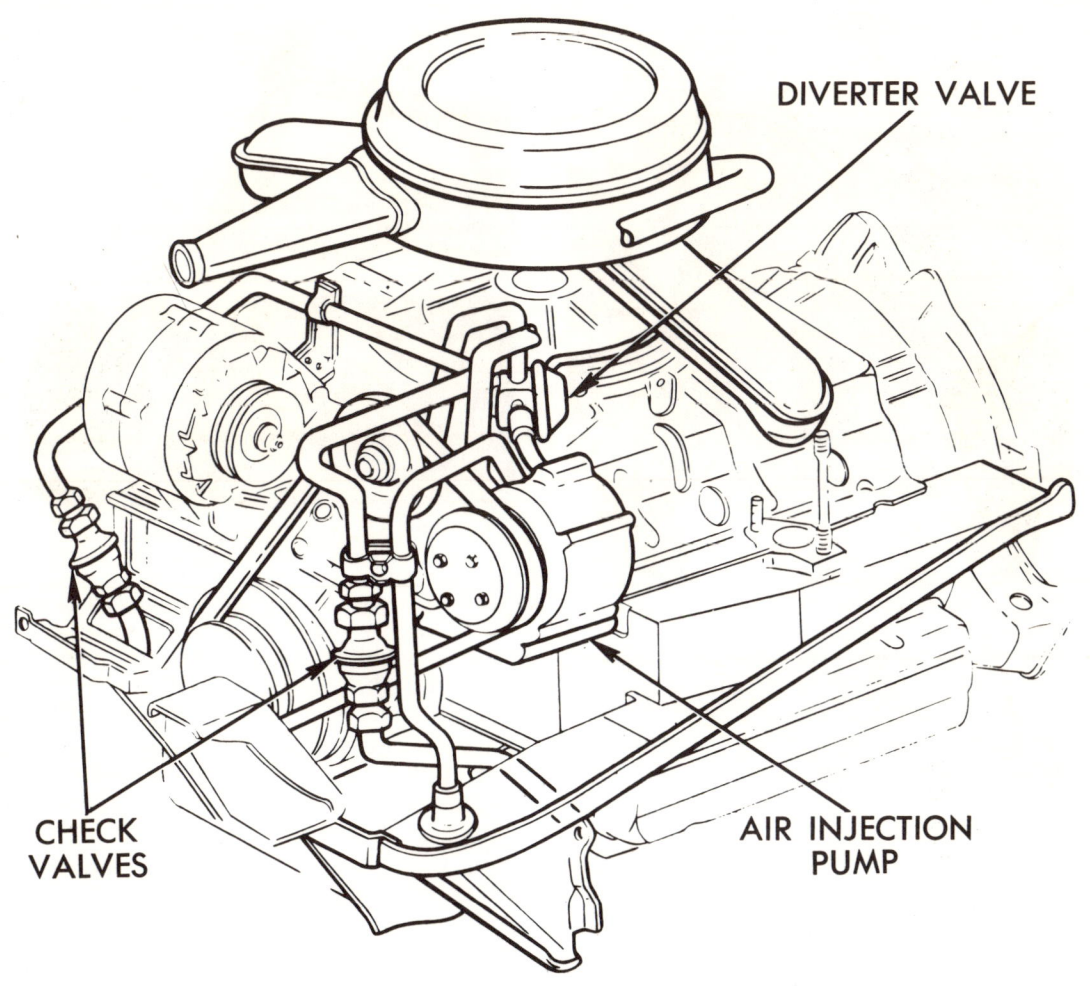

77

Air injection reactor system—1968-1969

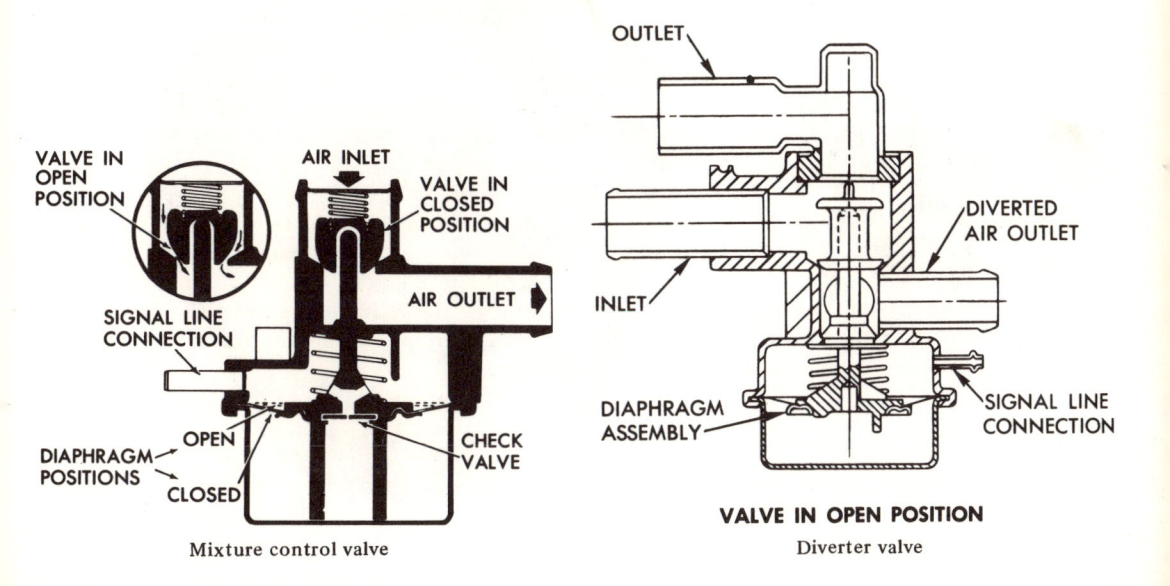

Mixture control valve

VALVE IN OPEN POSITION
Diverter valve

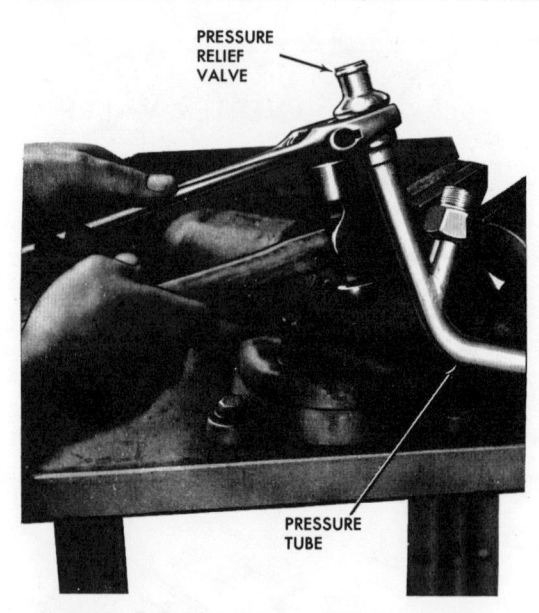

FUEL SYSTEM

Removing pressure relief valve

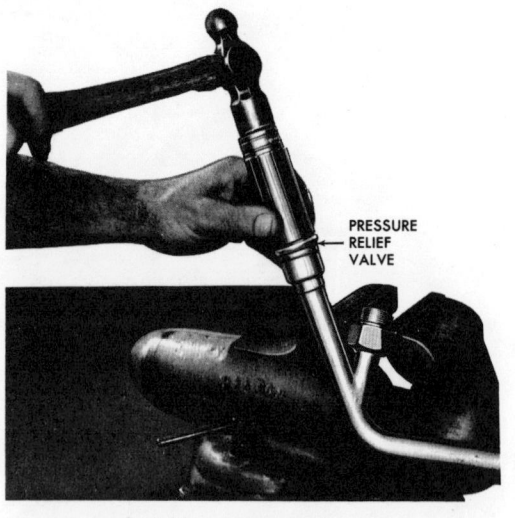

Installing pressure relief valve

shown fully disassembled. Check for bad bearings, excessive wear or grooving in the shoes, or wear to the pivot shaft on the cover.

Install the vane segments on a 3/8" rod and install the vanes, with the rod, in the pump with one vane against the "stripper" (the ridge on the pump bore marking the boundary between the inlet and the outlet). Install the vane shoes on each side of each vane and install the shoe springs under every other shoe as shown.

Check all parts for correct assembly as shown. Install the ring and bearing and the seal over the vanes and torque the screws to 37 in. lbs. Remove the 3/8" rod from the vane hinges and substitute the pivot shaft in the cover, lowering the cover into position. Torque the cover bolts to 10 ft. lbs.

Install the pump on the engine and bolt the pulley in place. Install and tighten the drive belt, then connect the hoses to the pump. Check the operation of the pump with the engine running.

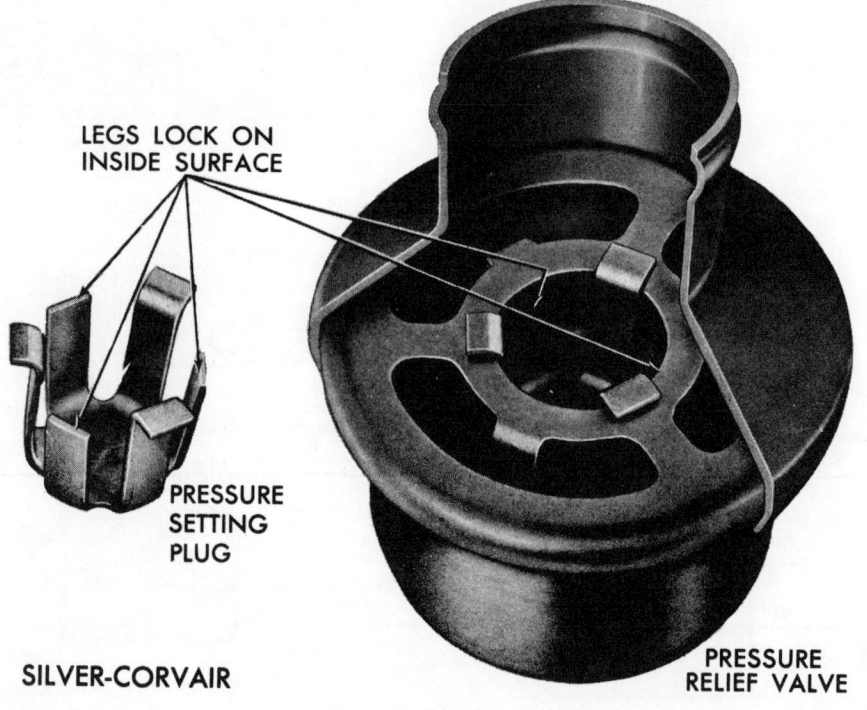

SILVER-CORVAIR

Pressure setting plug

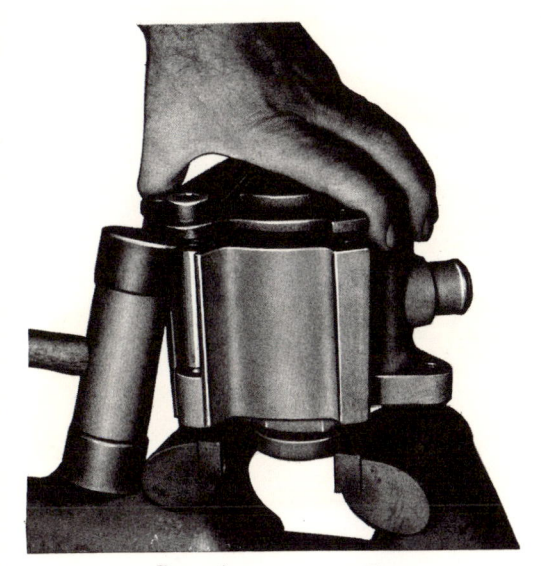

FUEL SYSTEM

Removing cover assembly

Installing vane assemblies

Removing vane shoes

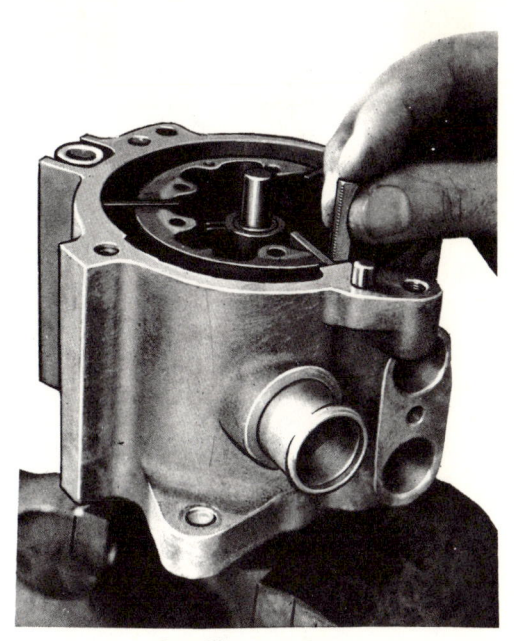

Installing vane shoes

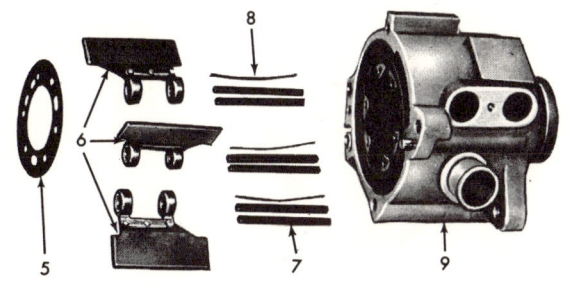

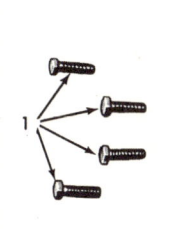

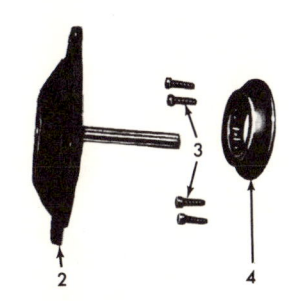

1 Cover attaching bolts
2 Cover assembly
3 Rear rotor ring screws
4 Rear rotor ring and bearing assembly
5 Rear carbon seal
6 Vane assemblies
7 Vane shoes
8 Shoe springs
9 Housing and rotor assembly

Air injection pump, exploded view

FUEL SYSTEM

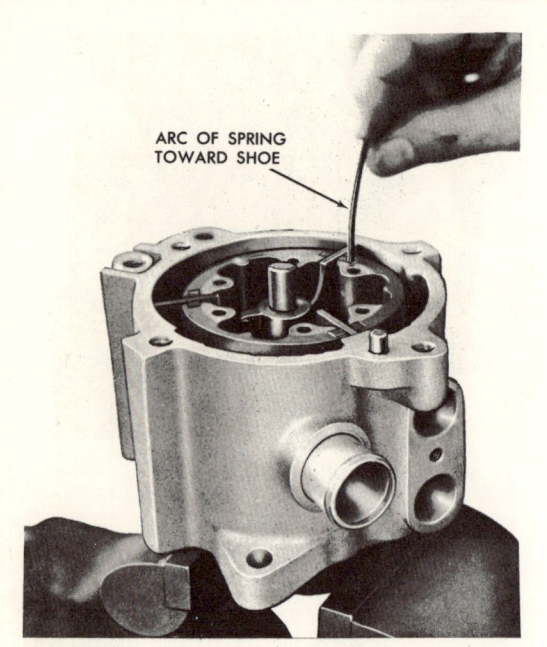

ARC OF SPRING TOWARD SHOE

Installing shoe springs

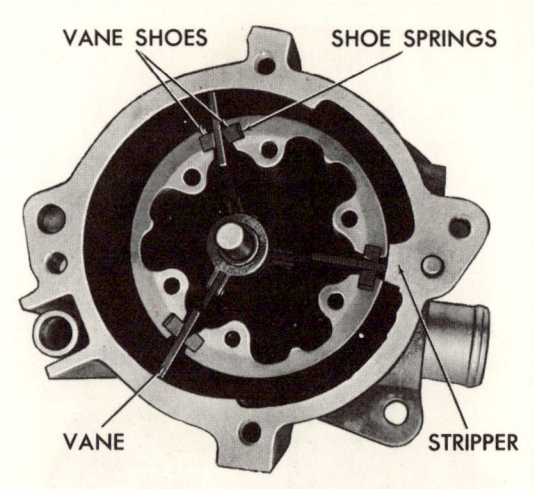

VANE SHOES   SHOE SPRINGS

VANE   STRIPPER

Vanes, vane shoes and shoe springs installed

5 • Electrical System

Battery and Charging System

Description

Corvairs are equipped with a conventional 12 volt DC system, utilizing a storage battery located in the engine compartment. Charging is accomplished by a DC generator (1960-1964) or alternator (1965-1969).

Battery

The battery depends on the correct amount and consistency of electrolyte for correct operation. This electrolyte is a dilute acid which, itself, never dissipates or decreases; the fluid level falls from time to time because of the evaporation of the water which dilutes the acid. For this reason, the electrolyte should be checked periodically and refilled (up to the level of the split ring in the filler ports in most batteries) with *water only*. The electrolyte level should be checked regularly, depending on the driving conditions. For example, during the hot summer months, the level should be checked every time you buy gas, because the battery is heated by the engine and may lose water very quickly. In winter the battery may lose water from excessive charging because of heavy cranking loads, rather than because of high outside temperatures.

The surface cleanliness of the battery is more important than many drivers realize. Dirt entering the cells by careless refilling can contaminate the electrolyte and cause it to deteriorate. Be careful when the filler caps are off and add only distilled or demineralized water.

Buildup of corrosion on the cables and clamps causes a breakdown of conductivity between the battery terminals and the cables. Occasionally the lights and accessories of a vehicle can be made to work, but not the starter; this condition is often mistaken for a dead battery, when actually it is a "thermocoupling" phenomenon wherein the stronger current drawn by the starting motor heats up the small area of contact left by a dirt film between the terminal and cable clamp, melts it slightly, and breaks the connection.

The cure for such trouble is better battery cleanliness. The terminals should be clean, dry, and tight when installed, preferably with a light coat of chassis grease, petroleum jelly, or spray lacquer applied to the terminals *after* they have been installed and tightened. A two-way wire brush, one side to scour out the inside of a clamp, the other to clean a terminal post, is commonly available and is a good investment.

Battery Condition Check

A great deal can be learned about a battery by observing it during operation. The electrolyte should be clear at all times, even under load (heavy discharge for starting, lights, etc.). If after recharging or heavy usage the electrolyte is cloudy or murky, this indicates that the battery is deteriorating and needs to be replaced.

ELECTRICAL SYSTEM

Testing the Electrolyte

Battery electrolyte is tested for specific gravity (indicating the strength of the acid solution) with a hydrometer as shown. With this instrument, a small quantity of electrolyte from each cell of a fully charged battery is sucked up into a column and the position of a float is read against its scale and corrected for the temperature of the electrolyte. This reading (corrected to 80°F.) should be between 1.250 and 1.290.

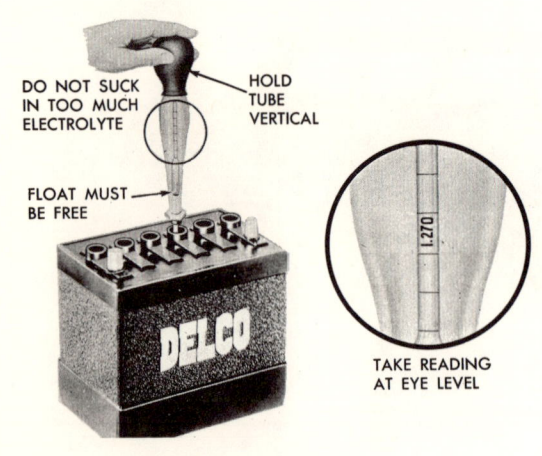

Testing specific gravity

Gas Discharge

A storage battery produces hydrogen gas, which is explosive when mixed with air. In most cases this gas is safely vented through the battery caps and escapes without burning, but a certain hazard exists, especially in an older battery. On some Corvairs a gas vent cap system is attached to the battery, which vents vapors through tubing to the outside of the engine compartment. This is an added safeguard and is worth maintaining; if the battery is equipped with this system, check these tubes when checking the battery and make sure they are clear and in good condition.

Starting from Another Vehicle

With the advent of alternator charging (1965 and later), a complication arises with regard to "jump starting." With this newer system of charging it is vitally important that the current used to assist the disabled vehicle's system has the same polarity. The *positive* terminal of one battery should be connected to the *positive* terminal of the other; the *negative* terminal of one to the *negative* terminal of the other. A few seconds contact with the polarity reversed can damage the diodes in the alternator of one or both automobiles. Be sure that the positive and negative cables are correctly positioned when starting one vehicle from the battery of another.

Charging System

Generator—1960-1964

The generator used in Corvairs from 1960 to 1964 is illustrated. This unit is the common dynamo type in which an armature is rotated through a charged field, producing an electric current by induction. This current is tapped off in the form of direct current by brushes contacting a segmented commutator on the end of the armature. The generator is driven continuously by the blower belt but only produces current when the field winding is charged upon a signal from the voltage regulator.

Maintenance

The generator is easy to maintain and service. Oil caps are provided at each end of the housing to feed the armature bearings; these caps should be opened and filled with light engine oil at every lubrication.

Indications of generator malfunction are noise coming from the generator bearings or armature, a dashboard charging light that doesn't go out, or a battery that keeps running down (suggesting that the battery is not being charged). Before removing and disassembling

Battery and Starter Specifications

YEAR	MODEL	BATTERY Ampere Hour Capacity	Volts	Terminal Grounded	STARTERS Lock Test Amps.	Volts	Torque Amps.	No-Load Test Volts	RPM	Brush Spring Tension (Oz.)
1960-61	Standard	35	12	Neg.	280-320	4.0	—	58-80	10.6	6,750-8,600	35
	Heavy Duty	40	12	Neg.	—	—	—	—	—	—	—
1962-64	All	42	12	Neg.	280	4.0	—	58-80	10.6	6,750-10,500	35
1965-66	All	44	12	Neg.	280	4.0	—	58-80	10.6	6,750-10,500	35
1967-69	All	45	12	Neg.	Not Recommended			69	10.6	6,750-10,500	35

ELECTRICAL SYSTEM

Generator and Regulator Specifications

Generators

Year	Model	Field Current In Amperes At 12 Volts	Brush Spring Tension (Oz.)
1960-61		1.50-1.62	28
1962-63	1102226/30A.	1.69-1.79	28
	1102227/30A.	1.69-1.79	28
	1105135/35A.*	2.73-3.00	28
	1105139/40A.	2.73-3.00	28
1964	1102336/35A.	1.69-1.79	28
	1105135/35A.	2.73-3.00	28

Regulators

Year	Cut-Out Relay Air Gap (In.)	Cut-Out Relay Closing Voltage	Current & Voltage Air Gaps (In.)	Current Regulator Setting (Amps.)	Voltage Regulator Setting (Volts)
1960-61	.020	11.8-13.5	.075	27-33	13.8-14.8
1962-63	.020	11.8-13.5	.075/.060	27-31	13.8-14.7
	.020	11.8-13.5	.075/.060	27-31	13.8-14.7
	.023	11.8-13.0	.075/.067	31.0-35.5	13.8-14.7
	.023	11.8-13.0	.075/.067	27.8-32.4	13.8-14.7
1964	.020	11.8-13.5	.075	31.0-35.5	13.8-14.7
	.020	11.8-13.0	.075/.067	31.0-35.5	13.8-14.6

1963 Cutout Relay Air Gap .020, Volt. Reg. Setting 13.8-14.6

Delcotron and AC Regulator Specifications

Alternator

Year	Model	Field Current Draw @ 12V.	Output @ Generator RPM 500	Output @ Generator RPM 1500	Model
1965-69	1100639	2.2-2.6	25	35	1119515
	1100698*	2.8-3.2	35	45	1119515

Regulator

Field Relay Air Gap (In.)	Field Relay Point Gap (In.)	Field Relay Volts to Close	Regulator Air Gap (In.)	Regulator Point Gap (In.)	Volts at 125°
.015	.030	2.3-3.7	.067	.014	13.5-14.4
.015	.030	2.3-3.7	.067	.014	13.8-14.8

*—with external field discharge diode.

ELECTRICAL SYSTEM

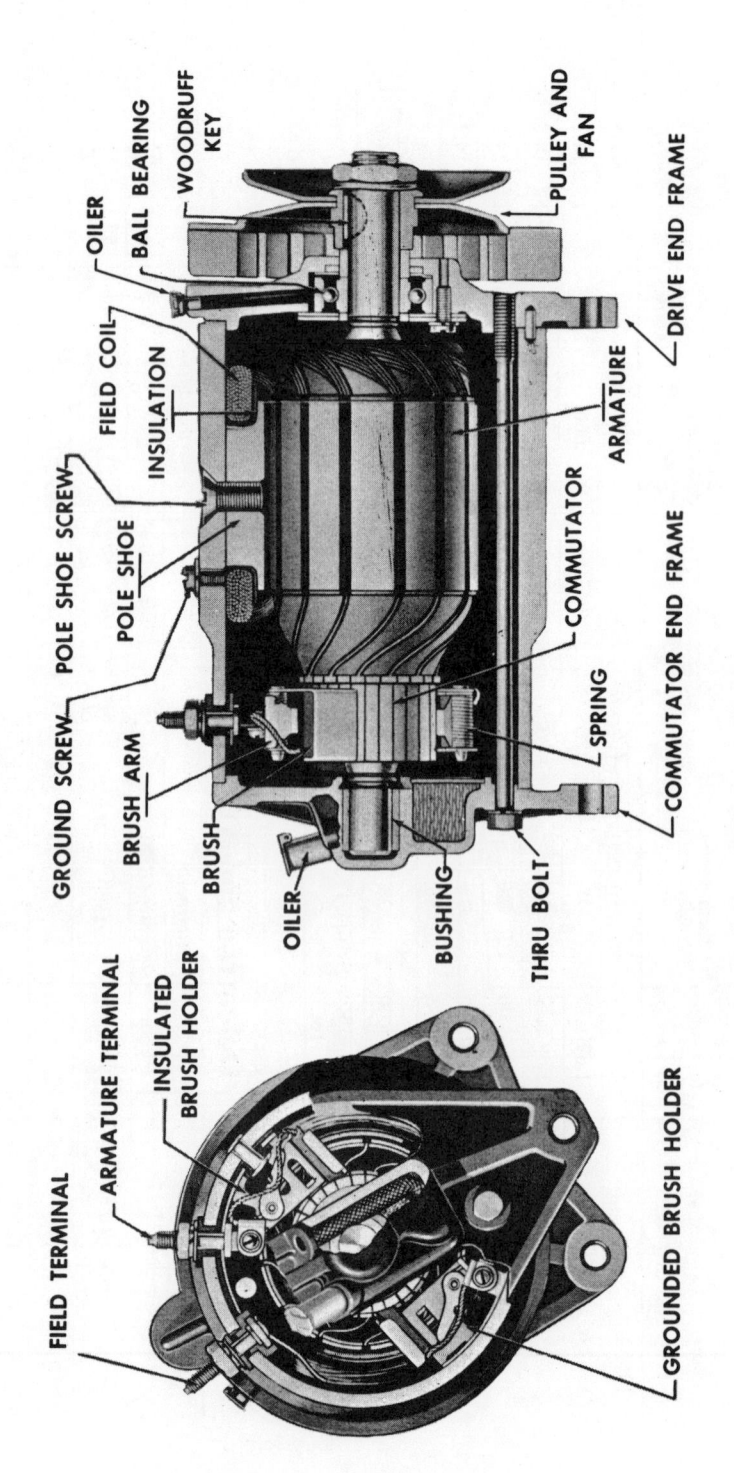

Generator, cross-section

the generator to find the trouble, perform the following checks:

1. With the engine running, check suspicious noises with a stethoscope or listening rod. If these noises seem to originate in the front or rear of the generator housing, a bad bearing may be misaligning the armature. A noise in the center of the housing may mean a broken and grounding armature or field wire.

2. Check the blower belt tension and adjust if necessary (see Chapter One).

3. Establish that the battery is in good condition. Inspect and tighten all electrical connections.

4. Check voltage regulator operation (see below).

If these checks do not resolve or pinpoint the problem, remove the generator and inspect it.

Generator Removal

Loosen the drive belt and slip it off the generator pulley. Disconnect the ground cable on the battery. Mark and disconnect the wires to the generator and unbolt and remove the generator.

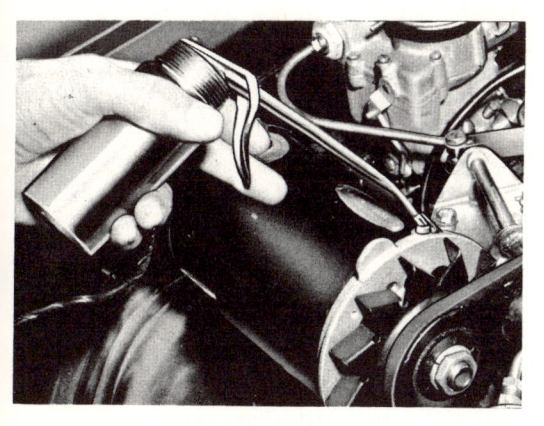

Oiling the generator

Disassembly

Remove the pulley from the end of the generator by unscrewing the locknut clockwise (left-hand thread). Immobilize the fan impeller on the pulley, if necessary, to remove the nut, but do not mar or bend the vanes or pulley. Remove the pulley and pull the woodruff key from the shaft before going on to the next step.

Clamp the generator on a bench and remove the outer frame bolts. Pull off the end frame and armature. Remove the front frame and inspect the brushes. If they are worn so short that they cannot contact the commutator reliably, unscrew and replace them.

When the leads have been disconnected, push on the tension springs to release the brushes and pull them from their channels. Replace them with new brushes and connect the leads securely. If no symptoms were found to suggest additional trouble in the generator, assemble the armature and end frame assembly and install the generator on the engine. Connect the wires to the generator and battery and test the generator.

If additional disassembly is required, remove the armature as before, and remove and disassemble the end frame to remove the bearing.

The generator is shown fully disassembled. It is usually unnecessary and inadvisable to remove the field coils, terminals, or pole shoes, unless inspection reveals obvious rubbing or shorted wires on their surfaces. Clean all small parts and end frames in solvent; do not clean the generator fields or armature beyond wiping off surface grime and do not use any solvent on the windings.

Check the ball bearing for damage or wear and check the fit of the armature shaft in the commutator end frame; the shaft should *not* be loose enough to slap back and forth in the bushing.

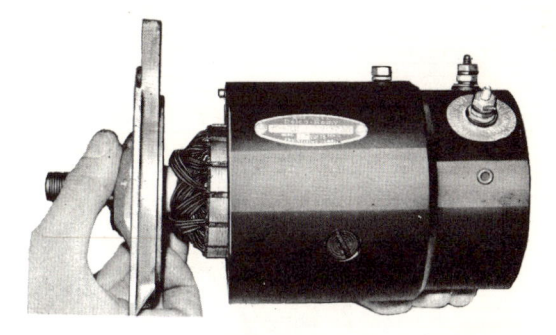

Removing end frame and armature from generator

Inspect the commutator surface. If it is rough, or if the brushes have worn a channel in it, it should be turned down to restore a flat, even surface. This can be done on a special spiral cutter fixture designed for the purpose, or the entire armature and shaft can be mounted in a bench lathe and a flat, sharp tool used to recut the surface flat and true. After turning down the commutator surface (cut only as far as necessary), undercut the mica insulation between the bars of the commutator to isolate these surfaces from each other electrically. A V-shaped tool, or a piece of hacksaw blade, is suitable for scraping down each groove until it is free of metal.

Armature and Field Coil Testing—General

The testing of the field and armature circuits in the generator is a simple matter, given a few

ELECTRICAL SYSTEM

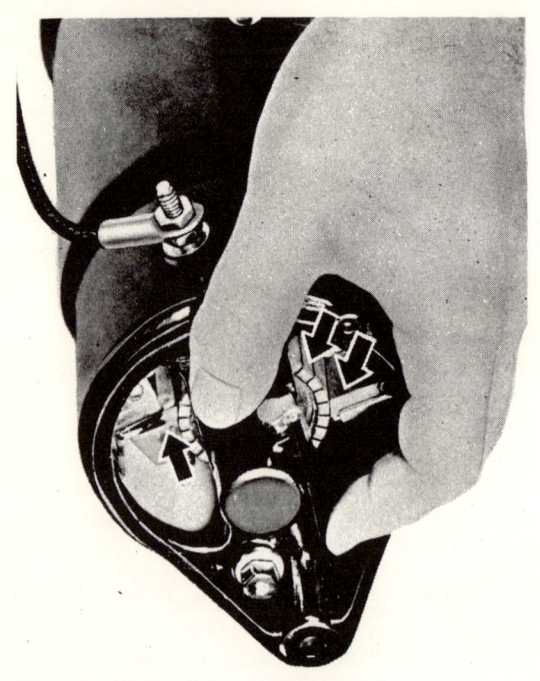

Removing the front frame and brushes from generator

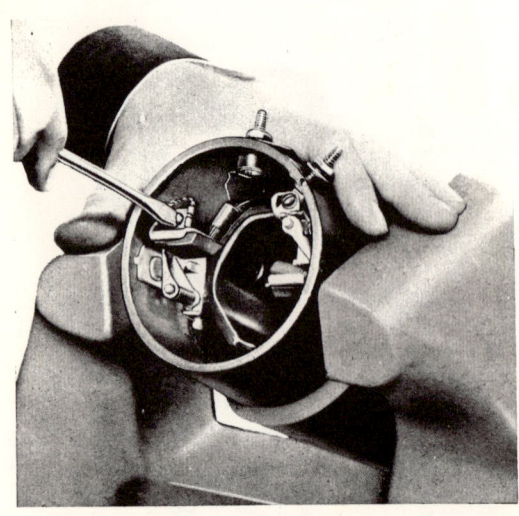

Removing brush leads

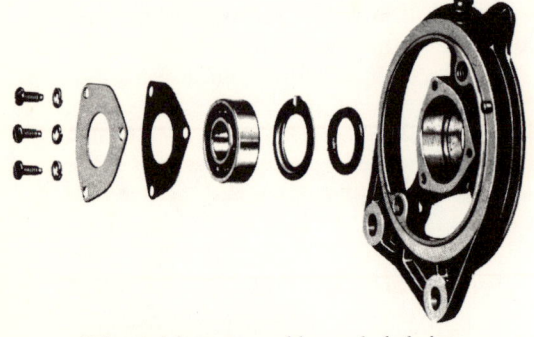

Drive end frame assembly, exploded view

simple testing devices. The simplest and most important is the test lamp or continuity light. This consists of a lamp (bulb) and socket with approximately two feet of suitable wire and a small battery, such as a six-volt utility battery. On one pole of the socket install about a foot of wire with a metallic probe or alligator clip at the other end. At the other end of the socket attach another foot of wire with a probe or clip, and interrupt the wire with the battery, so that when the two probes or clips touch, a circuit will be made and the lamp will light. This test lamp is a means of detecting conductivity through any object or assembly.

The "growler" mentioned in the armature test below is a common testing meter and should be found in any well-equipped service station.

The field windings, brush holders, and terminals should be left intact in the generator casing for the following inspection. In the field coil test for grounds or breaks; for instance, the field terminal must be effectively insulated from the generator casing, and all washers and insulators must be present and in the right order.

In any generator of this type, the electrical "ground" must be thought of in a special sense. Unlike the accessory and ignition circuits, where the "ground" side of the circuit is the engine and even the frame of the vehicle itself, the "ground" of the generator is an isolated electrical path, protected by insulators and terminating at the voltage regulator. The generator, being bolted to the engine, is a "ground" of the engine electrical system, but the only "ground" of the charging system is the field winding. This allows the positive side of the circuit (the commutator, armature, shaft, etc.) to touch the generator casing through its bearing and bushing without shorting any circuit.

Certain electrical faults in the fields and armature will be repairable. These include faulty insulation washers, frayed or broken wires, loose terminals, etc. These can be repaired by tightening, soldering, or replacement. As a general rule, if a fault is visible it is repairable. However, mysterious shorts and grounds inside a winding are usually impossible to locate or repair and the affected part should be replaced.

Armature Testing

The armature can be tested for short circuits with a "growler" fixture as shown. With the armature supported and rotated in the fixture and a hacksaw blade placed on the armature,

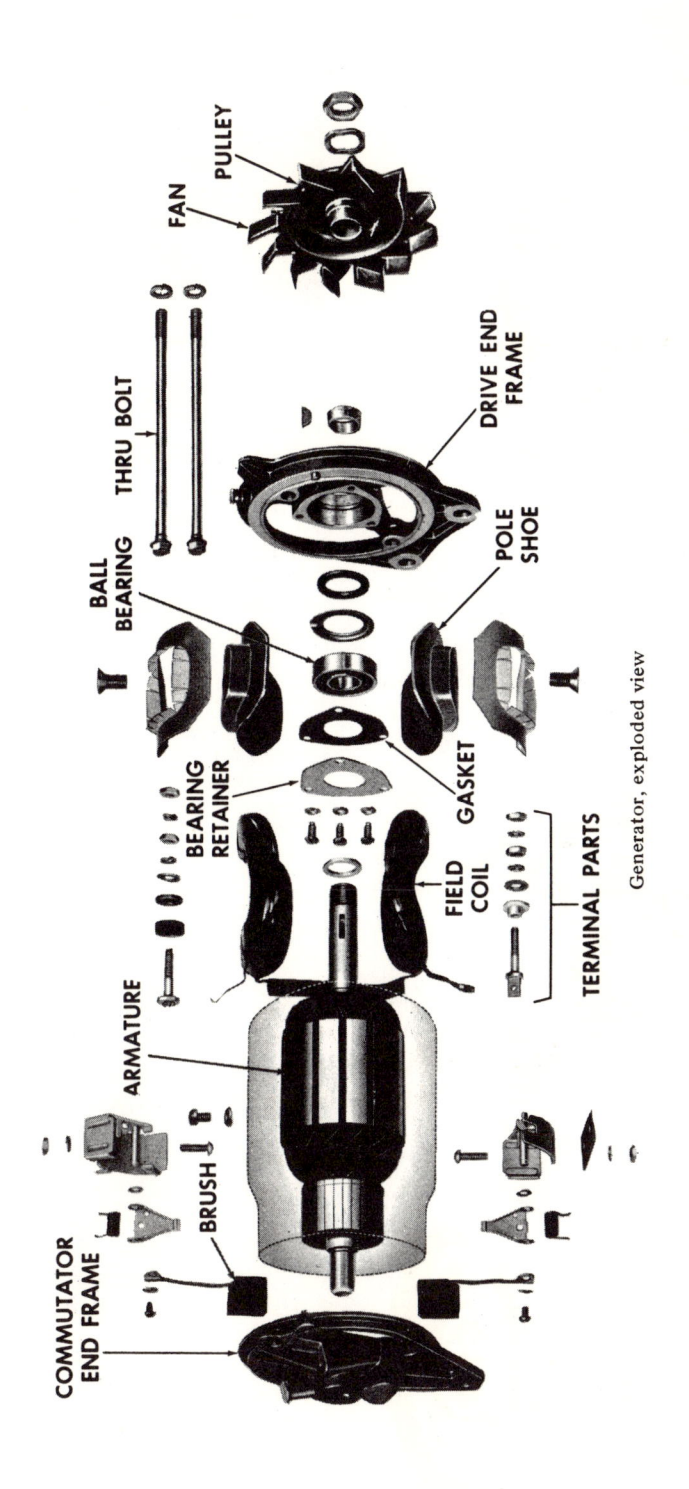

ELECTRICAL SYSTEM

87

Generator, exploded view

vibrations in the saw blade indicate a short circuit. If these symptoms persist after the commutator has been turned down and regrooved, the armature is beyond repair.

Test the armature for grounds as shown. If a continuity check with the probes of a test lamp indicates a short circuit across the bars of the armature and commutator, the armature has an internal ground and must be replaced.

Test for an open circuit. Check the circuits bar-to-bar across the commutator and reject the armature assembly if any poor or dead circuits are found.

Field Testing

The field windings (fastened inside the generator housing) are checked for their electrical relationship to the housing and to the brushes, as follows:

Test for an open circuit as shown, checking for continuity between the field terminal and the field coil brush terminal lead. If the test lamp does not light, there is a break in the field circuit.

Test for grounds between the generator housing and the field terminal (be sure the lead inside the casing is not touching the wall of the casing). If the lamp lights, the coils are grounded and the fields are unusable.

Test the positive terminal for ground between the positive terminal and the generator casing. Be sure the inside brush lead is not touching the casing. If the lamp lights, there is a short circuit into the generator frame through the terminal insulation.

Test the inside brush terminal between the brush holder and the generator casing. If the lamp lights, there is a short circuit across the brush holder insulation.

Armature test for ground

Assembly

When the generator parts have been checked out as described above, assemble them as follows.

1. Drive end frame group: install the washers, retainer, bearing, gasket, and plate as shown previously.

NOTE: Pre-lubricate the bearing with light oil before installation.

Install the spacer on the armature shaft (on the end with the keyway) and slide the shaft into the drive end frame. Coat the shaft *lightly* with oil to facilitate assembly.

2. Generator casing group: be sure all windings and coils are in place and secured. Tighten both terminal locknuts. Install new or serviceable brushes in the brush holders and secure the

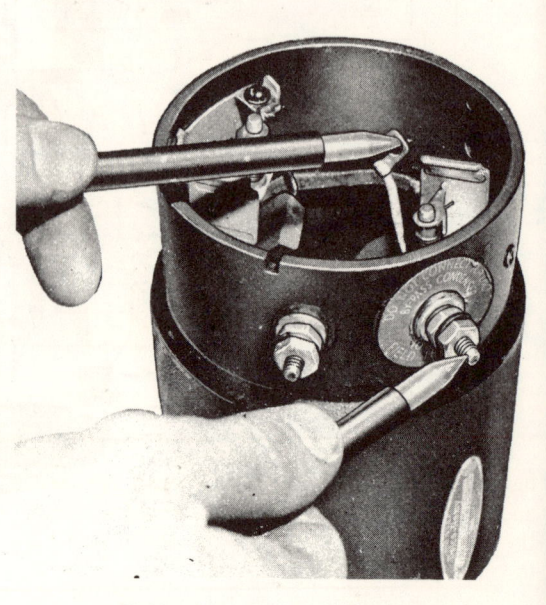

Armature test for shorts

Field coil test for open circuit

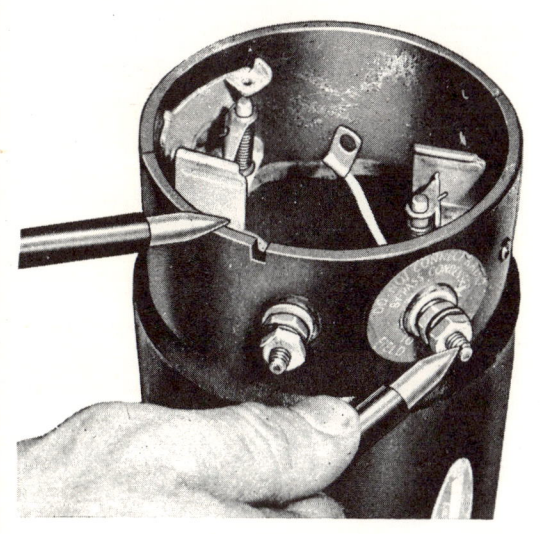

ELECTRICAL SYSTEM

Field coil test for ground

Positive brush test for ground

retaining screws. Check that the tension springs function.

Hold the brushes out with the fingers and insert the commutator end of the armature into the casing and between the brushes. Release the brushes against the commutator when the drive end frame has seated.

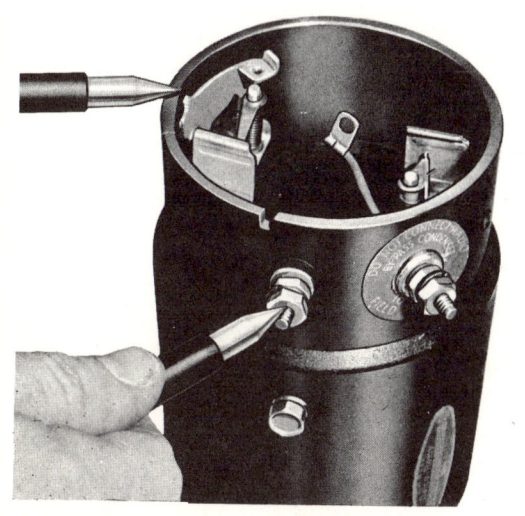

Positive terminal test for ground

Lubricate the commutator end frame bushing lightly, then install the frame onto the shaft and seat it against the generator casing. Align the end frames with the casing and install the through-bolts.

Press the pulley on as follows: install the woodruff key in its keyway on the shaft and install the pulley, being careful to engage the key smoothly in the pulley keyway. If the pulley is too tight to hand fit, it may be pressed on, provided an arrangement like that illustrated is used to support and protect the assembly.

NOTE: Woodruff keys, being semi-circular, have a tendency to rock out of their keyways if they are misaligned more than a fraction of an inch when the mating part is assembled. Watch the key closely when installing the pulley to be sure it is squarely in place and entering the keyway as it should.

When the pulley has seated, thread on the retaining nut *counterclockwise* (lefthand thread) and torque it to 50-60 ft. lbs.

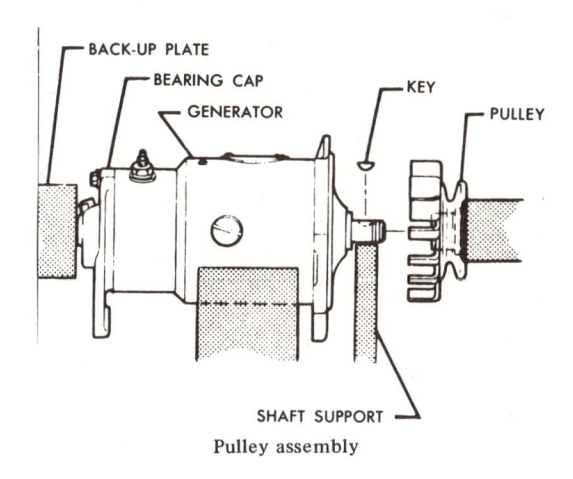

Pulley assembly

Installation

Install the generator on the engine, connect the drive belt and electrical connections and check charging operation. Fill the oil caps with oil.

NOTE: The radio condenser, if used, is attached to the armature (not the field) terminal.

Alternator—1965-1969

From 1965 on Corvairs were equipped with an alternator, as shown.

This unit, performing the same function as the generator it replaces, operates on a different principle, using components seemingly reversed in function from generator parts.

The basic alternator produces 12 volt alternating current, rectified by diodes into direct current. The roles of the standing and rotating parts are reversed from what they were in a DC generator; in a DC generator a wound armature rotates through a charged magnetic field (the field windings) inducing a current in the armature which is tapped off the commutator surface by carbon brushes. In an alternator, the rotating part (the "rotor") is a charged magnet which induces a current in the surrounding, stationary winding (the "stator"). The magnetic field in the rotor is created by current fed to the rotor windings through slip rings and brushes. The alternator represents a more advanced charging device because of its decreased bulk and greater output.

The advancement of the alternator over the DC generator has its price in terms of electronic complexity. The AC alternator uses diode rectifiers which must be protected from incorrect polarity when installing a new battery in the vehicle or when connecting jumper cables from another vehicle. All leads to and from the battery and voltage regulator must be in their correct positions.

Adjustment and inspection of an AC alternator requires such electronic testing equipment as a voltmeter and ohmmeter (available in combination as a "multitester"). If this equipment is not available, the alternator should be sent to a facility that does have it, as soon as the alternator is definitely suspected of causing trouble in the charging system. Very little beyond mechanical inspection and limited continuity checks can be accomplished without electronic analysis.

Output Test Using Voltmeter

Disconnect the four-terminal connector from the voltage regulator and pull out the F-R two-

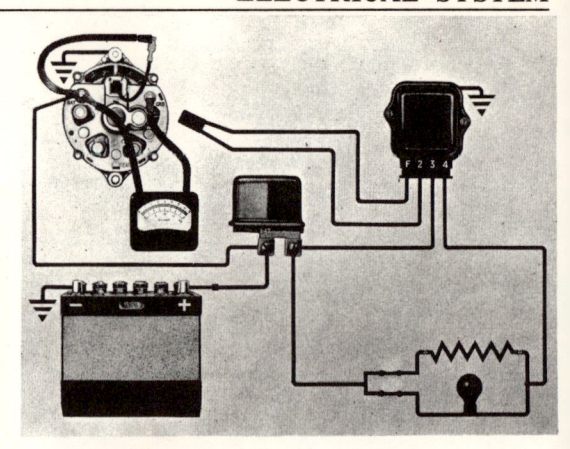

Output test connections, typical

terminal connector from the alternator. Connect a wire from the BAT terminal on the voltage regulator to the F terminal on the alternator to actuate the field winding. Connect a voltmeter from the alternator BAT terminal to the alternator GRD terminal as shown. Start the engine and turn on the high-beam headlights and the high-range heater blower. With the engine running at 1,500 rpm or higher, check the voltage output of the alternator on the meter. This should be in excess of 12.5 volts within a few minutes of operation.

CAUTION: Accelerate the engine cautiously: stop the engine if the voltage starts to exceed 16 volts.

Disconnect the voltmeter and reconnect the terminals in their proper locations.

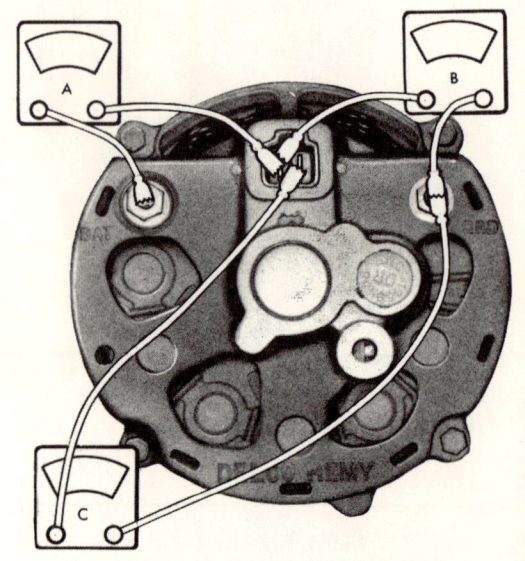

Delcotron alternator diode and field test

ELECTRICAL SYSTEM

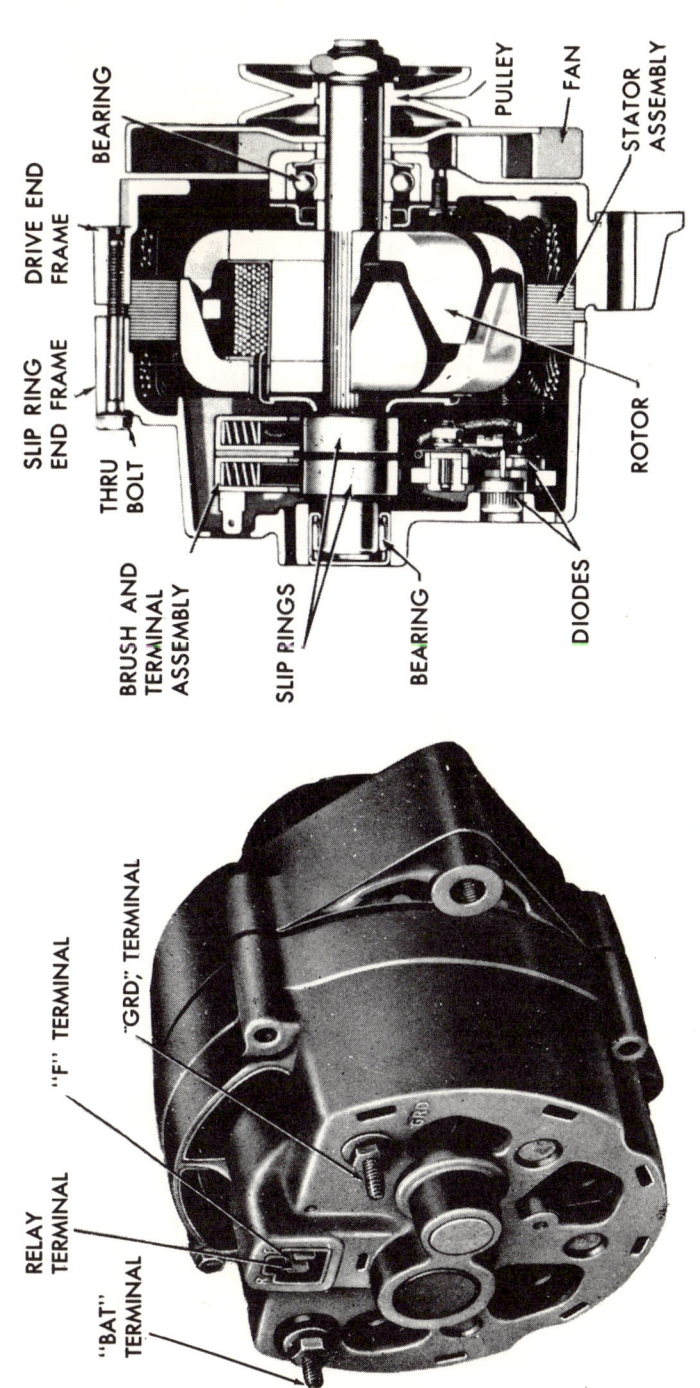

Alternator, cross-section

Diode and Field Test Using Ohmmeter

To detect a shorted diode or shorted or open field winding, disconnect the battery ground cable at the battery side.

Test A (positive diodes): Connect an ohmmeter between the R and BAT terminals on the alternator and take a reading, then reverse the leads and read again. The resistance reading should be high in one direction and low in the other.

Test B (negative diodes): Connect the ohmmeter between the R and GRD terminals and take a reading, then reverse the leads and read again. The resistance reading should be high in one direction and low in the other.

Test C (open field check): Connect the ohmmeter from the F to the GRD terminal and read the lowest range of the meter scale; this reading should be 7-20 ohms.

Field Excitation Check with Test Lamp

Connect a 12 volt test lamp at the following locations.

Test 1: Pull the four-way connector from the voltage regulator and connect one test lead to terminal 4 on the connector and the other test lead to a good ground on the regulator. Turn the ignition switch ON. If the lamp does not light, check for an open circuit between the switch and the regulator connector.

Test 2: Disconnect the Test 1 line and connect the test leads between the F and 4 terminals on the connector. With the ignition switch ON, if lamp does not light, check the wire between the F terminal and the alternator and regulator or the field windings.

Test 3: Disconnect the Test 2 line and connect it between the F terminals on the connector and on the alternator. With the ignition ON, if the lamp does not light, there is an open circuit in the alternator field.

NOTE: If the lamp does not go out at either Test 1, 2, or 3 test points when the engine is started, suspect the field relay in the voltage regulator, insufficient alternator output, or a shorted diode. Start the engine only momentarily with the alternator circuit open.

Alternator Removal

Disconnect the battery ground cable to prevent accidental short circuits. Disconnect the alternator leads and tag them for location to aid assembly. Slack off or remove the blower belt and remove the alternator.

Delcotron alternator assembly

Disassembly

Clamp the alternator to hold it steady and remove the pulley with a 15/16" box wrench and 5/16" hex-wrench.

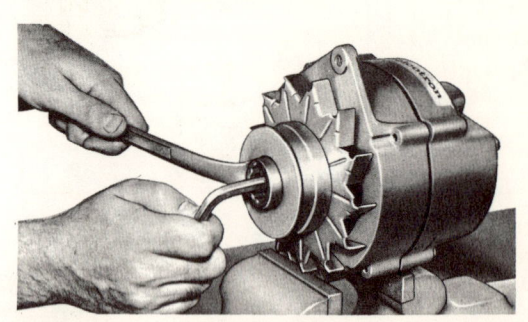

Pulley removal

Remove the through-bolts and separate the end frames. Remove the slip-ring side together with the stator, being careful to keep the spring-loaded brushes from popping out. Disconnect the stator leads and remove the stator from the frame. Remove the rotor and spacers from the drive end plate.

NOTE: If desired, the heat-sink may be removed from the slip-ring frame by removing the BAT and GRD terminals and the inside screw, then disassemble further.

Clean all small parts in solvent. Inspect the bearings for wear or damage. Do not clean the rotor or stator beyond light wiping with clean solvent on the friction surfaces. Inspect the brushes for wear which could prevent them from contacting the slip rings and replace them if necessary.

Rotor Inspection Using Ohmmeter

Perform the ohmmeter checks shown. Check for grounds between either slip ring and the

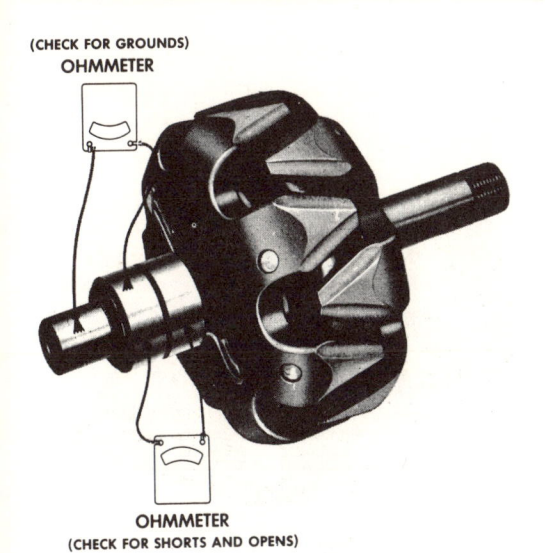

ELECTRICAL SYSTEM

(CHECK FOR GROUNDS)
OHMMETER

OHMMETER
(CHECK FOR SHORTS AND OPENS)

Checking rotor for grounds or open circuits

shaft. A low ohmmeter reading indicates a ground. Check resistance across both slip rings; high resistance indicates an open circuit.

Stator Inspection Using Ohmmeter or Test Lamp

Connect a 110-volt test lamp or an ohmmeter from any stator lead to the stator frame. If the test lamp lights or resistance is low, the stator winding is grounded to the frame.

Connect a test lamp or ohmmeter between any pair of stator leads. Failure of the lamp to light, or a high resistance reading, indicates an open circuit.

Diode Testing Using Test Lamp

Attach one lead of a 12 volt test lamp to the assembled heat sink and the other to a diode lead. Reverse the leads and compare results; a good diode will light the lamp *one* of the ways but not the other. If the lamp lights both ways or not at all, the diode must be replaced.

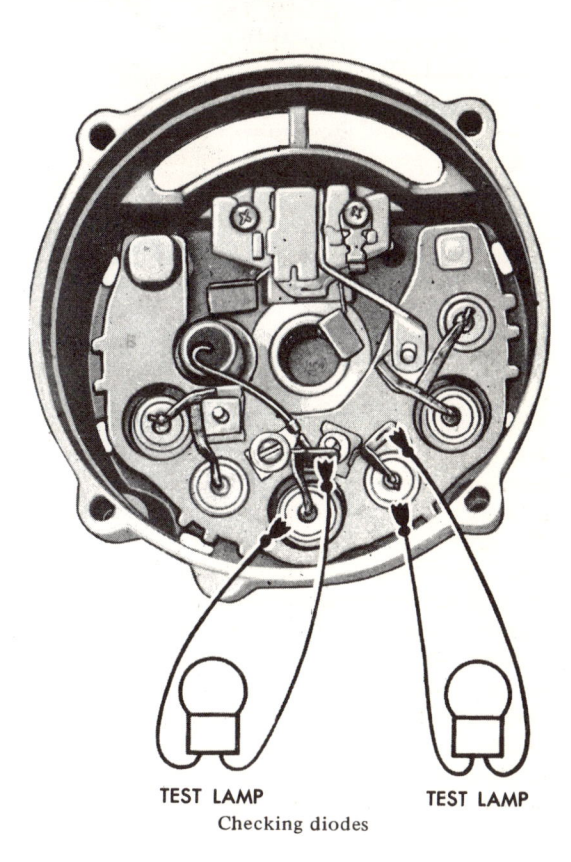

TEST LAMP   **TEST LAMP**
Checking diodes

OHMMETER
(Check for Opens)

OHMMETER   **OHMMETER**
(Check for Opens)   (Check for Grounds)

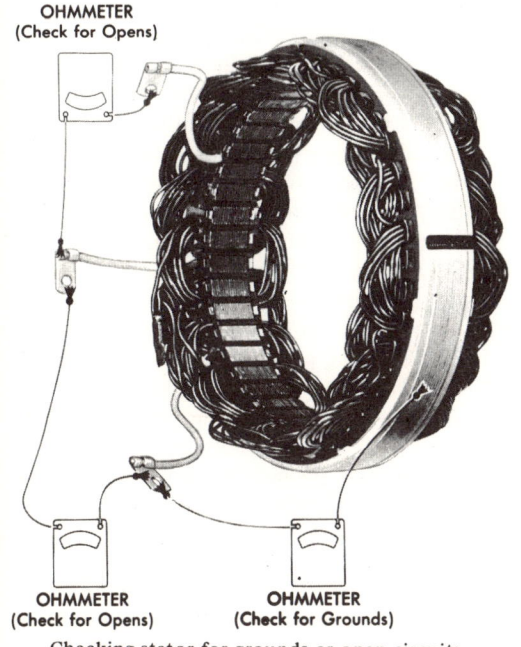

Checking stator for grounds or open circuits

NOTE: Replace the diodes by pressing them out of the end frame and pressing in new ones of the same color code (red-positive, black-negative). Press diodes in and out carefully to avoid damage.

Assembly

Assemble the alternator by first installing the rotor in the drive end frame. Install the stator in the slip-ring end frame and connect the diode leads. If the heat sink assembly was removed, install it and tighten the terminals. Assemble the end frames, being careful to guide the brushes onto the slip rings. Install the through-bolts. Install the pulley and tighten the locknut to 50-60 ft. lbs. using the tool arrangement shown. GM tool J-21501 can be duplicated by a

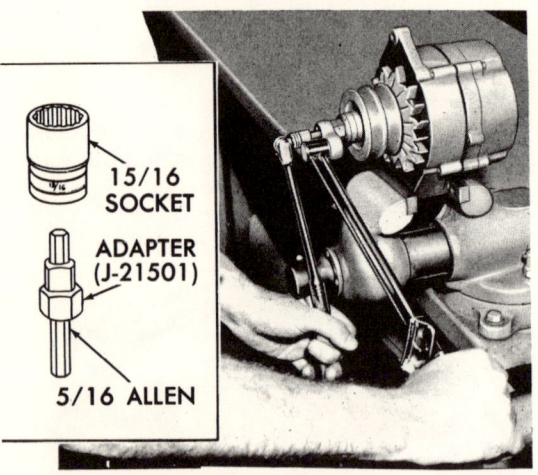

Torquing pulley nut

long 5/16" Allen wrench on a socket. Install the alternator on the engine; install and adjust the blower belt and connect all electrical leads in their proper locations.

Voltage Regulator

The "nerve center" of the charging system is the voltage regulator. This device activates the generator or alternator when the battery needs charging. This unit is usually reliable for the complicated job it does, but when the charging system fails for reasons not traceable to the generator or alternator or the battery, a malfunction in the regulator can be the cause. Suspect the regulator if the following symptoms are present:

1. The battery is in good condition but runs down repeatedly or is constantly weak.
2. The generator or alternator is in good condition but overheats from excessive operation.
3. The battery is observed to overcharge (heats up or boils over) or loses water rapidly.

Perform the various checks described below before attempting to disassemble or adjust the voltage regulator. A voltmeter or multitester (such as that called for in testing a generator or alternator) is a necessity for testing and adjusting a voltage regulator. If such devices are not available for checking the function of the regulator, it is best to take the regulator to a well-equipped shop for inspection and testing, or to replace the regulator with another one. Do not rely on mechanical adjustments alone.

Voltage Regulator—1960-1964

This regulator is used with the DC generator on Corvairs from 1960 to 1964. The electrical

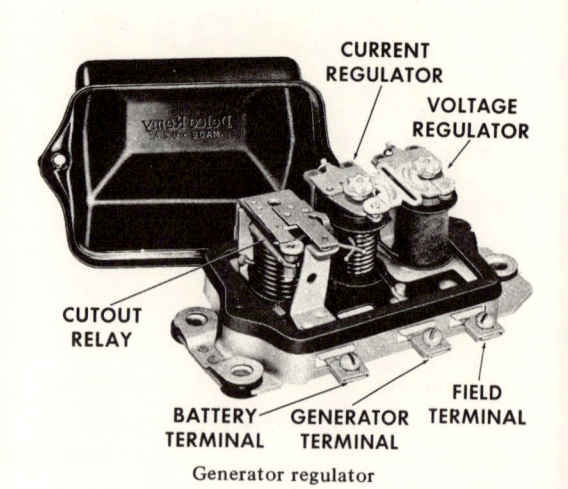

Generator regulator

schematic for the regulator and generator charging system is shown.

Checking the Voltage Regulator

Connect a voltmeter between the BAT terminal on the regulator and any good ground, and take a voltage reading first at idle, then at medium engine speed. The reading should increase as the engine speed increases.

Voltage specifications for the regulator are given in the chart. Temperature has an effect on the regulator's output. For this reason, all measurements of regulator output are meaningless unless the regulator cover is in place and fastened down and the engine is fully warmed up and running for five to ten minutes. The "ambient" temperature (the temperature of the regulator's air environment) can usually be assumed to be 40°F. above the air temperature in the working area. 125°F. is considered the normal operating range.

With the voltmeter connected as above, connect a tachometer and measure the voltage at 1600 rpm. If the voltage output is out of specification, it is permissible to remove the regulator cover and adjust the voltage regulator as shown. Increasing the spring tension (tightening the screw) will increase the voltage, and decreasing the tension (loosening the screw) will lower it.

NOTE: Make very small adjustments at first, especially in the increased-voltage direction to prevent accidental over-loading. Be sure the ad-

ELECTRICAL SYSTEM

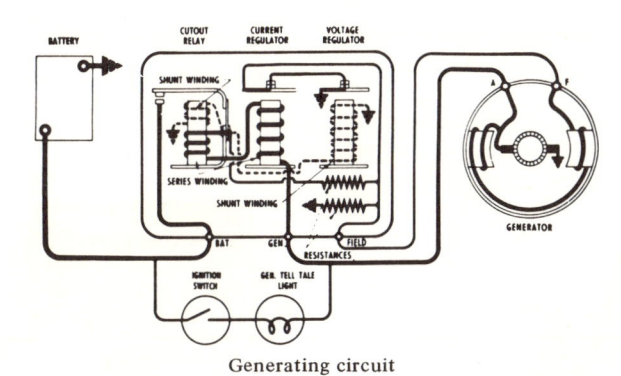

Generating circuit

Standard Regulator

VOLTAGE REGULATOR SPECIFICATIONS
vs
REGULATOR AMBIENT TEMPERATURE

REGULATOR AMBIENT TEMPERATURE	VOLTAGE LOW		HIGH
165° F	13.1	—	13.9
145° F	13.5	—	14.3
125° F	**13.8**	—	**14.7**
105° F	14.0	—	14.9
85° F	14.2	—	15.2
65° F	14.4	—	15.4
45° F	14.5	—	15.6

NORMAL SPECIFICATION RANGE
■ INDICATES PUBLISHED SPECIFICATIONS

Voltage regulator correction factors

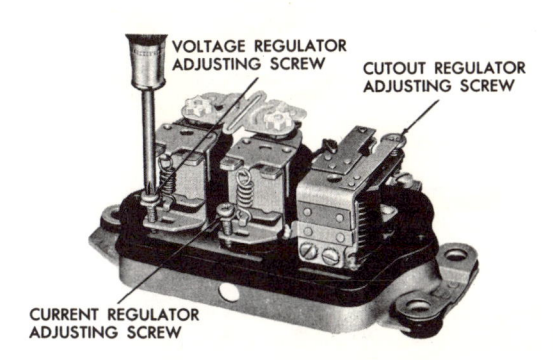

Regulator adjusting screws

justing screw is contacting the support as shown.

After any adjustment, replace the cover, start the engine, and take a voltage reading after a suitable warmup period.

Checking Cutout Relay

Connect the voltmeter between the GEN terminal and a good ground. Start the engine, allow it to idle, then slowly speed it up and note the closing voltage of the relay. This should be 11.8 to 13.5 volts but is acceptable anywhere at least 0.5 volt below the voltage read at the regulator in the preceding check. To adjust the relay voltage, remove the regulator cover and tighten (increase) or loosen (decrease) the spring tension. Replace the cover and retest the regulator.

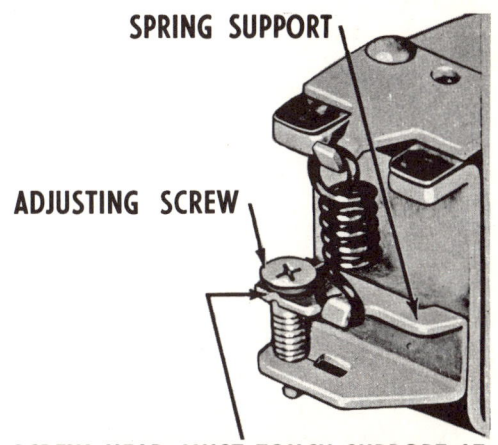

SCREW HEAD MUST TOUCH SUPPORT AT THIS POINT AFTER FINAL ADJUSTMENT

Contact between regulator spring support and adjusting screw

ELECTRICAL SYSTEM

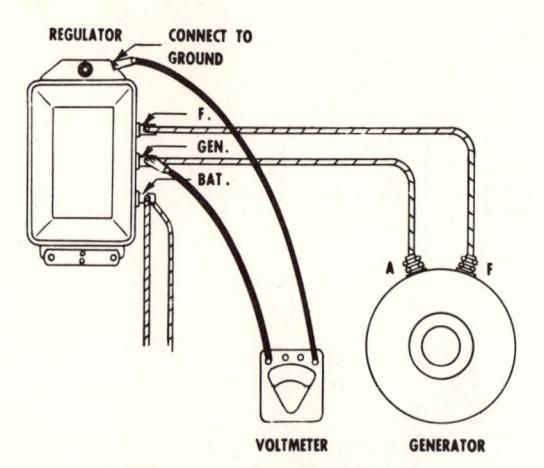

Checking cutout relay closing voltage

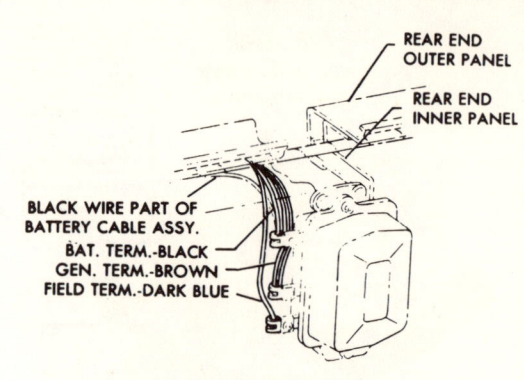

Regulator installed

Checking the Current Regulator

Disconnect the battery ground cable and the BAT wire at the regulator. Connect the voltmeter and an ammeter as shown, with a 25-watt capacity rheostat in the generator field wire to provide variable resistance. Connect the battery ground cable and start the engine. Warm up at 1600 rpm and cycle the generator (stop the engine and restart it). Note the current regulator setting and adjust it with the screw if necessary to bring the reading within the specifications previously given.

Removing and Cleaning the Regulator

Remove the regulator for checking and cleaning if the coils show erratic behavior during the electrical checks, indicating dirty contacts. Remove the regulator from the wall of the engine compartment, being sure to mark and separate the wires. Tape off or otherwise insulate the battery terminal wire to keep it from shorting against the body of the vehicle.

Clean the contact points of the voltage regulator coils just enough to remove surface pitting

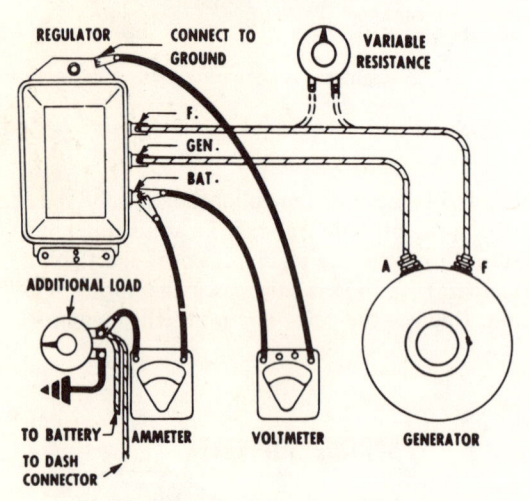

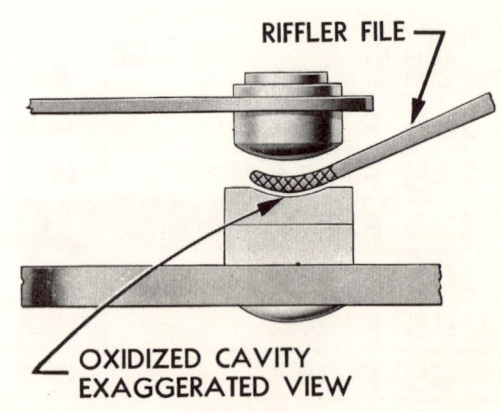

Checking current regulator setting

Use of the riffler file

or oxides. A spoon-shaped "riffler" file is best for this purpose.

NOTE: Do not use sandpaper or emery cloth, which will leave conductive deposits.

Clean the cutout relay contacts with crocus cloth (fine abrasive cloth) only, not a file, emery cloth, or sandpaper. Wipe all contacts clean after removing surface faults with alcohol or acetone.

Adjusting Air Gaps

Adjust the cutout relay air gap to 0.020" as shown while pressing lightly on the armature to close the contact points. Raise or lower the armature as required, loosening the adjuster screws to free the armature. After adjusting the air gap, adjust the point opening distance to 0.020" as shown, by carefully bending the armature stop.

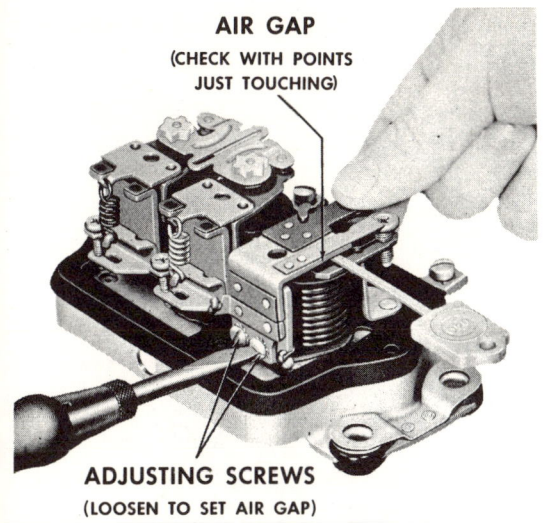

ELECTRICAL SYSTEM

Adjusting cutout relay air gap

Adjusting regulator air gap

Adjust the voltage regulator air gap to 0.075" with the contact points just touching, by turning the nut above the regulator coil.

Adjust the current regulator air gap in the same fashion, to 0.075".

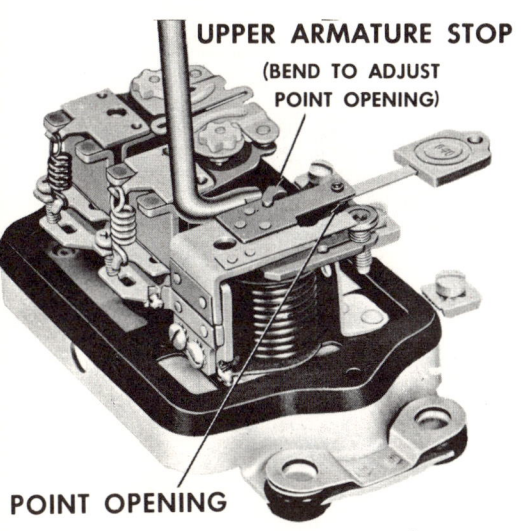

Adjusting cutout relay point opening

After adjustment of the regulator coils, check the voltage output, closing voltage, and current after the regulator is installed in the vehicle.

Voltage Regulator—1965-1969

The two unit voltage regulator used with the AC generator (alternator) on Corvairs from 1965 to 1969, is shown. The electrical schematic for the charging system is shown.

NOTE: On heavy-duty alternator installations, an extra diode will be found on the regulator.

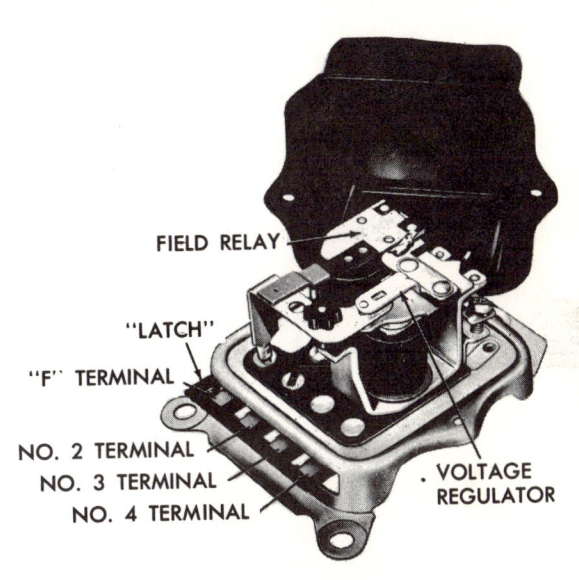

Two unit voltage regulator

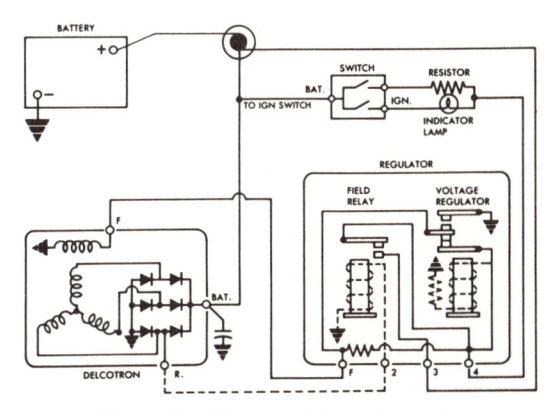

Two unit voltage regulator, schematic

ELECTRICAL SYSTEM

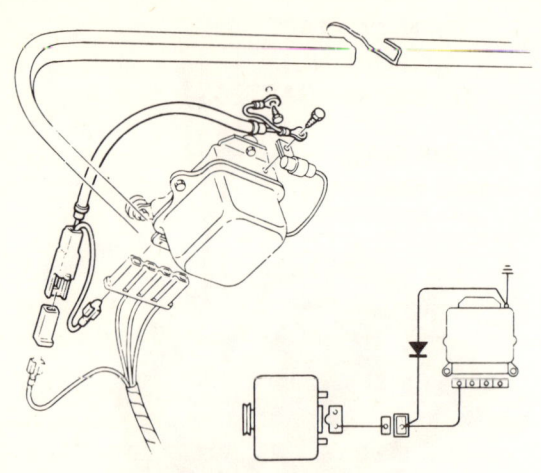

External field discharge diode

Checking Voltage Setting

Connect a jumper wire between the front junction block on the horn relay and the regulator base, and a ¼-ohm, 25 watt resistor between the junction block and wire 12-B. Warm up the engine for at least 15 minutes at 1500 rpm, then quickly disconnect and reconnect the regulator plug (to cycle the voltage control), and read the voltage. If the voltage is not between 13.5-15.2 volts, proceed as follows: disconnect the regulator plug, and remove the regulator cover. Reconnect the plug, and adjust the voltage to 14.2-14.6 volts. Disconnect the plug, install the cover, reconnect the plug,

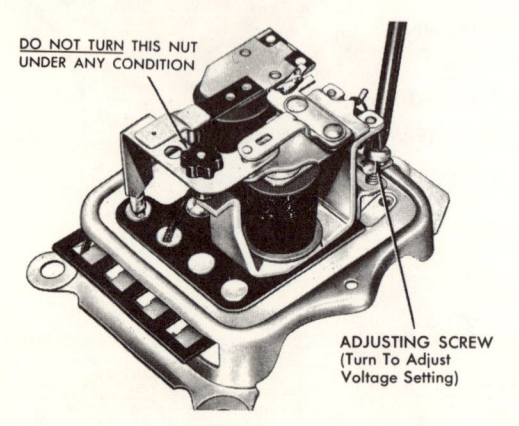

Adjusting voltage setting

and test as above. Do not allow the voltage to exceed 16 volts while the engine is running.

Checking Field Relay

Disconnect the plug from the regulator. Connect a voltmeter between the No. 2 terminal of the regulator and ground, and a 50 ohm variable resistor between the No. 3 terminal of the plug, and the No. 2 terminal of the regulator. Slowly decrease resistance of the resistor, and note the closing voltage of the relay. If this voltage is not between 1.5-3.2 volts, adjust by slightly bending the heel iron of the relay.

Contact Point and Air Gaps

Set the air gap under the voltage regulator as shown, turning the nut to adjust the gap to

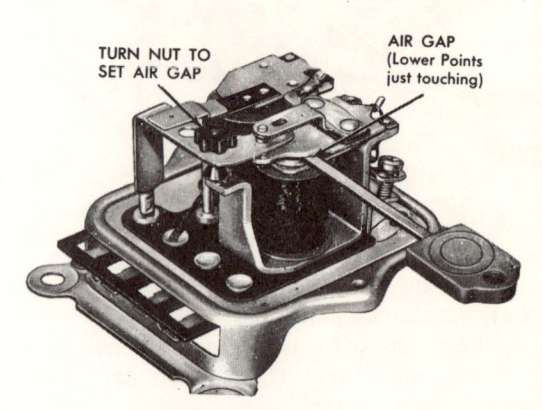

Checking voltage regulator air gap

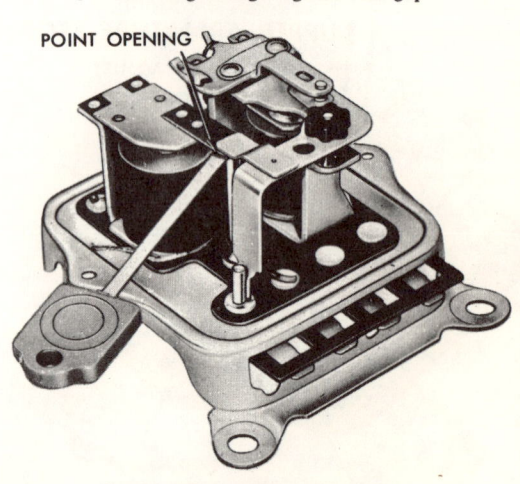

Checking field relay point opening

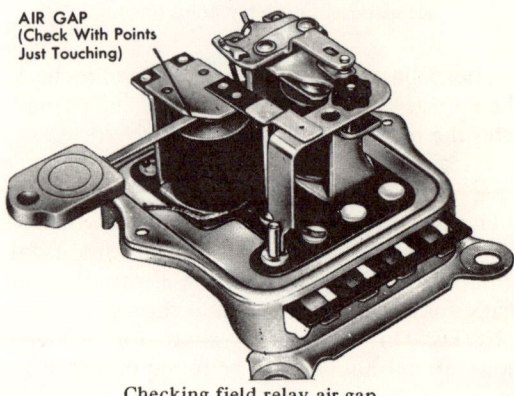

Checking field relay air gap

ELECTRICAL SYSTEM

0.067″. At this setting the point gap should be 0.014″; bend the arm to obtain this distance.

Adjust the field relay point opening to 0.030″ and the air gap to 0.015″, as shown.

Check the voltage output and closing voltage of the regulator on the vehicle after these adjustments have been made.

Starter

Description

The starting motor used on Corvairs is similar to a DC generator in construction, having a wound armature and a commutator ring. This unit, however, runs under reversed current from that in a generator, so that the armature is motorized and can be used to transmit power to the engine flywheel with a pinion gear. The operation of the Corvair starting motor is shown. Turning on the starter switch activates the solenoid, a wound coil which creates a strong magnetic field when energized. This magnetic force works axially on the plunger, pulling on the shift lever and sending the pinion gear into mesh with the flywheel. At this point, when the gear is safely engaged, full battery power is supplied to the armature and the motor cranks the engine. Ordinarily, the engine, after starting, would drive the pinion gear until the driver released the starter switch, thus cutting the armature and solenoid power; however, an overrunning clutch is provided on the pinion shaft, which engages spiral splines on the shaft and pulls the pinion gear out of mesh with the flywheel when the engine starts to spin the gear, preventing damage to the starter from overspeeding.

Common Starter Problems

1. The starter cranks slowly or not at all: check the tightness and cleanliness of battery and starter connections. Check the battery for condition and charge.

2. Solenoid clicks but no cranking occurs: check the battery charge and connections. Inspect the "hold-in coil" portion of the starter solenoid.

Removal and Disassembly

Disconnect the battery ground cable and the starter electrical connections. Jack up and support the vehicle and unbolt and remove the starter.

Remove the field connector on the solenoid (nearest to the starter body) and unscrew and remove the solenoid; remove the through-bolts holding the starter together. Turn the solenoid clockwise to release its mounting flange from the parting surfaces of the starter body and remove the solenoid. Remove the end frame and remove the shift lever by pulling out the hinge pin. Pull the armature from the field frame and disassemble: remove the collar, snap-ring, and retainer from the pinion gear end of the shaft and pull off the gear and the clutch assembly.

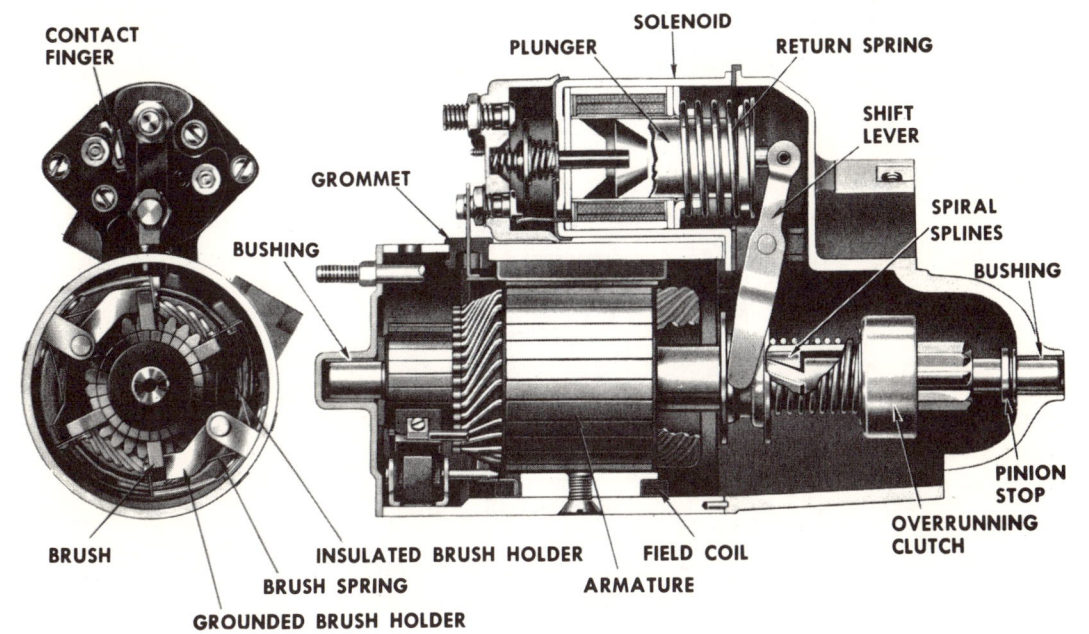

Starting motor cross-section

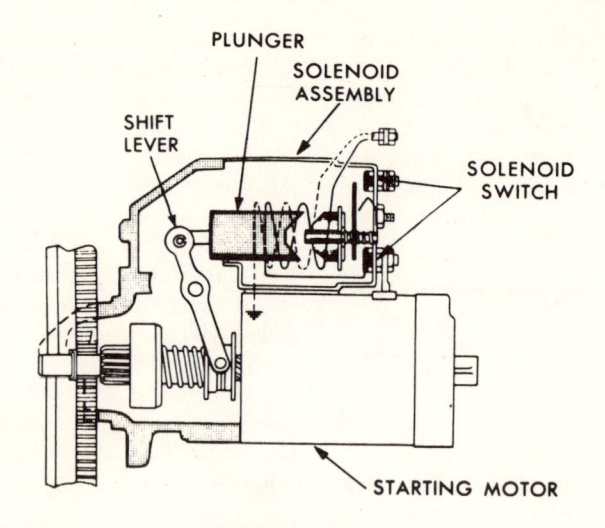

DISENGAGED

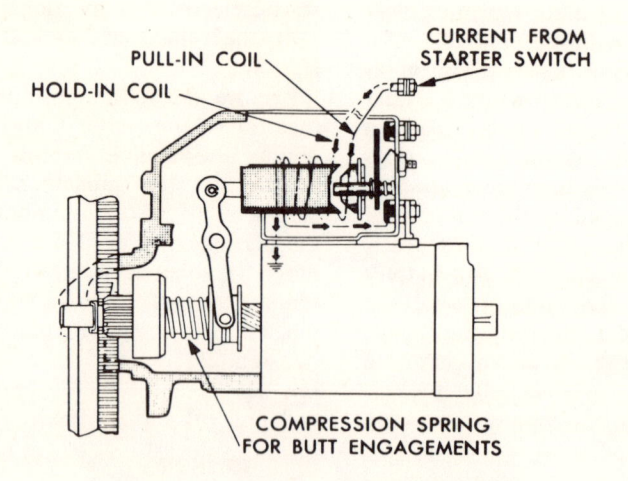

PINION PARTIALLY ENGAGED

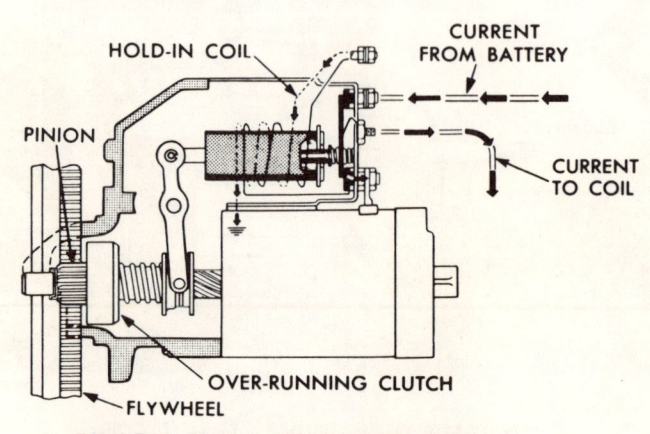

PINION FULLY ENGAGED AND STARTING MOTOR CRANKING

Solenoid operation

ELECTRICAL SYSTEM

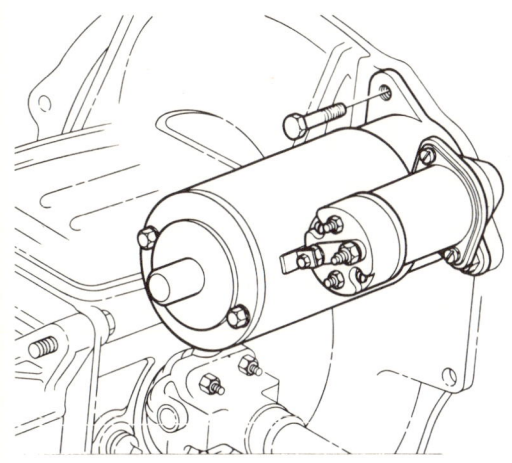

Starting motor installed

NOTE: On early-production assemblies, there will be a helper spring between the clutch and the armature winding. Slip off this spring after the clutch has been removed.

The starter is shown fully disassembled.

Ordinarily it is not necessary to disassemble the starter beyond its major groups and the brushes, but other parts (brush holders, etc.) may be removed if damaged or faulty, as proved by electrical checks.

Clean all small metallic parts in solvent. Do not immerse the clutch assembly in solvent; it is prepacked with grease which solvent would remove. Do not immerse the armature assembly or the field windings in solvent.

Inspect the commutator for damage (roughness, grooves, etc.) and turn the commutator surface down on a lathe to remove such damage. Hold such machining to a minimum, cutting away only enough to restore a true surface

to the commutator. Afterward lightly sand or stone the turned surface to remove tool marks. Recut the grooves between the commutator bars to remove copper chips and accumulated dirt.

Check the armature on a "growler" machine for short circuits as shown. See the Generator Section for a description of this instrument. Short circuits which cannot be remedied or traced are cause for rejection of the armature.

Use a test lamp and probes to check for grounds between the armature and commutator

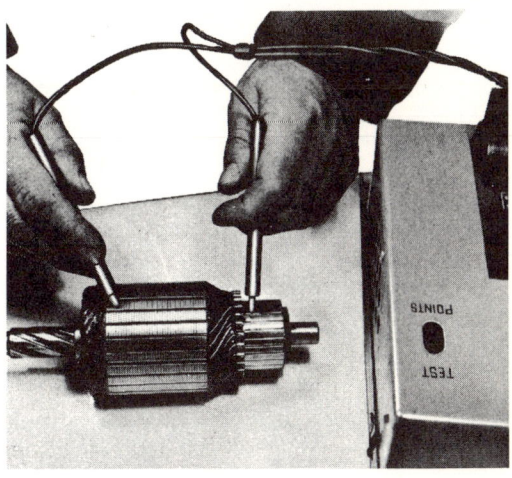

Armature ground test

bars; the test lamp should not light when applied in this manner.

Inspect the fields for rubbing damage on the surfaces, and for frayed wires. Use the test lamp to check for open circuits between the field

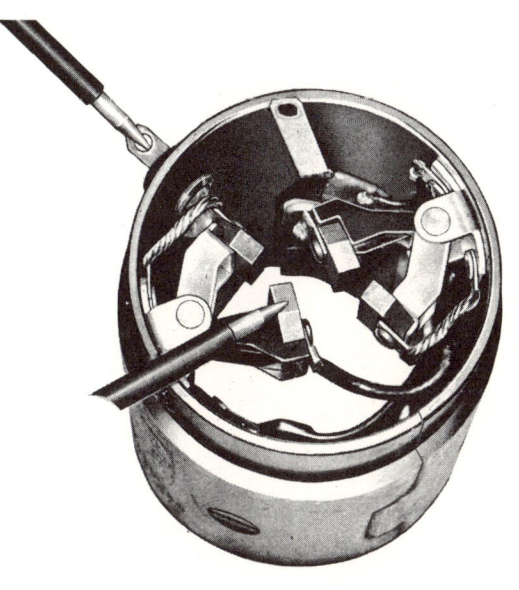

Armature short-circuit test

Field coil open circuit test

ELECTRICAL SYSTEM

1 Drive housing
1A Gasket
2 Shift lever boot
3 Shift lever nut and lockwasher
4 Pin
5 Shift lever
6 Solenoid plunger
6A Solenoid return spring
7 Solenoid case
8 Screw and lockwasher
9 Grommet
10 Field frame
11 Through bolts
12 Thrust collar
13 Snap-ring
14 Retainer
15 Overrunning clutch assembly
16 Spring
17 Collar
18 Snap-ring
19 Assist spring (early production)
20 Armature
20A Brake washer
21 Commutator end frame
22 Brush springs
23 Washer
24 Insulated brush holders
25 Grounded brush holders
26 Brush
27 Screws
28 Field coils
29 Insulators
30 Pole shoes
31 Screws

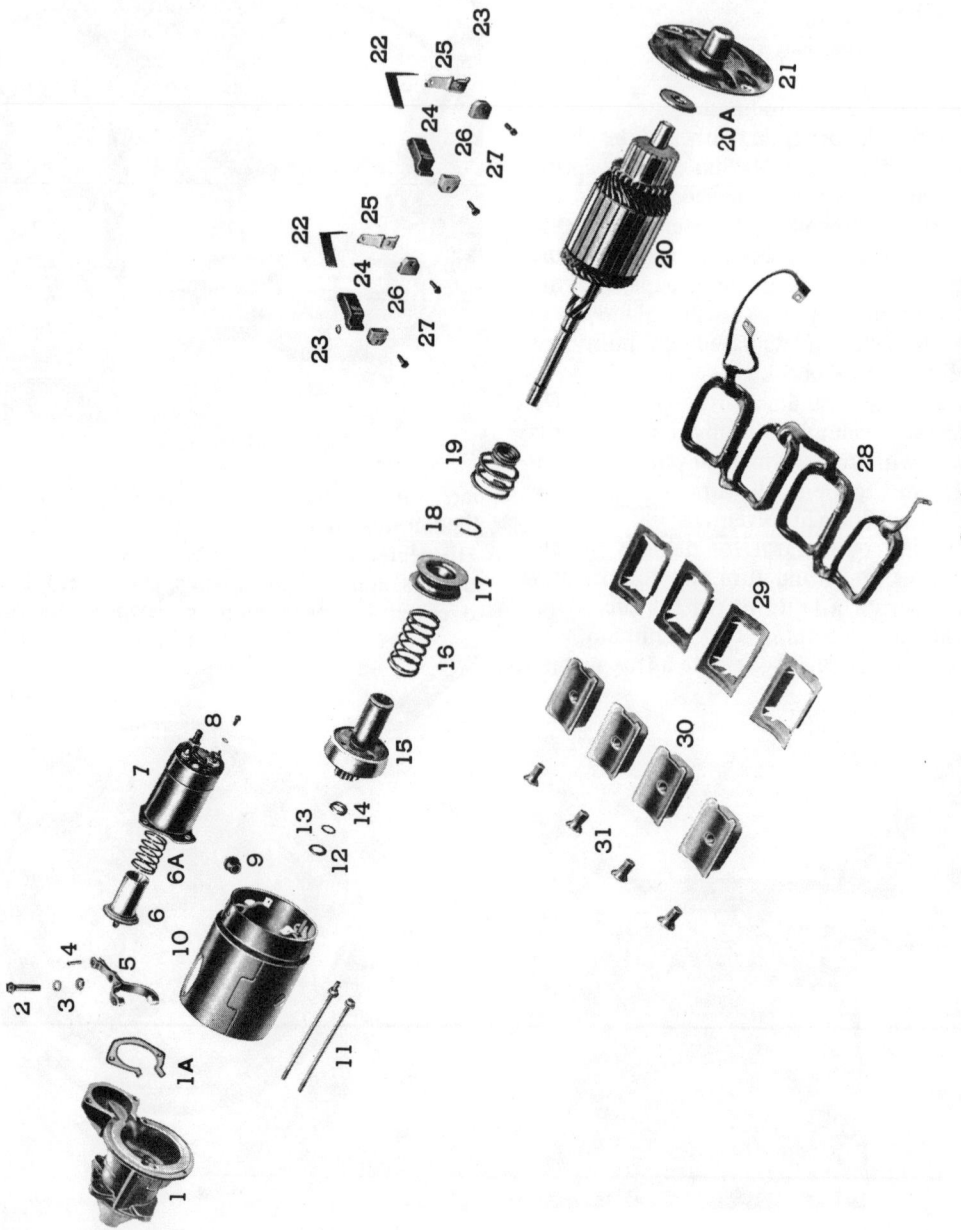

Starting motor parts layout

ELECTRICAL SYSTEM

connector on the outside of the starter body and each insulated brush. The test lamp should light in this test; if it does not, the circuit is broken and the terminals should be checked.

Check for grounds in the field coils as shown. The test lamp should not light; if it does, check

Field coil ground test

for visible short circuits or faulty insulation between the brush holders and the starter body.

Repair all visible short circuits, damaged insulation, or worn wires. Replace worn brushes.

Solenoid

Disassemble and inspect the solenoid to check for the cause of a malfunction: remove the retaining screws and pull off the end cover. Check parts for signs of burning, short circuits, or dirt binding the plunger. Assemble the solenoid and

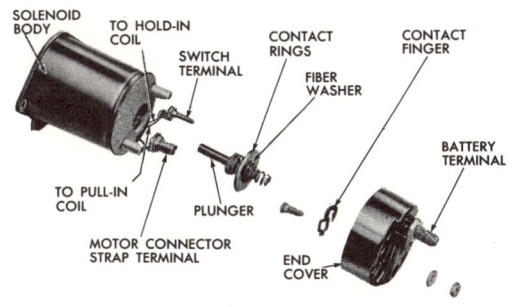

Solenoid, exploded view

test it with battery current to verify its operation.

Clutch

Check the clutch assembly for correct action: rotate the front clutch against the gear in each direction; the clutch should turn freely in its overrunning direction but not in the reverse direction. Check the pinion gear for worn or broken teeth.

Assembly

Assemble the starter in its major groups: field frame and brushes, armature and clutch assembly, and end frame and solenoid. Assemble the clutch assembly to the armature shaft (be sure the helper spring is in place, if it is used, with the smaller end toward the winding). Install the retainer, snap-ring, and collar on the shaft to retain the clutch and squeeze them together on the shaft to insure that they are seated together.

Install the shift lever in the end frame; coat the commutator end of the shaft lightly with oil to lubricate it in the bushing and install the armature assembly in the field frame, holding the brushes apart until the commutator passes between them.

Coat the pinion gear end of the shaft lightly with oil to lubricate it in the end frame and install the end frame loosely on the field frame and armature. Install the solenoid and position its flange against the end frame with its gasket (later-production models) in place. Thread in the through-bolts and tighten them, and install the field coil connector at the inner front of the solenoid.

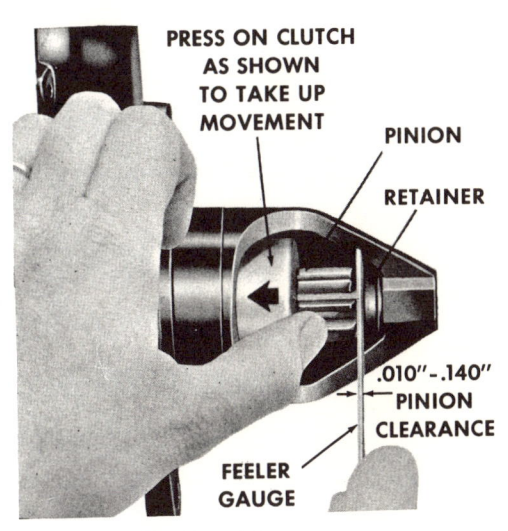

Checking pinion clearance

Fuses and Circuit Breakers

1960–65

Light circuits (except following)	15 Amp. CB
Tail, stop, dome lamp and cigar lighter	10 Amp. Fuse
Glove comp. lamp and heater blower	10 Amp. Fuse
Back-up lamp and total heater system	20 Amp. Fuse
Radio	4 Amp. Fuse
Instrument lamp, radio panel lamp, heater control panel	3 Amp. Fuse
Electric windshield wiper	20 Amp. Fuse
Air conditioner	15 Amp. Fuse

1966–69

Light circuits (except following)	CB
Radio	10 Amp. Fuse
Instrument lamps	4 Amp. Fuse
Gauges & back-up lamps	10 Amp. Fuse
Clock, lighter, courtesy lamps, and hazard flasher	20 Amp. Fuse
Stop, tail/side marker and tail lights	20 Amp. Fuse
Wiper motor	20 Amp. Fuse
Heater & air conditioner	25 Amp. Fuse

Light Bulbs

1960–63

Headlamp (outer)	4002; $37\frac{1}{2}$–50 W
Headlamp (inner)	4001; $37\frac{1}{2}$ W
Parking, tail, stop and dir. signals	1034; 4–32 CP
Back-up lamps	1073; 32 CP
Instrument lamps	1816; 3 CP
Radio dial lamp	1891; 2 CP
Indicator lamps, glove compartment lamp	57; 2 CP
High beam indicator, heater control panel	53; 1 CP
Dome lamp	211; 15 CP
Courtesy lamp	89; 6 CP
License plate lamp	67; 4 CP

1964–69

Headlamp (outer)	4002; $37\frac{1}{2}$–50 W
Headlamp (inner)	4001; $37\frac{1}{2}$ W
Parking, tail, stop and dir. signals	1157; 4–32 CP
Back-up lamps	1156; 32 CP
Instrument lamps	1816; 3 CP
Directional signal, headlamp beam, heater control panel indicator lamps	1445; 1 CP
Temperature, oil, generator indicator and glove compartment lamps	1895; 2 CP
Dome lamp	211; 12 CP
Courtesy lamp	631; 6 CP
License plate lamp	67; 4 CP
Radio dial lamp	1893; 2 CP

Check the pinion gear clearance as shown, using feeler stock. This clearance, between the retainer and the gear face, should be from 0.010-0.140", measured while pressing lightly on the clutch face to take up the initial play of the parts only (do not attempt to compress the clutch against its spring). If this clearance is out of specification, disassemble the starter again and check for misassembled or faulty armature parts or shift lever.

Installation

Bolt the starter in place on the engine and reconnect the starter and battery wires.

6 • Power Train

Clutch

Description

The clutch used in Corvairs equipped with manual transmissions is illustrated. It consists of a dry single-plate unit between a bent-finger, diaphragm pressure plate and the flywheel of the engine. A conventional throwout bearing transfers the thrust of the clutch fork to the fingers of the pressure plate. The Corvair clutch disk has no damper springs because the torsional flexibility of the long input shaft from the transmission to the disk absorbs sufficient vibration.

Actuation of the clutch is by foot pedal and control cable from the driver's compartment, pulling the arm of the clutch fork forward to release the clutch when the pedal is pressed.

Turbocharged Corvairs are equipped with a heavy duty clutch, identifiable by its six broad, flat mounting flanges on the pressure plate assembly.

Servicing

The Corvair clutch is easily adjustable by changing the length of the control cables and rods which connect the pedal system to the clutch fork. Adjustment to compensate for clutch disk wear is therefore possible.

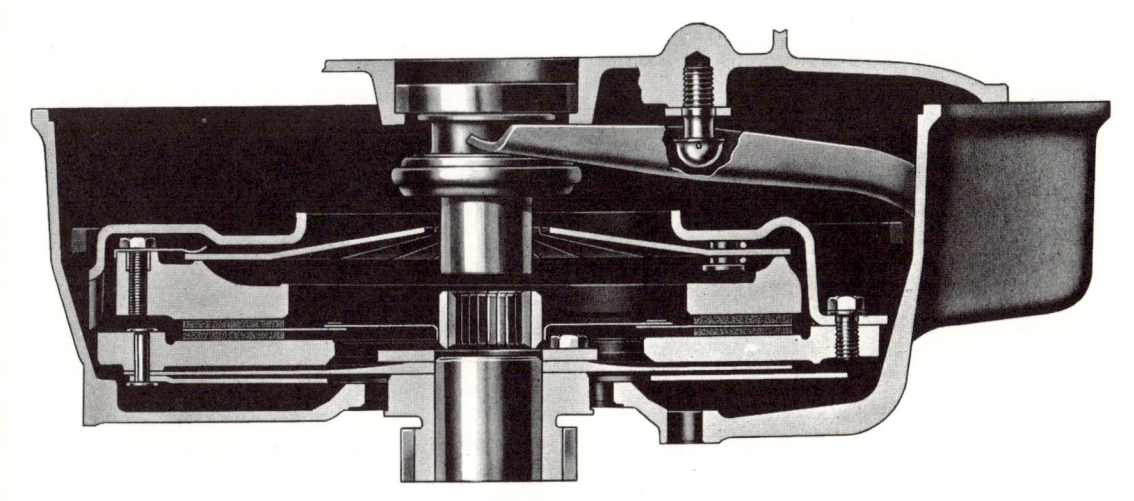

Clutch cross-section

Hi-performance clutch

The clutch assembly is bolted to the flywheel of the engine.

Adjustment

The "remote control" aspect of the Corvair clutch demands a different approach to clutch adjustment than that used on front-engine vehicles. Instead of a one or two-lever linkage from pedal to clutch fork, a control cable from the Corvair's clutch pedal transmits *pull* to a cross-shaft at the transmission front crossmember and from there to the clutch fork at the right side of the flywheel housing.

When adjusting the Corvair clutch it is best to check *all* the variables and not merely adjust the nearest swivel and consider the job done. For instance, if the cross-shaft is left too close to the transmission crossmember after adjustment or after extensive wear to the clutch disk, it will not be able to travel far enough to release the disk and the clutch will not function.

The three steps in clutch adjustment for any Corvair, in order, are:

1. Establishment of the cross-shaft to transmission crossmember distance.
2. Adjustment of the cable from the foot pedal to the cross-shaft to allow for the distance in Step 1.
3. Adjustment of the pull rod from the cross-shaft to the clutch fork.

Adjustment—1960-1961

Remove the cross-shaft return spring to release the tension on the shaft. Remove the spring clip holding the clutch fork pull rod swivel in the cross-shaft and pull out the swivel.

Establish the 1/8 to 3/8″ distance between the cross-shaft outboard lever and the nearby transmission crossmember; this can be done by cutting a block of wood to the correct thickness and keeping it pressed in place between the lever and the crossmember while making the other adjustments.

1 Locknut
2 Cable clevis
3 Control cross-shaft and outboard lever
4 Return spring

Adjusting clutch cable

While keeping the 1/8 to 3/8″ distance from lever to crossmember, take up on the cable (or loosen it, as necessary) by slacking off the locknut and threading the cable connnector in or out, with the cable pulled taut with the hands, until the connector fits in the cable clevis. Tighten the locknut to approximately 10 ft. lbs. and check the cable by pulling the clevis rearward and checking the crossmember distance.

Pull the clutch fork forward to push the throwout bearing in the clutch against the pressure plate fingers. With the rod pulled out by hand as far as it will go, thread the pull rod swivel in or out until it mates with the *upper* hole in the outboard lever when the cable and clevis are pulled rearward (tensioning the cable). After the pull rod has been adjusted in this manner, *lenghthen* it by three full turns of the swivel to "unload" the linkage slightly. Install the swivel in the outboard lever and install the spring clip to retain it. Install the return spring on the cross shaft (in the *lower* hole on the outboard lever).

Check the pedal free play in the driver's compartment; this travel should be at least 3/4″. To obtain lesser or greater pedal travel, adjust the *pull rod swivel*, not the cable.

POWER TRAIN

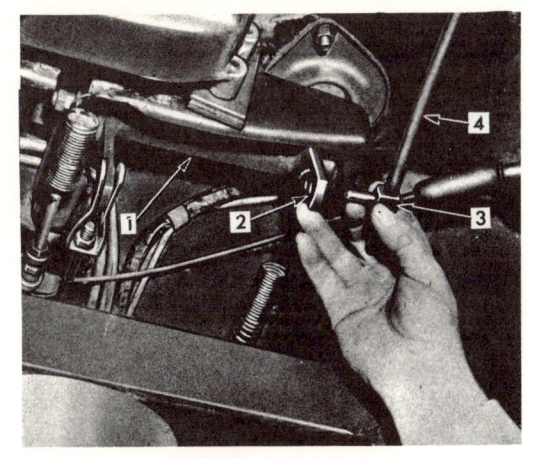

1 Control cross-shaft assembly
2 Control cross-shaft outboard lever
3 Clutch fork pullrod swivel
4 Clutch fork pullrod

Adjusting clutch fork pull rod

Adjustment—1962 and 1963

Adjust these models in the same way as above, but with a cross-shaft to crossmember distance of 3/8 to 5/8".

Adjustment—1964

Adjust this model in the same way as above, but with a cross-shaft to crossmember distance of 1/2 to 5/8".

Adjustment—1965

Remove the cotter pin and washer from the cable swivel and disconnect the swivel.

Establish a 7/8" distance between the *cable* (inboard) lever and the transmission crossmember.

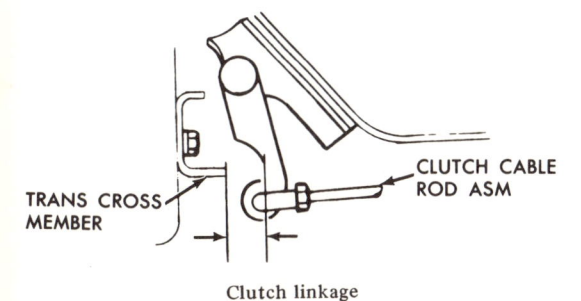

TRANS CROSS MEMBER
CLUTCH CABLE ROD ASM

Clutch linkage

Tighten the cable with the hands to approximately 15 lbs. tension and line up the cable swivel with its hole in the inboard lever. Turn the swivel in or out to adjust it and install it with its washer and cotter pin. Check the crossmember distance with the cable pulled taut.

Remove the spring clip on the pull rod swivel and remove the swivel.

NOTE: The return spring has been relocated to the cable lever on this and later models.

Thread the swivel in or out to match the hole in the pull rod lever; lengthen the rod three turns after this adjustment to "unload" the linkage. Install the swivel with its spring clip.

Adjustment—1966-1969

Adjust these models in the same manner as for 1965, but with a crossmember distance of 3/8" and *two* "unloading" turns on the pull rod swivel.

Removal of the Clutch

Method 1: Remove the engine alone from the vehicle and service the release bearing and clutch fork on the transaxle.

Method 2: Remove the entire engine and transaxle from the vehicle and unbolt and separate the transaxle from the engine on the ground.

NOTE: See Chapter Three for removal of the engine and/or transaxle from the vehicle.

Loosen the bolts holding the clutch assembly to the flywheel of the engine, one turn at a time until the spring pressure of the pressure plate is released. Mark the position of the pressure plate, the flywheel, and its cover in relation to each other; remove the six bolts and pull the pressure plate from the engine. Remove the three bolts holding the cover to the pressure plate and remove the cover.

Inspect the pressure plate for any scratches or scoring on the pressure face which could shorten the life of the next clutch disk installed. If the last clutch disk wore through the rivets on the pressure plate side, the plate may be scored too badly for use and should be replaced.

NOTE: If the clutch wore through its rivets on the flywheel side, the flywheel may have to be refaced if it is significantly scored.

Remove the release bearing from the clutch fork attached to the differential carrier by removing the retaining spring attaching the fork to its ball joint. Remove the bearing with the fork. Roll the bearing's rotating surface and check for roughness. Replace it if any roughness or obvious wear is present.

NOTE: Installing a questionable release bearing with a new clutch is false economy if the new bearing fails before the disk is due to be replaced. Replace the bearing if there is any evidence at all of its having deteriorated or if its prepacked grease supply has dried up.

Wipe out the pilot bearing recessed into the end of the crankshaft. Be sure it is smooth and

Clutch fork assembly

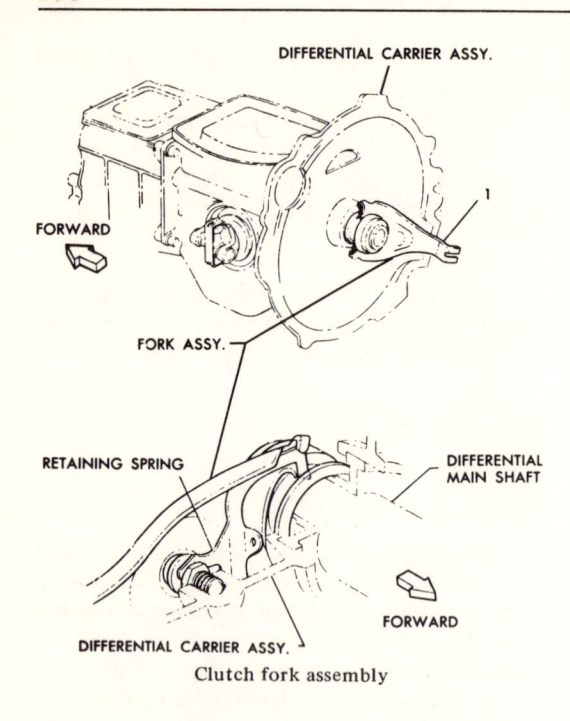

not excessively worn. Clear it of all foreign matter before reassembling the clutch.

Assembly

Install the new clutch disk against the flywheel, short hub inward (the inner side may be stamped "flywheel side").

The clutch disk must be positioned against the flywheel concentric with the pilot bearing so that the input shaft of the transmission can be installed in the disk spline without its pilot being off center, causing interference. The easiest way to achieve this alignment is to obtain a conventional, short, splined transmission input shaft from a dealer or junkyard for use as a pilot when installing the disk. If the splines on the shaft fit the clutch splines (the dimensions are common) and the pilot fits in the crankshaft the input shaft will work.

Install the disk on the face of the flywheel with the dummy shaft through its splines and locating in the crankshaft pilot bearing.

Bolt the cover onto the pressure plate in its original position. Torque the bolts to 15-20 ft. lbs.

Install the assembled cover and pressure plate over the clutch disk and thread in the six bolts until they just begin to contact the cover. Tighten them down evenly, until the plate is secured to the flywheel against its own spring tension. Torque the bolts to 15-20 ft. lbs.

Assemble the new or serviceable thrust bearing on the input shaft with the fork and retain them with the retaining spring as previously shown. Clean off the spline of the input shaft; *do not oil it.*

Remove the dummy shaft from the center of the clutch disk and assemble the transaxle to the flywheel housing, inserting the input shaft carefully until it is felt to mesh splines with the clutch disk. Jog the shaft by turning one of the universal joint yokes on the transaxle to aid in meshing the splines. Torque the housing bolts to 20-30 ft. lbs.

Install the power train in the vehicle and adjust the clutch as described in this section.

Transmission

Manual Transmission

Description

The Corvair three-speed transmission is a conventional synchromesh unit. Power from the engine is transmitted through a long, solid clutch shaft into a clutch gear in the transmission and from there through a countergear and into the gear train proper. Output power is through a hollow mainshaft inside which the input shaft turns. The mainshaft is splined to the pinion shaft in the differential. The transmission shares gear lubricant with the differential through passages around the mainshaft seal.

Shifting is accomplished by a single sliding and turning rod connected to the driver's shifting lever. Motion of the rod forward and rearward selects a gear, and rotation of the rod selects the fork for each pair of gears (reverse-first, second-third).

Maintenance

Transmission lubrication is accomplished with a supply of gear lubricant, maintained as described in Chapter One.

Shift Linkage

The linkage from the shift lever to the transmission consists of a control rod which transmits axial and turning force on the shifter shaft in the transmission. An adjusting clamp is provided at the rear of the shaft. This clamp should be adjusted so that all gears can be engaged without interference of the shift lever with the driver's seat, and without the need for excessive reaching by the driver. To adjust the linkage, shift the transmission into first gear as a refer-

POWER TRAIN

ence point, then loosen the clamp and pull the control rod rearward by hand to take up the slack in the linkage. Move the linkage forward or rearward as required until the shift pattern at the lever is in the right relationship to the driver and to the surrounding interior of the vehicle. A typical linkage is shown.

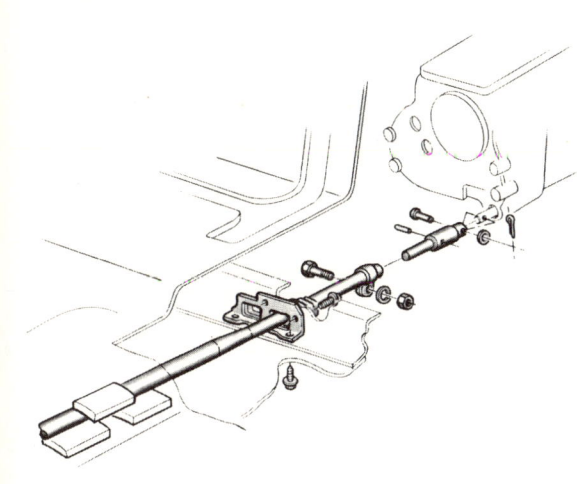

Control rod and linkage

Transmission Removal

If hard shifting, excessive noise, or loss of function in any gear indicates gear problems not related to the linkage, the transmission must be removed from the vehicle and overhauled.

If desired, the transmission may be removed from the differential carrier while the carrier and engine remain in the vehicle; disconnect the fuel lines and throttle linkages to the engine. Jack up the vehicle so that the rear wheels are off the ground and support the vehicle securely on jackstands. Disconnect the shift linkage at the transmission clamp and disconnect the clutch pull rod from the clevis at the transmission crossmember.

Remove the rear grille; support the weight of the drive train with a floor jack positioned securely under the differential.

Loosen the rear mount and disconnect the front mount. Lower the front (transmission) end of the drive train. Unbolt the transmission mounting flange and pull the transmission *straight* away from the differential carrier.

NOTE: The clutch input shaft will have to pull out of the clutch gear in the transmission and stay in the clutch driven disk; if it seems to hang up, do not force the transmission off, or the clutch release bearing seal on the differential may be damaged. Remove the clutch gear cover on the transmission and tap the end of the shaft out of the clutch gear with a dowel while drawing the transmission off.

As an alternate method of removal, drop the entire drive train out of the vehicle as directed in Chapter Three. Separate the engine from the transaxle at the flywheel housing and pull the input shaft out of the clutch release bearing shaft on the differential. Unbolt the transmission from the differential carrier front side and separate the two components straight apart, until the mainshaft is clear of the differential pinion shaft.

Remove the transmission crossmember from the front of the transmission and place the transmission on a bench.

Transmission Overhaul—General

Corvair manual transmissions are covered here in three sections, three-speed transmissions from 1960 to 1965, four-speed transmissions from 1960 to 1965, and both three and four-speed units from 1966 to 1969.

The fully synchromesh three and four-speed transmissions used in the Corvair from 1966 on are quite similar, and the overhaul procedures on them differ only in the placement of certain mainshaft components.

Three-Speed Transmission—1960-1965

Disassembly

Drain the transmission of any remaining lubricant. Mount the unit in a level place, preferably on a clean bench. Unbolt and remove the front cover and remove the clutch gear bearing snapring.

Pull the clutch bearing and gear from the transmission after spreading the retaining ring holding the outer race of the bearing. Use a puller which will hold the snap-ring groove on the end of the clutch gear securely.

Remove the top cover on the transmission; remove the mainshaft snap-ring at the rear of the unit, behind the mainshaft bearing, and push or drive the mainshaft frontward and out of the transmission case.

Remove the thrust washer retaining the second-speed gear and remove the second-speed gear, sliding gear, and clutch from the case through the top hole.

The mainshaft bearing may be removed by expanding its snap-ring and tapping the bearing into the case.

Remove the countergear shaft by driving it out from the rear and removing it from the front of the case. Use a dummy shaft duplicating the countershaft's outer diameter to drive

POWER TRAIN

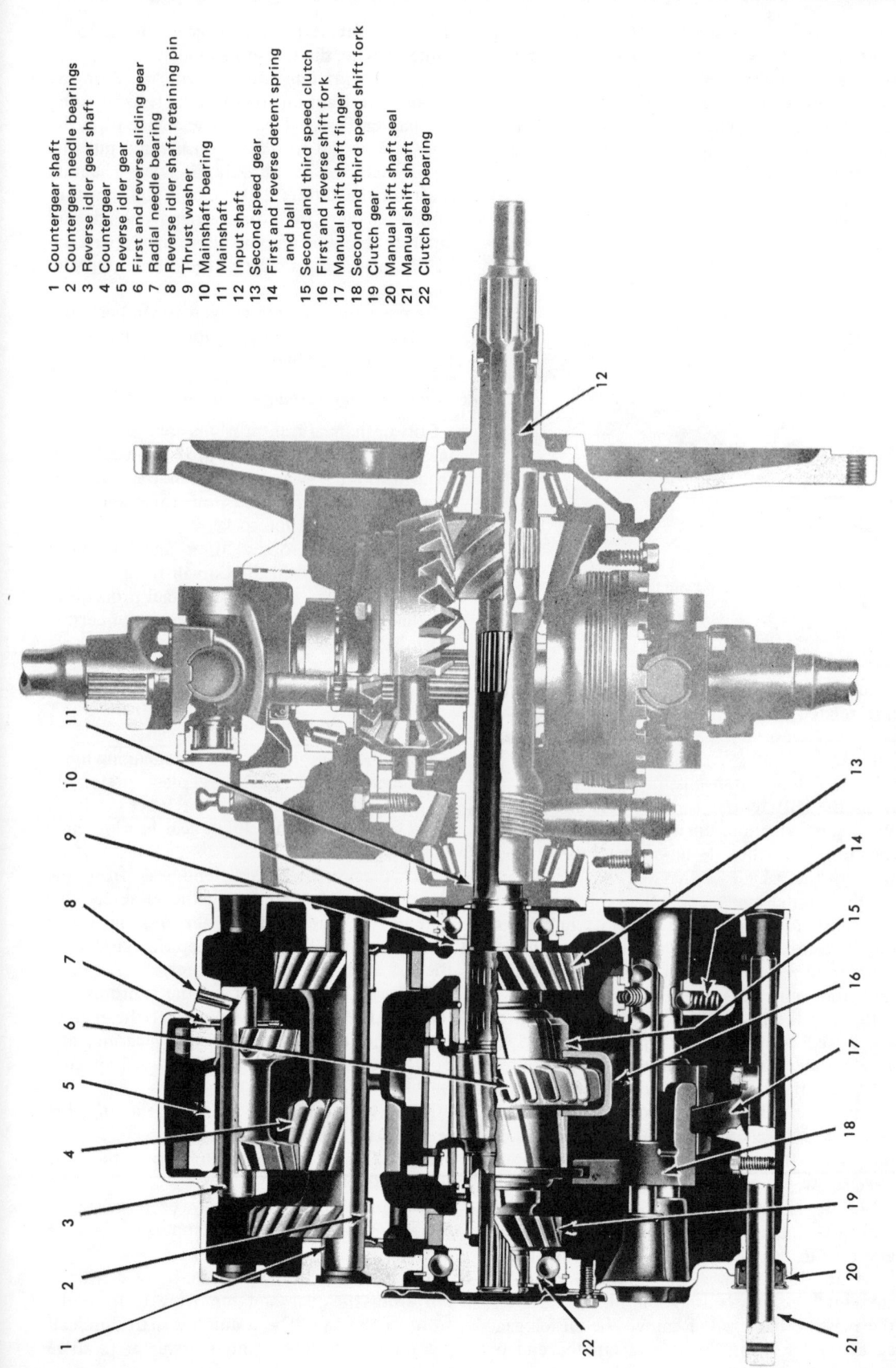

1 Countergear shaft
2 Countergear needle bearings
3 Reverse idler gear shaft
4 Countergear
5 Reverse idler gear
6 First and reverse sliding gear
7 Radial needle bearing
8 Reverse idler shaft retaining pin
9 Thrust washer
10 Mainshaft bearing
11 Mainshaft
12 Input shaft
13 Second speed gear
14 First and reverse detent spring and ball
15 Second and third speed clutch
16 First and reverse shift fork
17 Manual shift shaft finger
18 Second and third speed shift fork
19 Clutch gear
20 Manual shift shaft seal
21 Manual shift shaft
22 Clutch gear bearing

Transaxle, cross-section

Power Train 111

out the shaft, or the needle bearings in the countergear will fall out. Remove the countergear through the top hole.

To remove the reverse idler shaft and gear, drive the idler shaft retaining pin *into* the shaft then drive out the shaft from front to rear. Knock out the plug in the front of the case to allow the idler shaft to be removed this way. Remove the radial needle bearing and thrust washer from the rear of the reverse idler gear.

Remove the detent cover and the second-to-third gear detent spring and ball. Remove the second and third speed shift fork (toward the front of the case) by removing the retaining pin from the fork and driving out the shaft. Pull the interlock from the detent cavity in the case with a hook or magnet. Remove the other shift fork from its shaft by driving out the retaining pin and driving out the shaft. Remove the first and reverse detent ball and spring; remove the shifting shaft from the case by unbolting the shift finger and pulling the shaft from the case.

The three-speed transmission is shown fully disassembled.

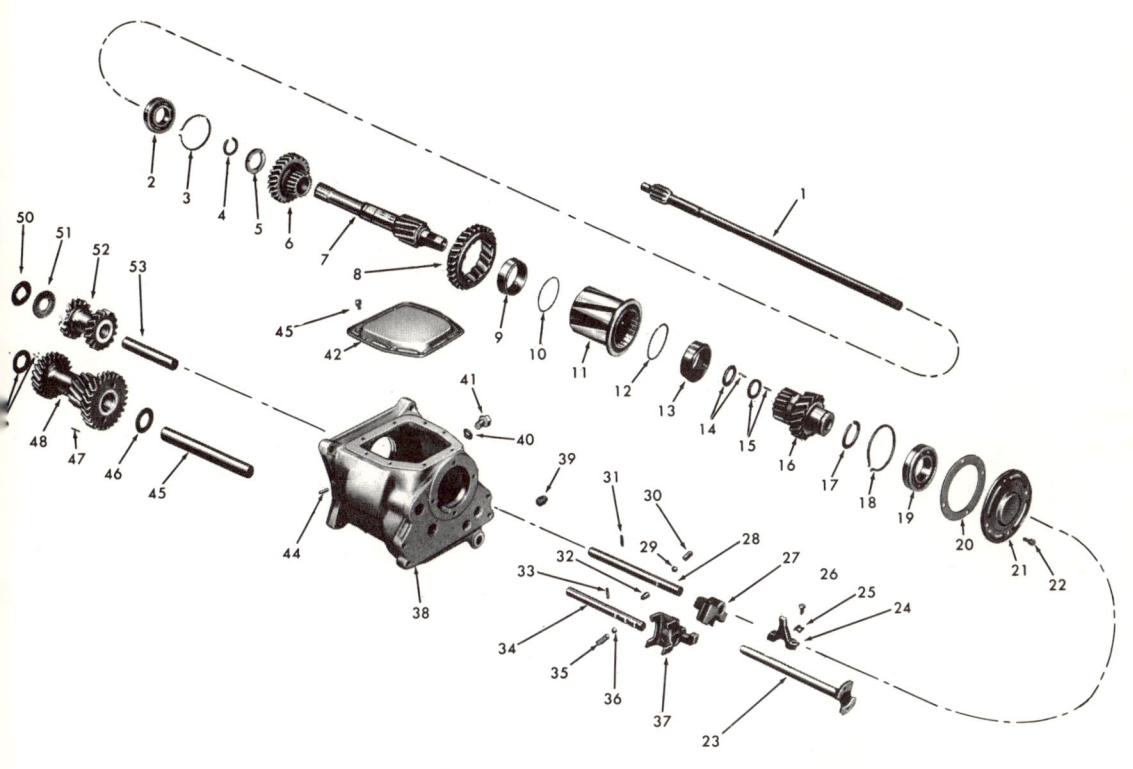

#	Part	#	Part	#	Part
1	Input shaft	19	Clutch gear bearing	37	First and reverse fork
2	Mainshaft bearing	20	Front cover gasket	38	Transmission case
3	Mainshaft bearing retaining ring	21	Front cover	39	Pipe plug (2)
4	Snap-ring (selective)	22	Front cover mounting bolt (4)	40	Detent cap gasket
5	Thrust washer	23	Manual shift selector shaft	41	Detent cap
6	Second speed gear	24	Shift finger	42	Top cover
7	Mainshaft	25	Shift finger bolt tab	43	Top cover screws (8)
8	First and reverse sliding gear	26	Shift finger bolt	44	Reverse idler gear shaft lock pin
9	Synchronizer ring	27	Second and third speed shift fork	45	Countergear shaft
10	Snap-ring	28	Second and third speed shift fork shaft	46	Countergear front needle thrust bearing washer
11	Second and third speed clutch	29	Detent ball	47	Countergear front needle bearings
12	Snap-ring	30	Detent spring	48	Countergear
13	Synchronizer ring	31	Roll pin	49	Countergear rear needle bearings and thrust washer
14	Mainshaft rear pilot bearings and spacer	32	Interlock	50	Reverse idler gear bearing race
15	Mainshaft front pilot bearings and spacer	33	Roll pin	51	Reverse idler gear bearing
16	Clutch gear	34	First and reverse shift fork shaft	52	Reverse idler gear
17	Snap-ring	35	Detent spring	53	Reverse idler shaft
18	Clutch gear bearing retaining ring	36	Detent ball		

Manual transmission, exploded view

Inspection

Clean all parts in solvent and check for significant wear or damage. Check the transmission case for cracks or damaged bearing surfaces; check the gears for damaged teeth and install them on the mainshaft to be sure they rotate freely. Install the idler gear on its shaft and check that it has 0.004" maximum clearance with the shaft. Drive the pin out of the idler shaft and save it for assembly.

Check the clutch gear bearing and replace it if necessary, tapping the old one off and a new one on (press or tap on the inner race only).

Inspect the clutch sleeve and synchronizer rings with special care; check the installed rings to be sure that there is not more than 0.030" play between the synchronizer cone and the snap-ring. Remove the rings as shown, expanding the snap-rings and pulling out the synchronizer rings. Check the rings for smoothness; the rings should fit evenly in the cones without any rocking. Any indications of serious wear in the rings or clutch will necessitate replacement of the entire synchronizer assembly.

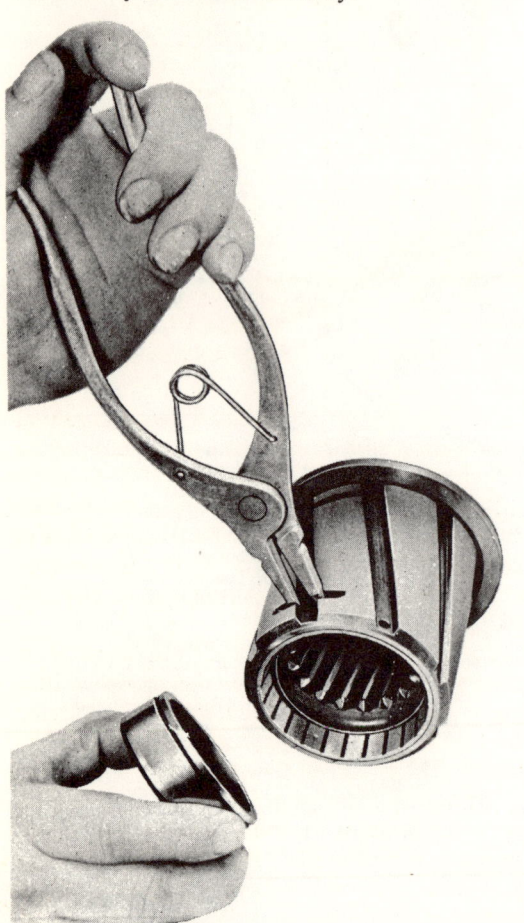

Install the synchronizer rings, if serviceable, in the clutch sleeve and retain them with the snap-rings. Be sure they are free to revolve behind the snap-rings.

Assembly

Assemble the transmission with the shifter shaft and the shift forks and shafts first: bolt the shift finger to the shifter shaft inside the case. Starting from the outside of the case, install the detent spring, *then* the detent ball. Install the first and reverse shaft in the case and install its fork, secured with its pin. Install the interlock pin in the detent cavity in the case, then install the second and third shaft in the case and slide on its fork; turn the shaft's interlock groove 90° from the interlock, then engage the interlock with the shaft when the shaft is fully installed in the case. Pin the fork to the shaft when this has been accomplished. Install the detent ball and spring for the second and third speed fork, then cover the detent cavity in the case with the plug and gasket. The transmission case is shown at this stage of assembly.

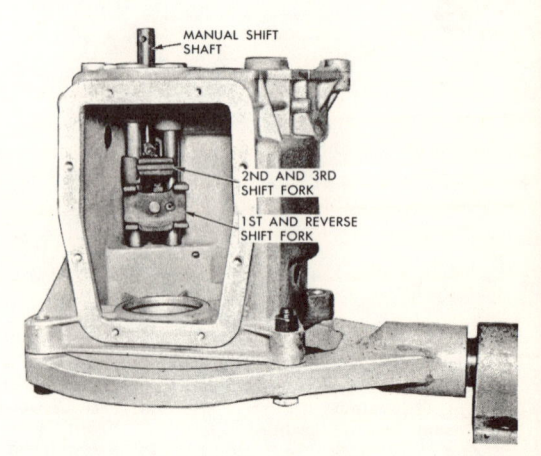

Shift forks installed

Assemble the countergear by assembling the needle bearing rollers in each end, retaining them with heavy grease. Install the dummy shaft in the gear to hold the rollers in place. Install the thrust washers at each end of the countergear (units from 1964 on). Install the countergear in the transmission case and push the countergear shaft into the case, displacing the dummy shaft and pushing it from the case at the other side. Check the thrust washers (later production) to be sure their tabs are engaged in the notches in the case at each end of the gear.

Removing synchronizer ring

POWER TRAIN

Position the thrust washers and bearing on the reverse idler shaft against the chamfered-tooth side of the idler gear. Install the reverse idler gear assembly in the case with the bearing side rearward. Line up the lockpin shaft hole with the hole in the case, with the holes at the same angle, and drive in the lockpin approximately 1/16" below the level of the case.

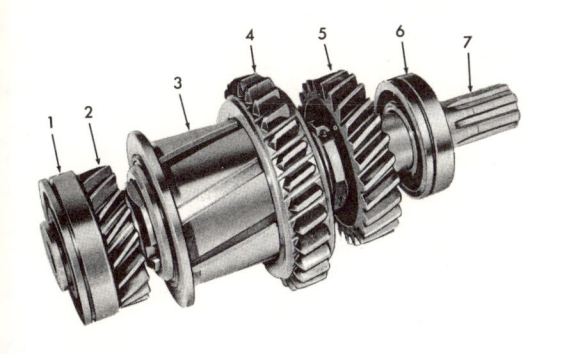

Mainshaft components

Assemble the mainshaft group in the order shown; assemble the sliding gear on the clutch with the second-speed gear in the rear end of the clutch. Place the clutch group in the case and install the mainshaft from the front of the case through the center of the clutch group and through its bearing in the rear of the case.

NOTE: If the mainshaft bearing was removed, replace it before installing the mainshaft by pushing it into the case from the rear until the bearing contacts its retainer.

Secure the rear end of the mainshaft with its snap-ring when the groove is accessible.

NOTE: Check the clearance between the mainshaft rear snap-ring and the bearing race; this clearance must be 0.004" maximum. Obtain a thicker washer to achieve this limit. Four oversizes, up to 0.097" thickness, are available.

Assemble the mainshaft pilot bearing needles in the clutch gear and retain them with heavy grease. Install the spacer in the gear against the first set of rollers and install the outer set of rollers, held with heavy grease.

Install the clutch gear with its bearing, aligning the spaces in the clutch gear tooth pattern with the synchronizer lands, and install the smaller snap-ring. Seat the clutch bearing from the front of the case with a soft hammer and install the bearing retaining ring.

Install the front and top covers with their gaskets; press in the expansion plugs covering the holes opened for access to the reverse idler shaft and shifter shaft.

Four-Speed Transmission—1960-1965

Disassembly

Remove the clutch gear and side covers from the case. Remove the plug from the detent cavity in the left side of the transmission case and remove the detent spring and ball. Move the third-fourth gear fork served by this detent into its full-forward position (fourth gear) and remove the pin from the fork. Drive out the shaft and remove the fork from the case.

Remove the first-second gear detent (from the front of the case, near the shifting shaft). Move this fork also to the full-forward position (second gear), drift out the fork pin, and drive out the shaft. Remove the fork.

Remove the clutch shaft, clutch gear, and clutch bearing snap-rings from the front of the case. These rings are shown. Use a screw-type

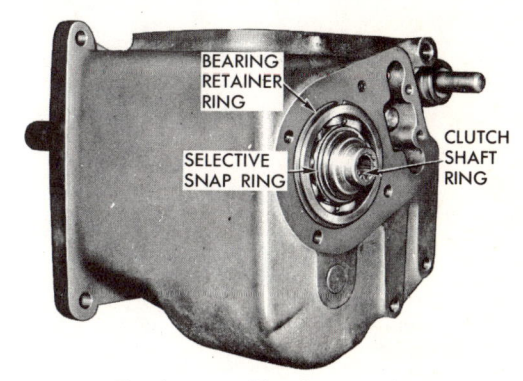

Clutch gear and bearing snap-rings

puller that will grip the clutch gear *securely* at the bearing snap-ring groove, and pull out the clutch gear bearing.

Remove the rear bearing retaining snap-rings and pull the entire, assembled mainshaft and gear cluster from the case. Shift the assembly from side to side on the way out to clear all parts.

The partly disassembled transmission is shown. Drive the pin from the reverse shifter head and remove the head and shaft, tapping the shaft out of the case and pulling out the head.

Drive out the reverse idler gear and reverse fork shafts, being careful to retrieve the woodruff key from the idler gear shaft. Remove the gear and fork, and remove the reverse shifter lever.

Remove the countergear by driving out the

POWER TRAIN

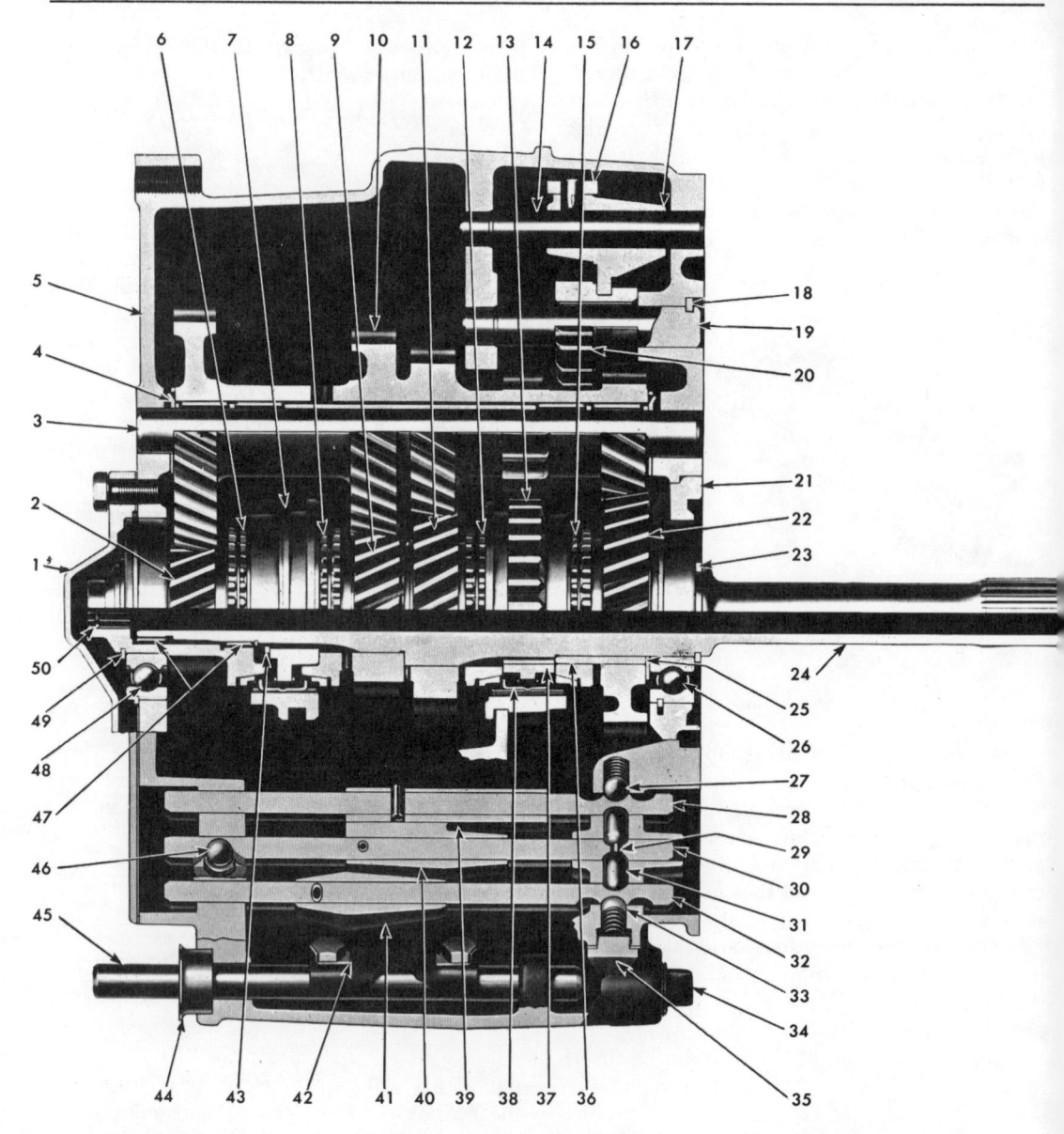

1 Clutch gear bearing cover
2 Clutch gear
3 Countershaft
4 Countergear thrust washer
5 Transmission case
6 4th blocker ring
7 3-4 shift collar
8 3rd blocker ring
9 Third gear
10 Countergear
11 Second gear
12 2nd blocker ring
13 1-2 shift collar (with integral reverse spur gear)
14 Reverse shift fork shaft
15 1st blocker ring
16 Reverse shifter lever
17 Reverse shift fork
18 Woodruff key
19 Reverse idler gear shaft
20 Reverse idler gear
21 Rear bearing retainer
22 First gear
23 Rear bearing selective snap-ring
24 Mainshaft
25 First gear thrust washer
26 Rear bearing
27 Reverse shifter head shaft detent ball and spring
28 Reverse shifter head shaft
29 Interlock pin
30 1-2 shift fork shaft
31 Interlock
32 3-4 shift fork shaft
33 3-4 shift fork shaft detent ball and spring
34 Drain plug
35 3-4 detent and interlock channel cap
36 First gear sleeve
37 1-2 Synchronizer hub
38 Synchronizer key
39 Reverse shifter head
40 1-2 shift fork
41 3-4 shift fork
42 Shift finger
43 Special snap-ring
44 Shifter shaft seal
45 Shifter shaft
46 1-2 shift fork shaft detent ball and spring
47 Mainshaft roller bearings
48 Clutch gear bearing
49 Clutch gear bearing snap-ring
50 Snap-ring (input shaft bottoming stop)

Four speed transmission 1960-64, cross-section

POWER TRAIN

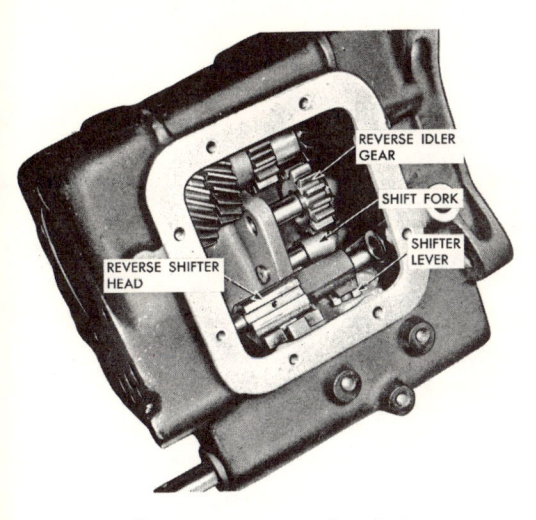

Reverse components installed

countergear shaft; use a dummy shaft to push out the shaft, so that the needle bearings in the countergear will not be displaced (a piece of 9/16" round stock 7" long will do). Drive the dummy shaft in, pushing the countergear shaft out the other side.

Remove the countergear, still on the dummy shaft, when the countergear shaft has been removed. Remove the thrust washers from the case with the countergear.

Remove the remaining interlocks (2), the pin, detent ball, and spring from the third-fourth gear detent cavity. Unbolt and remove the shift finger from the shifter shaft and drive out the plug opposite the shaft in the case wall to allow the shaft to be driven out of the case. Tap the shifting shaft out of this hole.

Disassemble the mainshaft by pulling off the clutch gear, carefully keeping the needle bearings inside from spilling.

Remove the front snap-ring from the mainshaft assembly and remove the third-fourth synchronizer and blocker rings, then the third speed gear.

NOTE: In transmissions prior to 1964, there is a needle thrust bearing between the second and third speed gears; lift out this bearing after removing the third speed gear. Remove the rear snap-ring, at the rear of the mainshaft, and remove the rear bearing and its retainer together.

Remove the first speed gear thrust washer, first speed gear, and blocker ring from the mainshaft; press the mainshaft out of the first-second synchronizer and first speed gear sleeve. Remove the second gear blocker ring and second speed gear.

Inspection

Clean all parts in solvent to remove lubricant and accumulated sludge. Inspect the transmission case for cracks and for scarred bearing contact surfaces.

Check the mainshaft and counter gear shaft for galling or circumferential wear.

Check the gears for chipped or broken teeth; inspect the bearings for smoothness.

Assembly

Assemble the mainshaft from the rear at first, installing the second speed gear and blocker ring, then the first-second synchronizer and first speed gear sleeve. Install the first-second blocker ring in the rear of the first-second synchronizer, engaging the ring slots in the keys of the synchronizer.

NOTE: The first-second blocker ring can be distinguished from the third-fourth ring by its slightly greater height.

Install the first speed gear and thrust washer on the rear of the mainshaft, followed by the rear bearing in its retainer. Secure the rear bearing with the bearing snap-ring. Check the clearance between the rear bearing and the snapring; this clearance should be 0.005" maximum. Select snap-rings as necessary to obtain this limit.

At the front of the mainshaft, install the third speed gear on the front of the shaft, seating the gear against the shoulder on the shaft.

NOTE: On transmissions prior to 1964, install the second-third gear thrust bearing between the third and second speed gears (on the surface of the second speed gear from the front side before installing the third gear).

Install the third-fourth blocker ring against the third speed gear, followed by the third-fourth synchronizer, mating the ring slots to the keys in the synchronizer. Install the fourth gear blocker ring on the synchronizer. Retain these parts with their snap-ring on the mainshaft.

Position the needle bearings inside the two inner diameters of the clutch gear and retain the rollers with heavy grease. Slide the gear carefully onto the mainshaft.

Install the shifter shaft in the case from the inside (through a cover port) to avoid damaging the seal. Bolt the shift finger to the shaft. Install the counter gear (on a dummy shaft, with the bearing rollers in place) in the case, with a thrust washer on each side. When the gear is lined up with its shaft hole, tap in the countergear shaft from the rear of the case until it is flush with the front of the case.

Install the reverse shifter lever, idler gear shift fork, and idler gear as shown. Install the woodruff key in the reverse idler gear shaft before seating the shaft into the case.

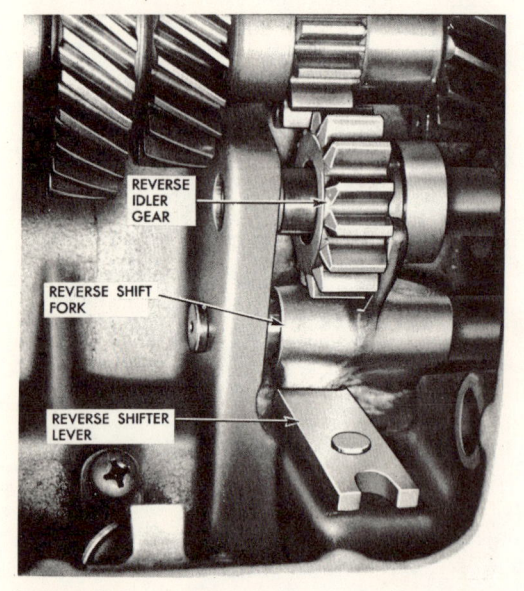

Installation of reverse shifter lever, shift fork, and reverse idler gear

The shift fork shafts are shown. Install the third-fourth detent spring and ball in their detent cavity; depress the ball with a long drift and install the reverse shaft part way in, against

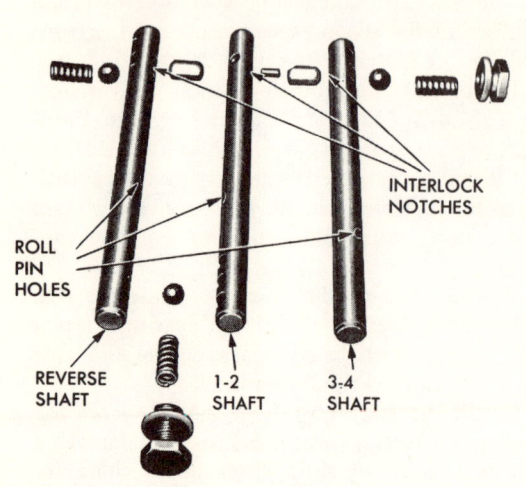

Shift fork shaft identification

the detent. Install the reverse shifter head and drift in the locking pin when the holes line up. The detent parts are shown.

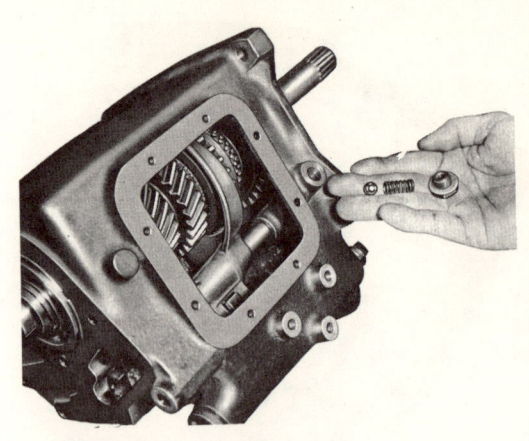

Removing 3-4 shift fork detent components

Install the assembled mainshaft in the transmission case from the rear (shift both synchronizers forward to gain access on the way in). When the assembly is seated at both ends, tap in the rear bearing to seat flush with the case. Install the bearing retainer and snap-ring.

Install the front bearing (with the larger snap-ring in place) in the front of the case over the clutch gear with the snap-ring touching the case. Install the snap-ring on the clutch gear bearing and install the smallest ring in the center of the clutch gear.

Move the two synchronizers to the neutral position to prepare for shift fork installation; install the interlock in the third-fourth detent cavity. Insert the interlock end of the first-second shaft in the case; engage the first-second shift fork in its synchronizer and pin it to the shaft when the holes line up. Tap the shaft rearward to position it.

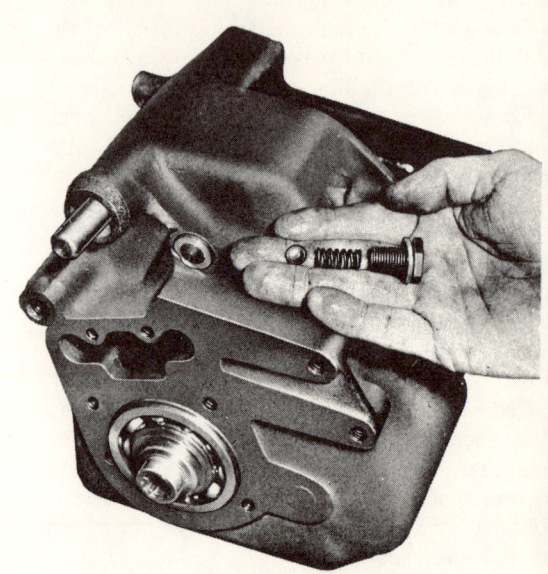

Installing 1-2 shift fork detent components

POWER TRAIN

Install the first-second detent ball and spring, then the plug and gasket, as shown. Install the pin and interlock in the third-fourth detent cavity, then partially install the third-fourth shift shaft. Slip on the fork and position the fork on the third-fourth synchronizer, then push the shaft the rest of the way in and pin the fork to the shaft when the holes line up.

Install the detent ball, spring, washer and cap in the third-fourth detent channel. Check the operation of the shifter shaft by gripping the shaft and moving it to actuate the gears.

Install the clutch gear cover and side cover with the cover gasket. Torque the bolts to 3-4 ft. lbs.

Three and Four-Speed Transmission—1966-1969

Disassembly

Remove the side cover with the shift forks attached. Unbolt and remove the clutch gear bearing cover and remove the snap-ring securing the clutch gear to its bearing. Tap the clutch gear bearing from the inside of the case to push

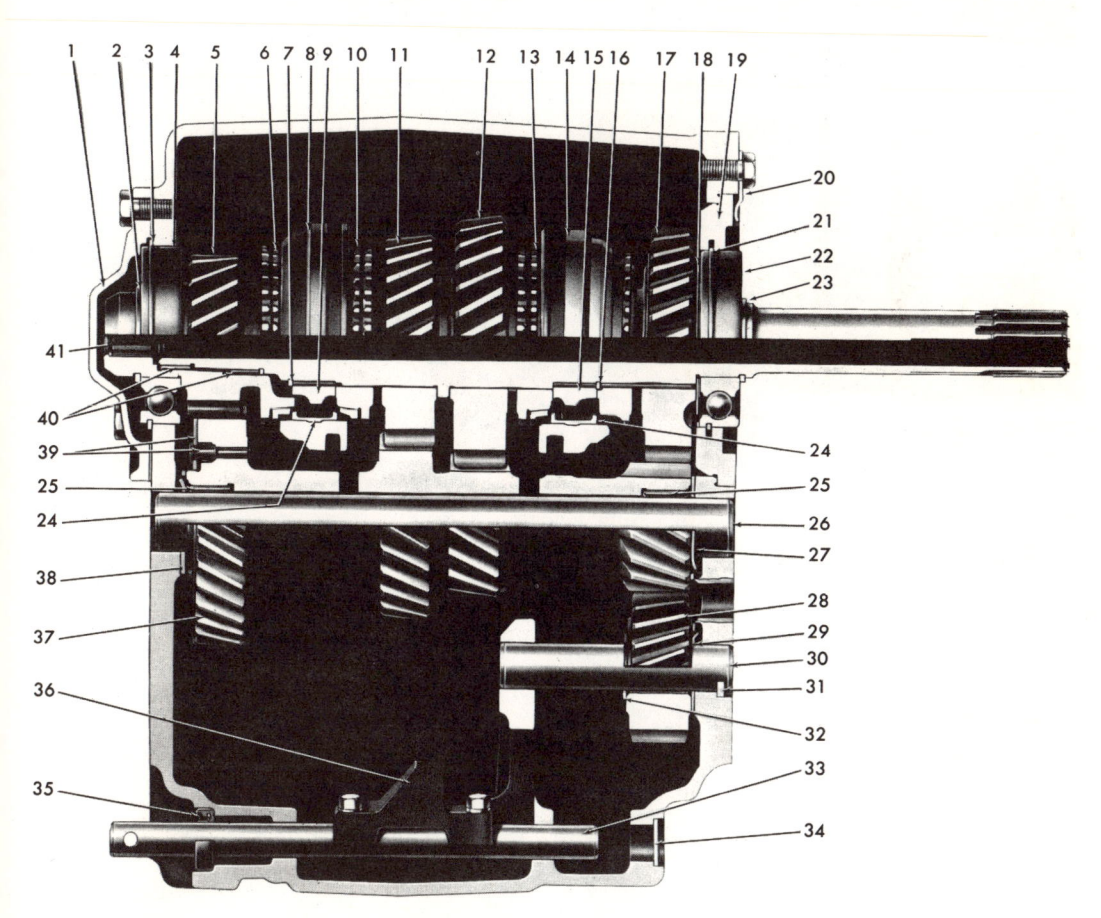

1. Bearing retainer
2. Snap-ring bearing to gear
3. Snap-ring bearing to case
4. Clutch gear bearing
5. Clutch gear
6. Third speed blocker ring
7. Snap-ring second to third synchronizer
8. Second to third synchronizer sleeve
9. Second to third synchronizer hub
10. Second speed blocker ring
11. Second speed gear
12. First speed gear
13. First speed blocker ring
14. First speed synchronizer sleeve
15. First speed synchronizer hub
16. Snap-ring first speed synchronizer
17. Reverse gear
18. Reverse gear thrust and spring washers
19. Rear bearing retainer
20. Retainer strap
21. Snap-ring rear bearing to retainer
22. Rear bearing
23. Snap-ring bearing to mainshaft
24. Synchronizer key
25. Countershaft roller bearings
26. Countershaft
27. Rear thrust washer
28. Reverse idler gear
29. Thrust washer (1966 only)
30. Reverse idler shaft
31. Woodruff key
32. E-ring retainer
33. Selector shaft
34. Welsh plug
35. Oil seal
36. Shift finger
37. Countergear
38. Front thrust washer
39. Anti-rattle plate assembly
40. Mainshaft pilot bearings
41. Snap-ring

Three speed transmission 1966-69, cross-section

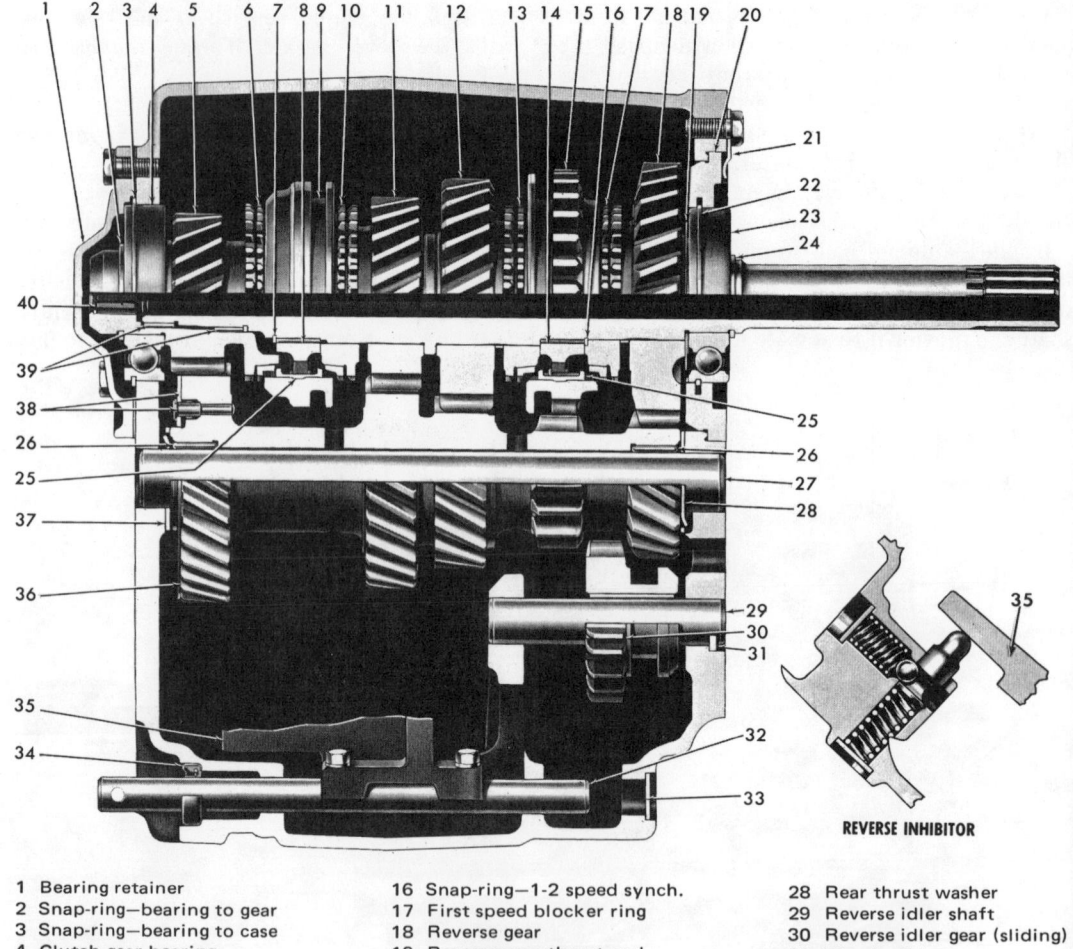

POWER TRAIN

REVERSE INHIBITOR

1 Bearing retainer	16 Snap-ring—1-2 speed synch.	28 Rear thrust washer
2 Snap-ring—bearing to gear	17 First speed blocker ring	29 Reverse idler shaft
3 Snap-ring—bearing to case	18 Reverse gear	30 Reverse idler gear (sliding)
4 Clutch gear bearing	19 Reverse gear thrust and spring washers	31 Woodruff key
5 Clutch gear	20 Rear bearing retainer	32 Selector shaft
6 4th speed blocker ring	21 Retainer strap	33 Welsh plug
7 Snap-ring—3-4 synch.	22 Snap-ring—rear bearing to retainer	34 Oil seal
8 3-4 synch. hub	23 Rear bearing	35 Shift finger
9 3-4 synch. sleeve	24 Snap-ring—bearing to mainshaft	36 Countergear
10 3rd speed blocker ring	25 Synchronizer key	37 Front thrust washer
11 Third speed gear	26 Countershaft roller bearings	38 Anti-rattle plate and rivet assembly (1966 only)
12 Second speed gear	27 Countershaft	39 Mainshaft pilot bearings
13 2nd speed blocker ring		40 Snap-ring
14 1-2 speed synch. hub		
15 1-2 speed synch. sleeve and reverse gear		

Four speed transmission 1966-69, cross-section

it out through the clutch gear port. Remove the clutch gear by pulling it straight out, being careful not to lose the pilot bearing rollers.

At the rear of the case, pull off the "E" ring (three-speed units) or the snap-ring (four-speed units) securing the reverse idler gear and unbolt the rear bearing retaining strap. Remove the rear bearing retainer and pull out the retainer and mainshaft (with all gears) as a unit. Shift the synchronizers as necessary to clear the countergear on the way out.

Tap the reverse idler gear out of the case from the inside, using a long drift. Pull the reverse idler gear from the case. On 1966 three-speed transmissions, remove the thrust washer from the reverse idler gear shaft after removing the gear.

Use a dummy shaft to drive out the countergear shaft from front to rear; the dummy shaft will keep the countergear needle bearing rollers from spilling out. Pull the countergear, bearings, and thrust washers from the rear of the case.

NOTE: 1966 transmissions have an anti-

POWER TRAIN

rattle plate secured to the front face of the countergear; this may be left in place on the gear.

The selector shaft may be removed by unbolting the shift finger and pulling the shaft from the front of the case. Remove the shaft seal also, if desired, by tapping or pulling it out.

Three-Speed Mainshaft Disassembly

Disassemble the mainshaft by removing the second-third speed synchronizer snap-ring at the front of the mainshaft. Remove the synchronizer, second speed blocker ring, and second speed gear from the front of the mainshaft.

At the rear of the mainshaft, remove the rear bearing snap-ring and press off the reverse gear, thrust washer and spring washer, and the rear bearing and retainer (support the gear cluster behind the reverse gear and press the shaft out of the reverse gear and associated parts). Expand the rear bearing retaining snap-ring and press the bearing from its retainer. Remove the first and reverse synchronizer snap-ring and pull out the synchronizer, first speed blocker ring, and first speed gear.

Four-Speed Mainshaft Disassembly

At the front of the mainshaft, remove the snap-ring retaining the third-fourth synchronizer and remove the synchronizer, third speed blocker ring, and third speed gear.

At the rear of the shaft, remove the rear bearing snap-ring and press off the reverse gear, thrust washer and spring washer, and the rear bearing and retainer (support the assembly behind the reverse gear on an arbor press and press the shaft out of the reverse gear and associated parts). Expand the rear bearing retaining ring and press the bearing from the retainer.

Remove the first-second synchronizer snap-ring and pull out the first speed blocker ring, first-second synchronizer, second speed blocker ring, and the second speed gear.

Inspection

Clean the transmission case in solvent and inspect for cracks and bad bearing surfaces. Wash the clutch gear bearing and rear bearing in solvent and check them for damage. Check the counter gear and reverse idler gear "needle" bearings for damage. Inspect the gears for chipped or broken teeth.

Inspect the synchronizers carefully, making sure they turn freely and without unevenness. Check for broken keys or springs inside the synchronizer units. When disassembling a synchronizer to replace a key or spring, mark the radial relationship of the hub and sleeve so that they will be reinstalled in the same position.

The three-speed and four-speed transmissions are shown fully disassembled.

Three-Speed Mainshaft Assembly

At the front of the mainshaft, install the second speed gear, clutching teeth outward; seat the gear against the shoulder of the shaft. Install the second speed blocker ring with its teeth against the second speed gear, then install the second-third synchronizer, seating it on its splines and aligning its keys with the slots of the adjacent blocker ring. Secure these parts with the synchronizer snap-ring.

At the rear of the mainshaft, install the first speed gear, clutch teeth outward, seating the gear against the mainshaft shoulder. Install the first speed blocker ring, teeth toward the first speed gear, then install the first-reverse synchronizer on its splines, aligning its keys with the blocker ring slots. Secure these parts with the synchronizer snap-ring.

Install the reverse gear, clutch teeth inward, and install its thrust and spring washers.

Install the rear bearing in its retainer by expanding the snap-ring; position the snap-ring groove on the bearing toward the retainer's inner (chamfered) side. Seat the snap-ring to secure the bearing. Press the rear bearing and retainer on the rear of the mainshaft and secure them with the rear bearing retainer snap-ring.

Four-Speed Mainshaft Assembly

At the front side of the mainshaft, install the third speed gear, clutch teeth outward, seating the gear against the shoulder on the shaft. Install the third speed blocker ring, clutch teeth against the third speed gear, then install the third-fourth synchronizer, seating it on its splines and aligning its keys with the slots of the adjacent blocker ring.

At the rear of the shaft, install the second speed gear, clutch teeth outward, seating the gear against the shoulder on the shaft. Install the second speed blocker ring, teeth toward the second speed gear, then install the first-second synchronizer on its spline, aligning its keys with the blocker ring's slots. Secure these parts with the synchronizer snap-ring.

Install the reverse gear, clutch teeth inward, and install the thrust and spring washers.

Install the rear bearing in the retainer by ex-

POWER TRAIN

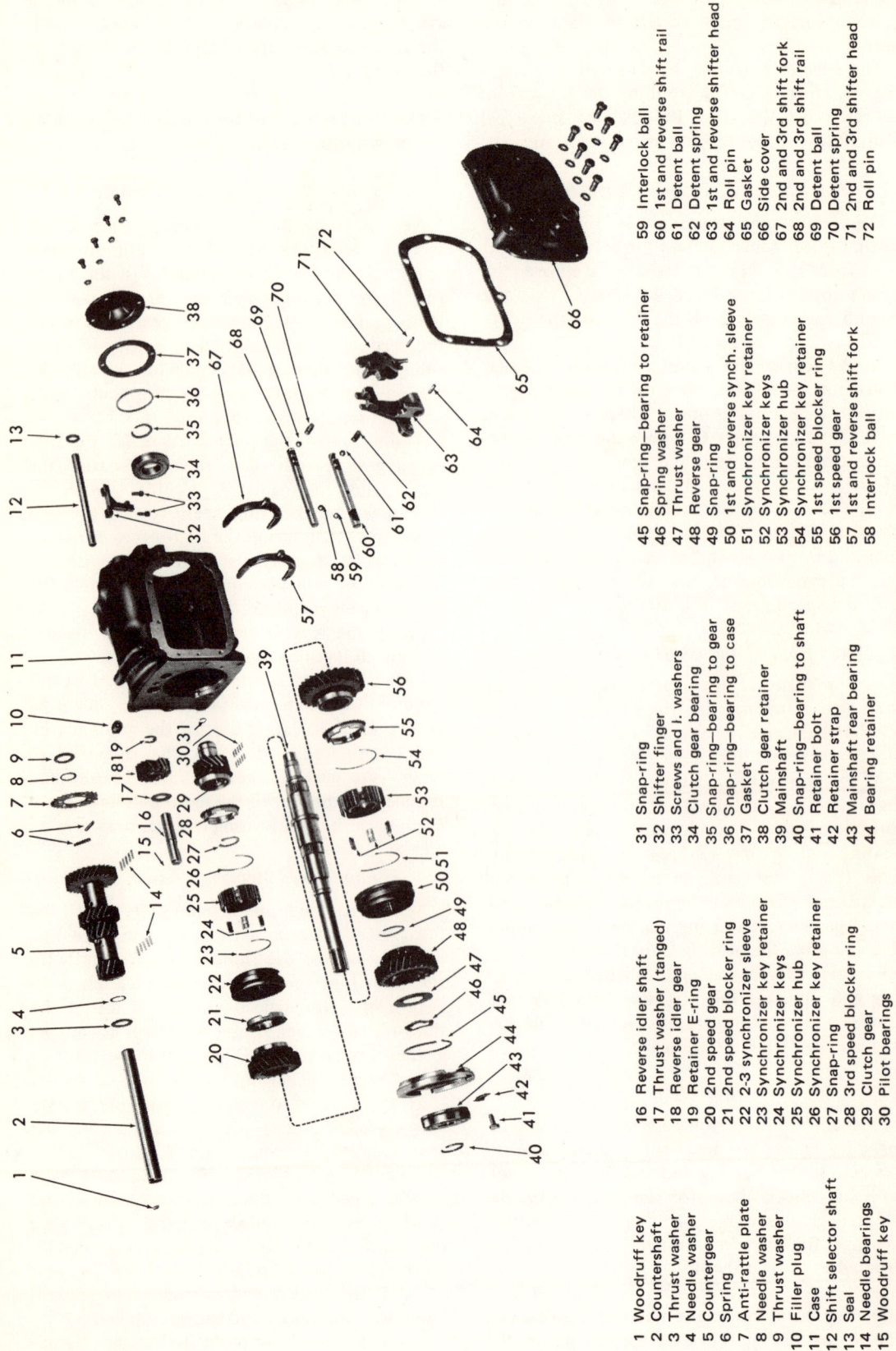

1 Woodruff key	16 Reverse idler shaft	31 Snap-ring	45 Snap-ring—bearing to retainer	59 Interlock ball
2 Countershaft	17 Thrust washer (tanged)	32 Shifter finger	46 Spring washer	60 1st and reverse shift rail
3 Thrust washer	18 Reverse idler gear	33 Screws and l. washers	47 Thrust washer	61 Detent ball
4 Needle washer	19 Retainer E-ring	34 Clutch gear bearing	48 Reverse gear	62 Detent spring
5 Countergear	20 2nd speed gear	35 Snap-ring—bearing to gear	49 Snap-ring	63 1st and reverse shifter head
6 Spring	21 2nd speed blocker ring	36 Snap-ring—bearing to case	50 1st and reverse synch. sleeve	64 Roll pin
7 Anti-rattle plate	22 2-3 synchronizer sleeve	37 Gasket	51 Synchronizer key retainer	65 Gasket
8 Needle washer	23 Synchronizer key retainer	38 Clutch gear retainer	52 Synchronizer keys	66 Side cover
9 Thrust washer	24 Synchronizer keys	39 Mainshaft	53 Synchronizer hub	67 2nd and 3rd shift fork
10 Filler plug	25 Synchronizer hub	40 Snap-ring—bearing to shaft	54 Synchronizer key retainer	68 2nd and 3rd shift rail
11 Case	26 Synchronizer key retainer	41 Retainer bolt	55 1st speed blocker ring	69 Detent ball
12 Shift selector shaft	27 Snap-ring	42 Retainer strap	56 1st speed gear	70 Detent spring
13 Seal	28 3rd speed blocker ring	43 Mainshaft rear bearing	57 1st and reverse shift fork	71 2nd and 3rd shifter head
14 Needle bearings	29 Clutch gear	44 Bearing retainer	58 Interlock ball	72 Roll pin
15 Woodruff key	30 Pilot bearings			

Three speed transmission 1966-69, exploded view

POWER TRAIN

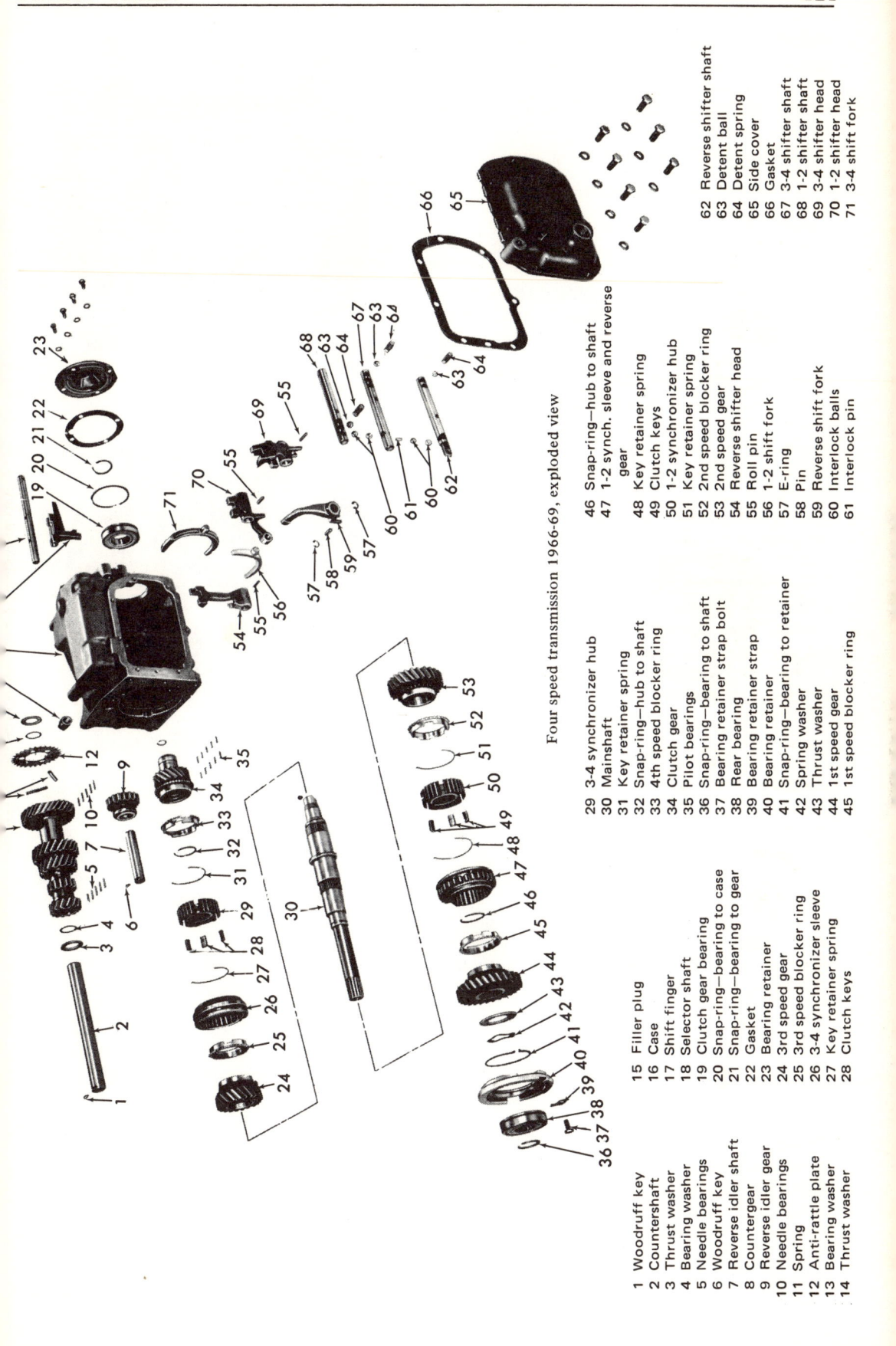

121

Four speed transmission 1966-69, exploded view

1 Woodruff key
2 Countershaft
3 Thrust washer
4 Bearing washer
5 Needle bearings
6 Woodruff key
7 Reverse idler shaft
8 Countergear
9 Reverse idler gear
10 Needle bearings
11 Spring
12 Anti-rattle plate
13 Bearing washer
14 Thrust washer
15 Filler plug
16 Case
17 Shift finger
18 Selector shaft
19 Clutch gear bearing
20 Snap-ring—bearing to case
21 Snap-ring—bearing to gear
22 Gasket
23 Bearing retainer
24 3rd speed gear
25 3rd speed blocker ring
26 3-4 synchronizer sleeve
27 Key retainer spring
28 Clutch keys
29 3-4 synchronizer hub
30 Mainshaft
31 Key retainer spring
32 Snap-ring—hub to shaft
33 4th speed blocker ring
34 Clutch gear
35 Pilot bearings
36 Snap-ring—bearing to shaft
37 Bearing retainer strap bolt
38 Rear bearing
39 Bearing retainer strap
40 Bearing retainer
41 Snap-ring—bearing to retainer
42 Spring washer
43 Thrust washer
44 1st speed gear
45 1st speed blocker ring
46 Snap-ring—hub to shaft
47 1-2 synch. sleeve and reverse gear
48 Key retainer spring
49 Clutch keys
50 1-2 synchronizer hub
51 Key retainer spring
52 2nd speed blocker ring
53 2nd speed gear
54 Reverse shifter head
55 Roll pin
56 1-2 shift fork
57 E-ring
58 Pin
59 Reverse shift fork
60 Interlock balls
61 Interlock pin
62 Reverse shifter shaft
63 Detent ball
64 Detent spring
65 Side cover
66 Gasket
67 3-4 shifter shaft
68 1-2 shifter shaft
69 3-4 shifter head
70 1-2 shifter head
71 3-4 shift fork

panding the snap-ring; position the snap-ring groove on the bearing toward the retainer's inner (chamfered) side. Seat the snap-ring to secure the bearing. Press the rear bearing and retainer on the rear of the mainshaft and secure them with the rear bearing retainer snap-ring.

Final Operations

Assemble the countergear needle bearings, retaining the rollers with heavy grease. Install the dummy shaft in the gear and position the gear in the case with a thrust washer (tang away from the end of the gear) at each end. Insert the countershaft from the rear of the case, displacing the dummy shaft. Install the keys in the shaft from outside the case.

Install the reverse idler gear and shaft (with a thrust washer, if used, between the gear and the case of a three-speed unit).

Install the clutch gear inner and outer needle bearings in the gear, retaining the rollers with heavy grease. Install the clutch gear carefully on the front of the mainshaft.

Install the assembled mainshaft in the case from the rear and secure the rear end with the strap and bolt (torqued to 10 ft. lbs.).

Install the snap-ring on the clutch gear bearing and install the small snap-ring in the center of the clutch gear. Bolt the retainer to the front of the case and torque the bolts to 20 ft. lbs.

NOTE: The oil hole on the retainer should face downward.

Install the reverse idler gear "E" ring (three-speed) or snap-ring (four-speed) on the shaft. Bolt the shift finger to the selector shaft and torque the bolts to 10 ft. lbs. (the right-angle lug on the shift finger faces the front of the case).

Shift the synchronizers to neutral and install the cover and fork assembly, with its gasket, aligning the shifting heads with the synchronizer grooves. Align the shift finger with the shifting forks. Torque the cover bolts to 20 ft. lbs.

Cover and Forks

The three-speed cover and fork assembly and the four-speed cover are illustrated.

If necessary, remove the forks and shafts by driving out the pins securing the forks to the shafts and pulling the forks and shafts from the mounting bosses on the cover. The detent springs and balls are located in the mounting bosses; after removing the shafts, the spring and ball in each boss may be removed and replaced if desired.

Position the synchronizer rings in the trans-

Side cover, shifter shafts, heads and forks, three speed

Side cover and fork assembly, four speed

mission in neutral, and the shift forks in the side cover on the neutral detents. Install the side cover on the transmission, and torque the mounting bolts to specifications. Check the action of the shift mechanism by inserting a punch in the hole in the shifter shaft, and operating the shaft manually.

Installation—All Manual Transmissions

Differential in the Vehicle

Install the front mount bracket on the front of the transmission and torque the bolts to 25 ft. lbs. Check the input shaft, protruding from the differential carrier, to be sure it is piloted into the clutch disk; push the shaft rearward to engage it in the clutch disk and crankshaft pilot bearing. Move the transmission into position against the front of the differential carrier, inserting the mainshaft into the pinion shaft and over the input shaft. As the units come together, rotate the transmission to mesh the mainshaft and pinion shaft splines and the

POWER TRAIN

input and clutch gear splines. When the transmission is seated against the differential carrier, bolt it in place and torque the bolts to 45 ft. lbs.

Lift the drive train back into place and secure the front mount (torqued to 70 ft. lbs.). Connect the fuel, throttle, and electrical linkages in the engine compartment. See Chapter Three.

Drive Train Out of the Vehicle

Install the transmission on the differential carrier, meshing the mainshaft with the pinion shaft. Install the input shaft through the rear of the carrier until it splines into the clutch gear in the transmission. Assemble the carrier to the engine as directed in Chapter Six, and install the drive train as in Chapter Three.

Automatic Transmission

The Corvair's optional automatic transmission is a standard, three-element torque converter adapted for a transaxle-type power train. The various unique features of this transmission include a plate-type reverse clutch and a torque converter with an integral ring gear. The torque converter is bolted to a flex plate on the front of the engine.

A low-range inhibiting device in this transmission prevents the unit from shifting into Low at speeds over approximately 55 mph, delaying such a shift, if selected, until the vehicle has slowed to this speed.

The driver's speed selection is by finger lever on the dashboard. A neutral safety switch is installed in the finger lever mechanism so that the starting circuit can only be activated when the transmission is in Neutral.

This transmission is shown. Service operations on this transmission are limited by the need for special tools and adequate facilities for rebuilding and checking an automatic transmission of any kind; disassembly and internal repair are beyond the scope of the amateur mechanic and are not covered here. The replacement of small controls and the adjustment of the shift linkage are valuable to know, and are described below.

Governor Replacement

The governor is located at the left rear of the transmission; this unit can be removed by unscrewing the lockscrew and pulling the governor out, turning it on the way out to clear the drive gear on the differential pinion shaft.

NOTE: This unit must be removed when the transmission and differential carrier are separated, so that the pinion shaft will clear the drive gear.

Install the governor by inserting with the same twisting motion. Make sure the O-ring seal is in place. Tighten the lockscrew to clamp the governor in place.

Vacuum Modulator Replacement

This unit is located on the right front side of the transmission housing and is connected to the vacuum balance tube of the engine. To replace this unit, disconnect the vacuum supply tube, then unscrew and remove the modulator diaphragm and the internal valve. Check the valve for nicks or scoring and check the diaphragm unit with a vacuum source for leaks. Replace both the diaphragm and the valve if either is unusable.

Removing vacuum modulator and valve

Shift Linkage

Shifting is accomplished with a single control cable running from the selector lever to a shifting link on the left side of the transmission. Adjust this cable, or connect it after the transmission has been replaced in the vehicle, as follows: shift the selector lever on the dashboard to "D." Disconnect the throttle rod at the transmission and rotate the throttle valve lever counterclockwise to its full limit. Install the throttle linkage; the lever should be below the fluid pan seam, as shown.

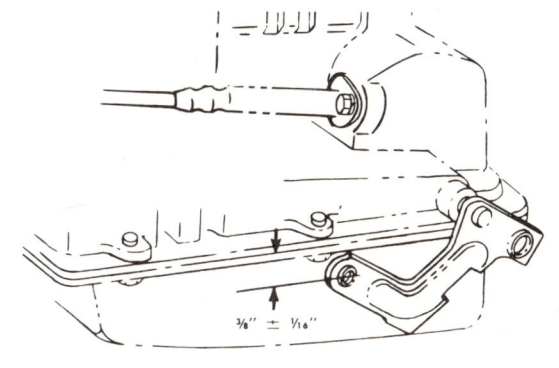

Cable installation check diagram

POWER TRAIN

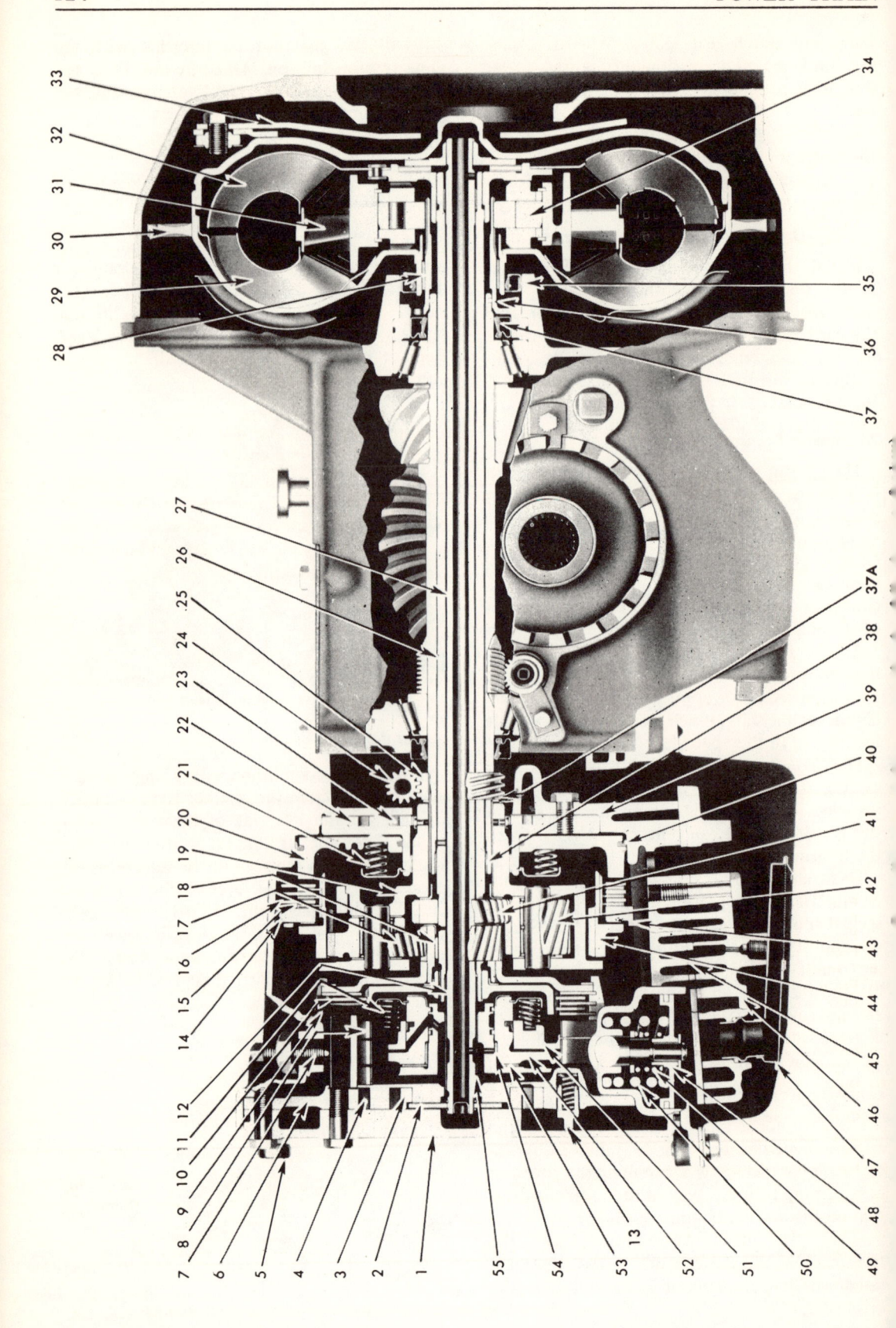

POWER TRAIN

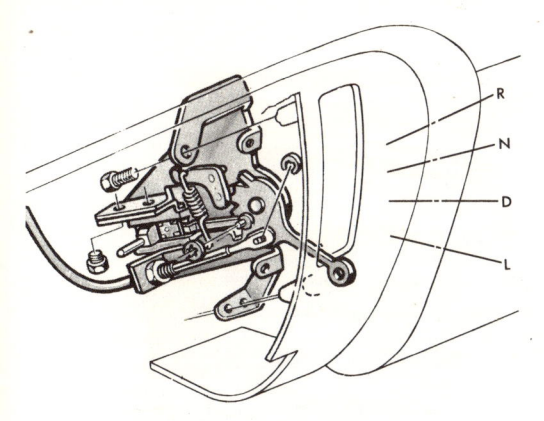

Neutral safety switch

Neutral Safety Switch

If the engine cannot be made to crank, or if the engine will crank in other control lever positions besides Neutral, adjust the neutral safety switch, located in the finger lever mechanism. Loosen the attaching screws and set the selector in "N" with the ignition switch turned to "Start." Move the safety switch back and forth until a "safe range" is found in which the engine will crank only in the "N" setting. Tighten the screws to freeze the setting.

Automatic Transmission Removal/Installation

Prepare the drive train in the same manner as for a manual transmission, described in this section. Use the same equipment and procedures to disconnect the engine linkages and mounts and to drop the rear of the drive train (differential installed in the vehicle) or to remove the entire drive train from the vehicle. Remove the transmission in either case by disconnecting the shifting linkage and unbolting the transmission from the differential carrier. Remove the governor, as directed above. Pull the transmission straight away from the differential to protect the turbine and pump shafts.

Install the transmission in reverse sequence, installing the transmission on the differential and mating the turbine and pump shafts in the torque converter splines. Torque the transmission-to-differential bolts to 45 ft. lbs.

---

1 Front pump cover
2 Front pump shaft drive hub
3 Front pump drive gear
4 Front pump driven gear
5 Transmission vent
6 Front pump body
7 Low band adjusting screw and locknut
8 Low band
9 Clutch drum reaction plate (3 used)
10 Clutch drum faced plate (2 used)
11 Clutch piston return spring (15 used)
12 Turbine shaft front bushing
13 Reverse clutch retaining ring clip
14 Reverse clutch front reaction plate (thick)
15 Reverse clutch faced plates (3 used)
16 Reverse clutch reaction plate (3 used)
17 Short pinion
18 Low sun gear bushing
19 Planet carrier hub (transmission output)
20 Reverse piston
21 Reverse piston return spring (17 used)
22 Rear pump driven gear
23 Rear pump drive gear
24 Governor driven gear
25 Governor drive gear
26 Turbine shaft
27 Front pump shaft
28 Converter hub bushing
29 Converter pump
30 Starter gear
31 Stator
32 Turbine
33 Engine flex plate
34 Stator cam race
35 Converter hub seal
36 Stator shaft
37 Pinion shaft rear oil seal
38 Pinion shaft bushing
39 Rear pump wear plate
40 Reverse piston outer seal
41 Planet carrier input sun gear
42 Long pinion gear
43 Reverse clutch plate retaining ring
44 Ring gear
45 Valve body ditch plate
46 Valve body
47 Oil pick-up pipe
48 Low servo piston
49 Low servo piston cushion spring
50 Low servo piston return spring
51 Clutch drum piston
52 Clutch drum hub
53 Clutch drum selective thrust washer
54 Clutch drum bushing
55 Front pump body bushing

Powerglide transmission, cross-section

7 • Rear Axle and Suspension

Description

The most radical difference between the Corvair and more conventional American cars is in its rear suspension and final drive. The Corvair features independent rear suspension with rear-drive through a transaxle located in front of the engine. The differential, which distributes power to the rear wheels, is located between the transmission (to the front) and the engine (to the rear). This arrangement is achieved by a long, solid input shaft from the clutch driven disk, across the rear axle, and into the transmission. Power from the transmission is led back (rearward) into the rear axle on a hollow output shaft inside which the input shaft turns. The output shaft terminates at the differential pinion gear.

Final drive is by a conventional hypoid differential rigidly attached to the vehicle; half-shafts linked to the differential side gears by universal joints lead to the rear wheels through double tapered roller bearings at the outer torque arms of the independent rear suspension.

The independent rear suspension consists of longitudinal torque arms to which the rear wheel spindles are fitted. Springing is by coil springs between the torque arms and the frame; in 1964 a single-leaf transverse spring was added; from 1965 on the suspension was completely revised to feature four-link, adjustable rear suspension with front and rear strut rods installed parallel to the axle and extending to the torque arms. Shock absorbers are fitted, one to each torque arm. The rear suspension is fully adjustable for toe-in at the torque arm front bracket and for camber at the outer end of the strut rod.

Maintenance

Maintenance of the Corvair rear axle and suspension is confined to lubrication of the differential and universal joints (when specially equipped with grease fittings).

The differential is lubricated with a supply of gear lubricant which is shared with a manual transmission (when so equipped). The rear wheel bearings consist of two opposing tapered roller bearings on each wheel spindle, lubricated by a sealed supply of wheel bearing grease. From 1965 on the wheel bearings may be disassembled to be repacked or to correct excessive axle end play.

Wheel Bearing Adjustment—1965-1969

The rear wheel spindle and brake drum group is shown. Similar to a front wheel bearing unit, the rear wheel bearing unit uses opposing tapered roller bearings. In addition, the end play (axial movement of the shaft spindle) is adjustable by selecting shims for installation behind the inner bearing. In service this end play

REAR AXLE AND SUSPENSION 127

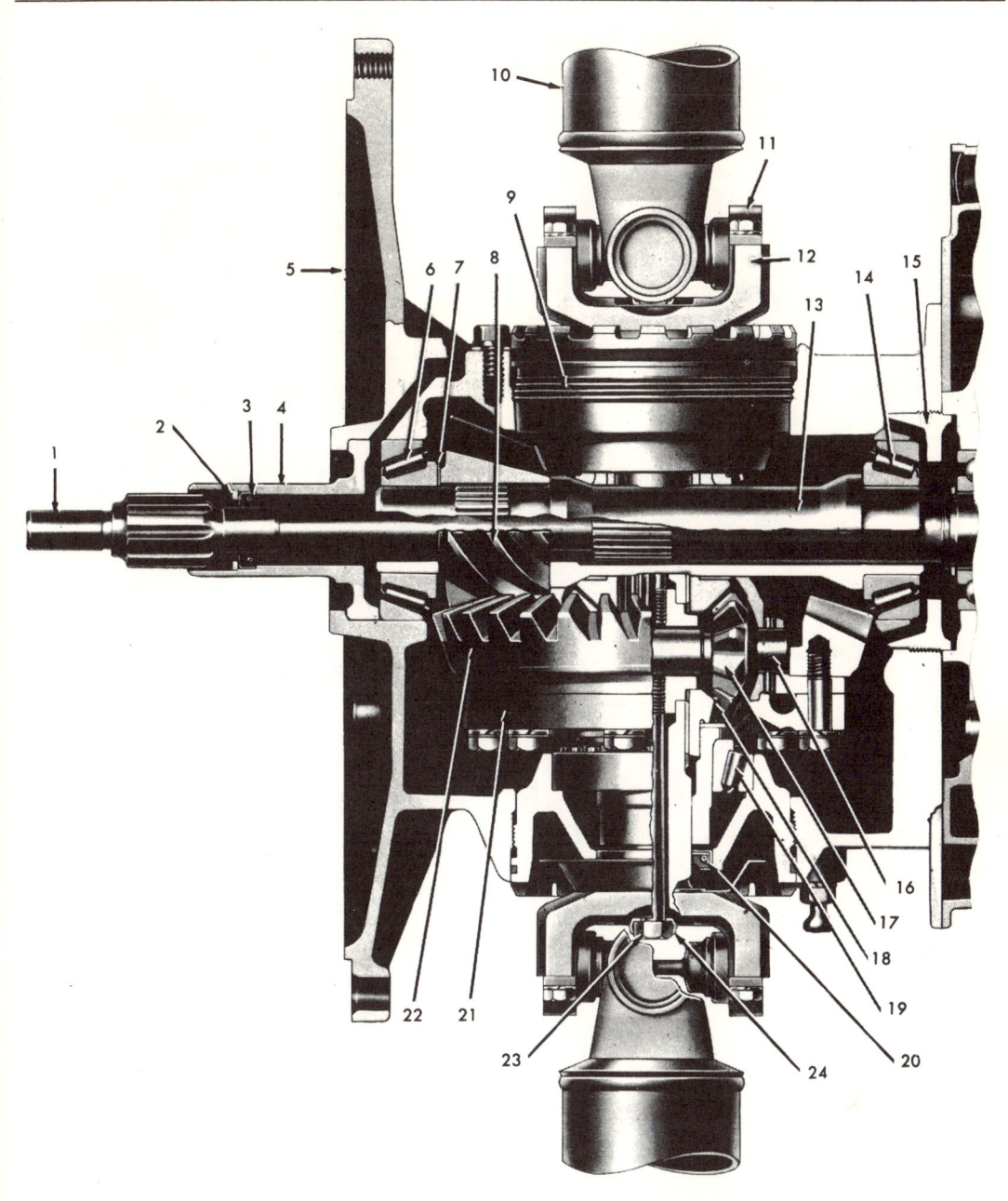

1 Clutch shaft
2 Washer
3 Clutch shaft seal
4 Clutch release bearing support
5 Differential carrier
6 Pinion rear bearing and race
7 Pinion depth shim
8 Pinion gear
9 Differential side bearing adjusting sleeve
10 Axle shaft
11 Drive shaft trunnion retaining strap
12 Differential side gear yoke
13 Pinion shaft
14 Pinion front bearing and race
15 Pinion bearing adjusting sleeve
16 Differential pinion gear shaft
17 Differential pinion gear
18 Differential side gear
19 Differential side bearing and race
20 Differential side bearing adjusting sleeve seal
21 Differential cover
22 Ring gear
23 Differential side gear yoke retaining bolt
24 Yoke retaining bolt lock

Manual transmission rear axle

REAR AXLE AND SUSPENSION

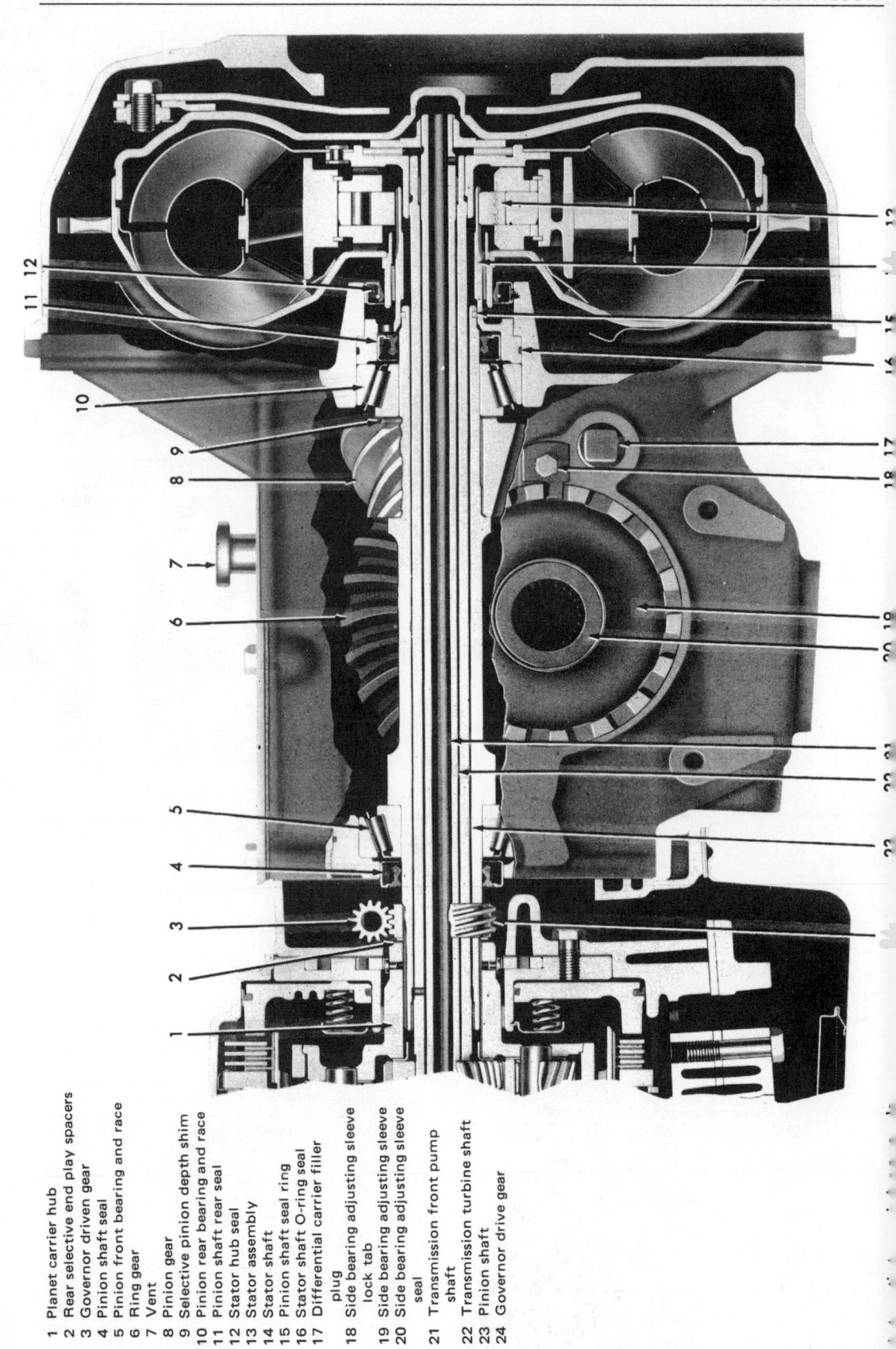

1 Planet carrier hub
2 Rear selective end play spacers
3 Governor driven gear
4 Pinion shaft seal
5 Pinion front bearing and race
6 Ring gear
7 Vent
8 Pinion gear
9 Selective pinion depth shim
10 Pinion rear bearing and race
11 Pinion shaft rear seal
12 Stator hub seal
13 Stator assembly
14 Stator shaft
15 Pinion shaft seal ring
16 Stator shaft O-ring seal
17 Differential carrier filler plug
18 Side bearing adjusting sleeve lock tab
19 Side bearing adjusting sleeve
20 Side bearing adjusting sleeve seal
21 Transmission front pump shaft
22 Transmission turbine shaft
23 Pinion shaft
24 Governor drive gear

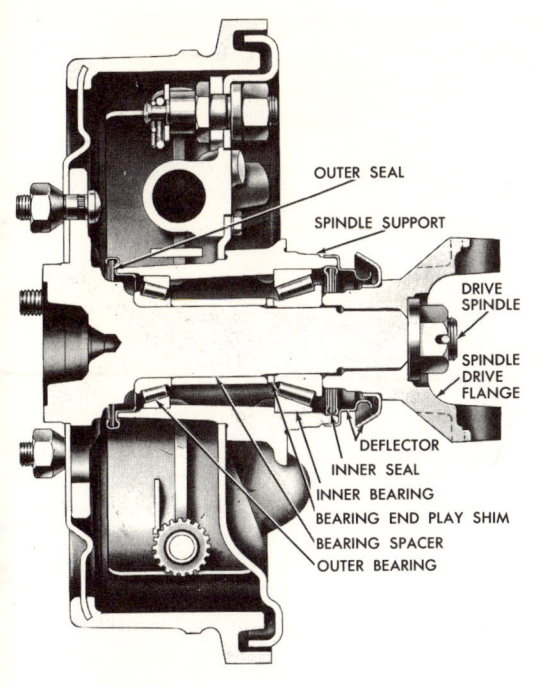

REAR AXLE AND SUSPENSION

Wheel spindle and support, cross-section

When the spindle drive flange is off, remove the spindle from the outer side and remove the shim. Measure it with a micrometer and compute the required thickness for a new one.

Clean the bearing on the spindle and repack it with a good grade of wheel bearing grease.

NOTE: Inspect the bearing for damage before repacking it. The bearing may be left in place on the spindle throughout this operation; removal will require an arbor press.

At the inner side of the spindle support, remove the deflector and seal and pull out the inner bearing rollers and inner race. Check it for damage after cleaning it in solvent, then repack it with wheel bearing grease and replace it, followed by a new grease seal and the deflector, tapped evenly and gently into place on the support.

Replace the spindle and bearing assembly from the outer side, seating it carefully through the inner bearing. Install the spindle drive flange, drawing it into place with its retaining nut.

NOTE: Do not drive the flange onto its spline; if desired, the flange may be heated in an oven to approximately 300°F., then installed while hot. Torque the nut to 100-150 ft. lbs.

Connect the universal joint and torque the yoke nuts to 100 ft. lbs. Attach the strut rod.

Wheel Bearing Replacement—1960-1964

The axle bearing assembly for these Corvair models is shown. The bearing unit is sealed and must be replaced if wear is evident.

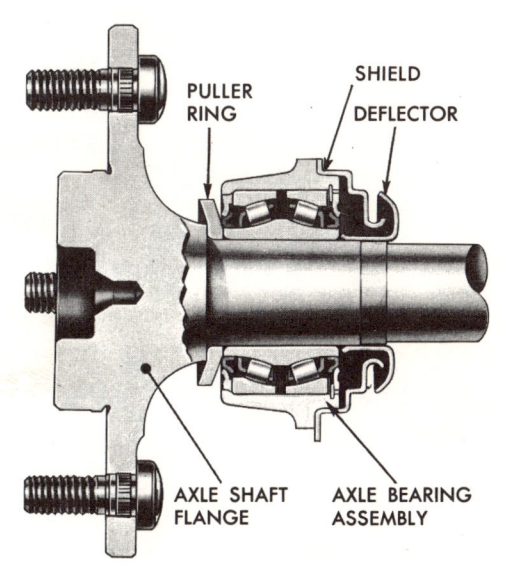

must be within 0.000-0.006" measured with a dial indicator as follows:

Jack up the rear end of the vehicle and support it securely on jackstands. Loosen the outer universal joint enough so that an end play reading for the spindle alone can be taken. Remove the brake drum and fasten a dial indicator to the brake backing plate so that the indicator can be made to touch the hub. Push the hub in and out and observe the total indicator reading.

If the reading is over 0.006" change the shim to bring it within limits: a new shim will be required which will be thinner than the existing one by an amount at least as great as the amount of excess play. For instance, if the end play is 0.013", 0.007" over the limit, the new shim will have to be at least 0.007" thinner than the old one. Determine the new shim required after the old one has been removed.

Disconnect the outer universal joint completely and drop the shaft down, out of the way. Check the universal joints for condition as described below. If the strut rod is in the way, disconnect it at the differential side and swing it down.

Remove the spindle drive flange, using a screw puller. Remove the retaining nut and pull off the flange using the center spindle shaft as a counterforce surface.

NOTE: Do not use a slide-hammer puller, or the bearings will be damaged.

Axle and bearing

Jack up the rear of the vehicle and support it securely on jackstands. Remove the brake drum on the side to be serviced. Insert a socket wrench on an extension through the access hole in the hub and unscrew the nuts retaining the axle and bearing assembly. Unbolt the universal joint at the inner end of the axle shaft and separate the joint.

Tug the axle outward and pull the shaft part way out of the brake backing plate. Unscrew the bolt retaining the universal joint yoke on the shaft inner end and pull the joint yoke from the splined end of the shaft as shown. Service the universal joint as directed in this section.

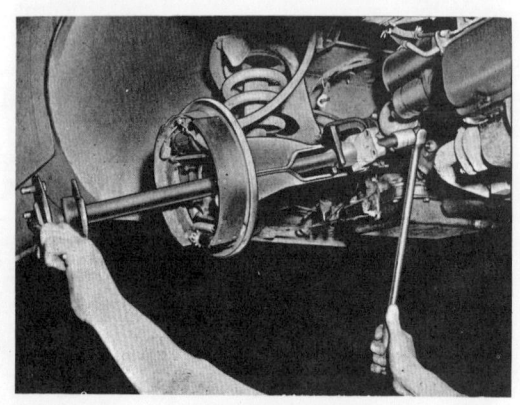

Removing U-joint yoke

NOTE: Use a suitable puller of the jackscrew type to remove the yoke, using the center of the shaft for counterforce.

Pull the shaft the rest of the way out of the backing plate and off the vehicle.

Pull off the deflector and bearing shield from the end of the bearing assembly. Support the shaft on an arbor press, hub-end down, with a support ring behind the puller ring. Press on the end of the axle shaft to push the shaft down and out of the bearing assembly.

Install the new bearing assembly by inverting the shaft on the bed of the press with the bearing assembly supported and the puller ring installed and facing up; press on the hub end of the shaft to push the shaft down into the bearing and seat the bearing on the shaft. Install the shield and deflector, after wiping a generous quantity of wheel bearing grease around the inside of the lip of the deflector to act as a dust seal.

NOTE: Corvair van axles have a longer, cylindrical bearing shield which is installed in the same way as the sedan axle's shield.

Install the axle shaft through the brake backing plate and install the universal joint yoke and draw the yoke down onto its spline with its retaining bolt.

Slide the shaft the rest of the way into position, securing the bearing assembly retaining bolts at the backing plate and rejoining the universal joint at the inner end. Install the brake drum and adjust the brakes if necessary.

Universal Joints

The universal joints used on all Corvair axle shafts are of the strapped-yoke, trunnion type, with "needle" bearings (thin, uncaged cylindrical rollers). From 1960 to 1964 one joint was used, at the inner end of each axle shaft on the differential side gear connection. From 1965 on, outer universal joints were fitted, at the wheel spindle.

These units are sealed and are not intended to be lubricated on a regular basis, although replacement units may be equipped with standard grease fittings which may be used to service the joints along with the rest of the chassis parts. If the axle shafts are loosened or removed for any reason, it is best to disassemble the joints involved for inspection and repacking. Check the joints for condition while they are still installed; check for wear by moving the flange and yoke of each in opposite directions, back and forth, to detect play in the trunnion bearings.

NOTE: Rotating the wheels back and forth will not pinpoint universal joint problems because of the multiplication of tolerances throughout the drive line. The best check is to move one part of the joint against another to detect wear.

Replacement—1960-1964

Remove the axle shaft part way from the vehicle to pull the universal joint and side gear connector from the differential as follows: remove the brake drum and unbolt the axle bearing retaining nuts (at the outer side). Pull the axle out to free the side connector. Unbolt the straps on the universal joint and complete the removal of the joint from the connector on a bench.

Replacement—1965-1969

Remove the axle shafts from the vehicle by unbolting the trunnion straps and removing them; have an assistant push each wheel outward, or slack off the strut rod adjust cams, until the shaft can be dropped downward. Remove the joints on a bench.

REAR AXLE AND SUSPENSION

Disassembly

As soon as the joints are disconnected from their yokes, tape or wire the trunnion cups temporarily in place to prevent the cups from falling off and spilling the bearing rollers.

Remove each joint from its attaching flange as follows: remove the lockring from each end of the shaft or connector flange. Press out each bearing cup, one at a time, in a vise or an arbor press. For instance, place the joint in a vise with a deep socket between one side of the joint and vise jaw, as shown, and an extension pushing

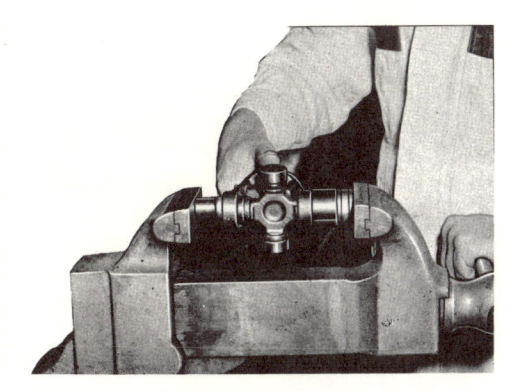

Removing bearing caps

against the other side of the joint. Squeeze the joint in the vise, pushing the trunnion and bearing cups to one side, only far enough to drive one cup into the deep socket. Remove this cup and its bearing rollers, then move the trunnion to one side and pull off the other cup and bearing rollers. Pull the trunnion out of the yoke.

NOTE: Do not interchange parts between arms on a trunnion; keep the bearing cups and rollers separated in sets and be sure to replace them on the same arm from which they are taken.

Clean the trunnion well and assemble the rollers and cups, lightly lubricated. The cups should fit over the bearing rollers with no looseness or grittiness when rotated. If any damage or significant wear is evident, replace the joint. If the joint is acceptable, assemble each arm of the trunnion with the cups and rollers packed with wheel bearing grease and a new grease seal at the inner side of the cup. It will be necessary to assemble the shaft or connector-mounted arms while they are being installed in the shaft or connector, as follows: install one cup part way into the shaft or connector and arrange the rollers in the cup; install the trunnion at the inner side of the flange and position the arms in the flange bores. Press the cups in place from both sides, being careful not to bind or jam the rollers. When the cups are seated and the trunnions are centralized between the flanges on the shaft or connector, install the lockrings over each cup.

Install the shaft between the wheel spindle and differential (later models), or insert the side gear connector in its spline on the differential (earlier configuration). Install the retaining straps over the remaining trunnion arms to secure them to the yoke of the joint.

Shock Absorbers

Replace the rear shock absorbers if a bouncing or rolling rear end indicates that they are no longer effective. Raise the rear end of the vehicle to give adequate access to the lower shock absorber mounts.

NOTE: From 1960 to 1964 the rear shock absorbers were located inside the coil springs; from 1965 to 1969 they angle rearward from the torque arm to the frame, outside the spring.

Remove the upper mounting nut for each shock absorber unbolt the lower end of each unit and pull it down and out of the vehicle. Install the new units in reverse order, inserting the upper piston rod through the upper mounting hole, securing the lower end, and installing the nut at the upper end.

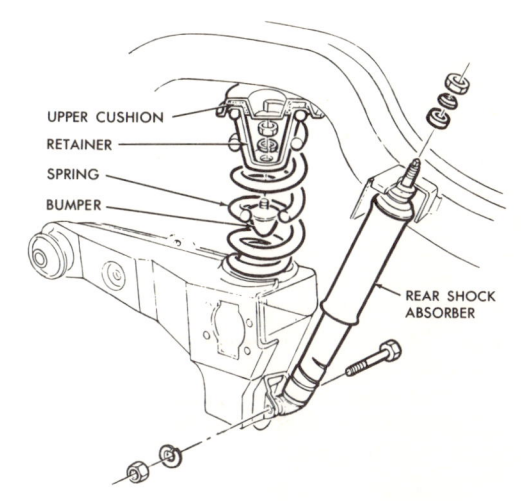

Spring and shock absorber installation

NOTE: A floor jack exerting slight pressure on the torque arm to compress the coil spring will aid installation and removal of the shock absorbers.

Rear End Alignment—1965-1969

The rear suspension is adjustable for camber and toe-in, using the following procedures. See the wheel alignment chart in Chapter Nine for figures. These adjustments must be carried out using the appropriate wheel alignment fixtures to gauge the exact degree of alignment.

Camber

Loosen the bolt at the outer end of each strut rod and move the cam until the camber is from 0° to −1°.

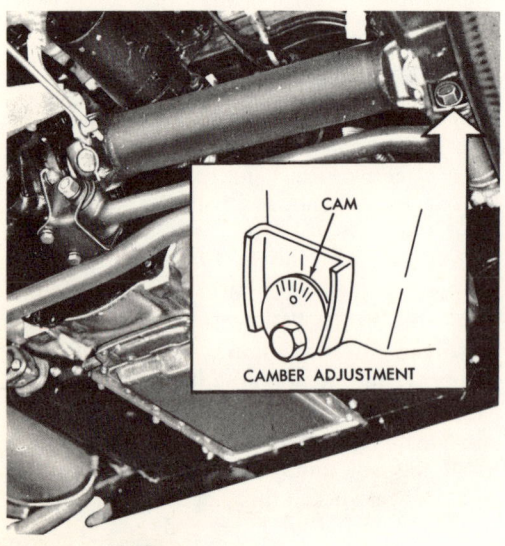

Camber adjusting cam location

Toe-In

Locate the elongated attachment holes in the front ends of the torque arms and loosen the bolts securing the arms to the frame. Adjust the toe-in to specifications.

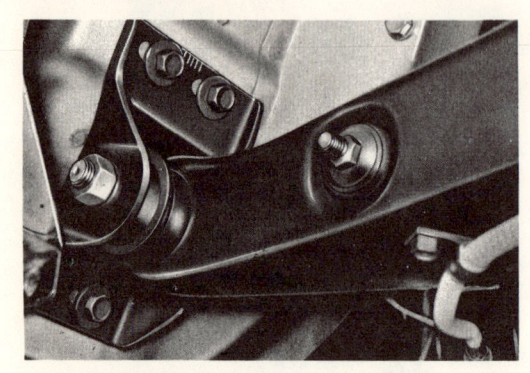

Toe-in adjusting bracket location

Differential

Removal

Remove the engine and transaxle from the vehicle, as directed in Chapter Three. Support the engine on a level surface and separate the engine from the transaxle at the flywheel housing by unbolting the flange and pulling the transaxle straight away from the engine.

On manual transmission units, unbolt the transmission and pull it away from the front of the differential carrier. On automatic transmission units, unbolt and remove the torque converter from the rear of the carrier. Pull the turbine shaft carefully out of the carrier and transmission. Remove the governor lockscrew and pull the governor out of the transmission. Unbolt the transmission and pull it from the front face of the carrier.

Removing governor

Inspection of the Assembled Differential

Perform gear backlash checks on the differential assembly before disassembling it, to detect specific faults which would be hard to find later. The following checks are recommended.

General Condition

Rotate the pinion and ring gears and "feel" for indications of bad bearings (such as grittiness from flattened rollers). Inspect the gear teeth for unusual wear or damage and push the gears from side to side to check for extreme bearing wear.

Pinion and Ring Gear Backlash

Install a dial indicator on the carrier with the point against the back of one ring gear tooth, then move the gear from one end of its lash (free play) to the other while holding the pinion gear steady. This backlash should be 0.005 to 0.008″ total.

Reduce the backlash by moving the ring gear and differential assembly toward the pinion (or increase the lash by moving it away from the pinion) by rotating the side bearing sleeves in or out.

NOTE: The side gear gearings must remain a fixed distance apart, so that the sleeves must be

REAR AXLE AND SUSPENSION

Measuring ring gear to pinion backlash

turned equally in the same direction (left one tightened one slot, right one loosened one slot, etc.) or the differential gears will lose or have excessive preload.

Check the lash after each small adjustment until the correct value is achieved.

Turning Torque

Check the torque required to turn the differential pinion, by attaching a low-range torque wrench to the pinion. With no force applied to the ring gear, this turning torque at the pinion should be 12 to 14 in. lbs. If the torque is out of specification, turn the side gear adjusting sleeves equally in the *opposite* direction themselves (left one loosened one slot, right one loosened one slot, etc.) until the turning torque is within limits.

Measuring pinion turning torque

Tooth Contact Analysis

This check analyzes the way in which the pinion and ring gear teeth contact each other, and should be performed after the bearing load and gear backlash have been adjusted as directed above. The backlash and load could be within limits as observed, but the teeth of the gears could still be in the wrong relationship to each other.

The nomenclature of gear teeth is shown.

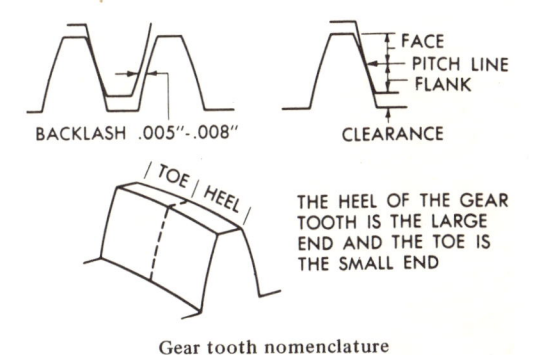

Gear tooth nomenclature

Gears mesh efficiently only on certain portions of the tooth surface; gear tooth design provides for maximum thrust area and wear resistance on a specific area of the tooth pressure face; if the teeth of two mating gears mesh out of the design area, increased wear and noise will result. The nomenclature chart shows the different parts of a gear tooth and the relationship of mating teeth; on the Corvair's beveled hypoid gears, the "heel" of a gear tooth is its larger, higher end, and the "toe" is its smaller end.

The tooth contact area on the principal gears can be observed by coloring one gear with dye and meshing it with its mating gear; the color will transfer at the actual contact surfaces, which can then be compared with the ideal surface.

Clean the pinion and ring gear contact surfaces well with solvent, rotating the gears and wiping each tooth with a solvent-moistened rag until the surfaces are free of lubricant.

Coat the *ring gear* teeth with a light, even coat of a suitable dye such as blue layout dye or special iron oxide gear marking compound. Block the ring gear lightly with a rag or a piece of wood to act as a brake, then rotate the pinion gear against the ring gear with a wrench. Roll the pinion gear back and forth to produce a visible, consistent dye transfer onto its teeth.

Compare the dye pattern on the teeth with the illustration. Pattern "A" shows the ideal contact area. Patterns "B" and "C" indicate faulty backlash which should be corrected as follows.

Pattern B: Increase the backlash by moving the ring gear away from the pinion; loosen the

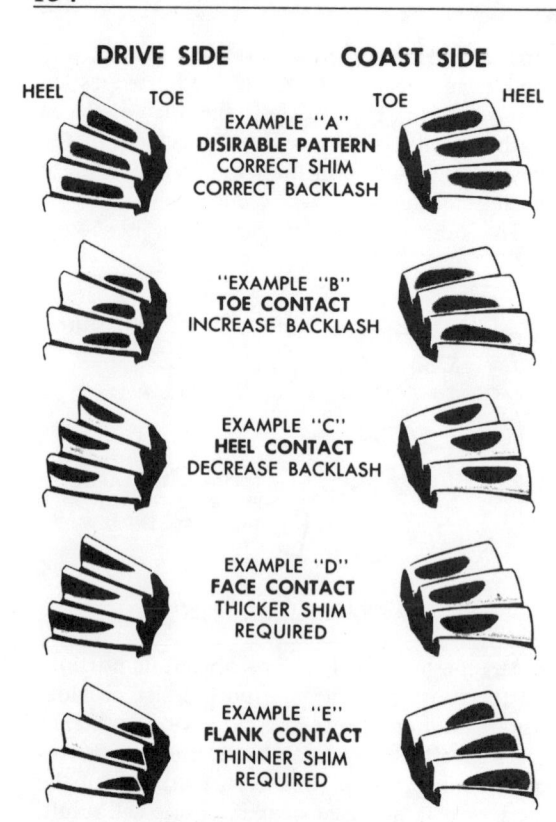

Ring gear contact patterns

DRIVE SIDE — **COAST SIDE**

EXAMPLE "A"
DESIRABLE PATTERN
CORRECT SHIM
CORRECT BACKLASH

"EXAMPLE "B"
TOE CONTACT
INCREASE BACKLASH

EXAMPLE "C"
HEEL CONTACT
DECREASE BACKLASH

EXAMPLE "D"
FACE CONTACT
THICKER SHIM
REQUIRED

EXAMPLE "E"
FLANK CONTACT
THINNER SHIM
REQUIRED

left-hand adjusting sleeve and tighten the right-hand sleeve an identical amount. Recheck with dye to verify the adjustment.

Pattern C: Decrease the backlash by moving the ring gear into the pinion; loosen the right-hand sleeve and tighten the left-hand sleeve an identical amount. Recheck with dye to verify the adjustment.

Pattern "D" and "E" indicate faulty gear position, to be remedied as follows.

Pattern D: The pinion is too far out of mesh with the ring gear; install a thicker shim between the rear bearing and the gear as described below.

Pattern E: The pinion is too far into the ring gear; install a thinner shim between the rear bearing and the gear as described below.

Replace the pinion bearing shim as directed, then assemble and check the gears. While assembling the differential in the carrier, be sure to adjust the backlash with a dial indicator as described above.

Differential Overhaul

General

The Corvair differential is shown fully disassembled. Disassemble this unit only as far as necessary. This unit should only be disassembled under the right working conditions and using proper tools; do not attempt to remove bearings or seals without screw-type pullers which will remove these parts without damage. Do not install parts unless they are perfectly clean and in good condition. Full-width drifts and installing tools are not essential for replacing bearings and seals, but if flat punches are used, be sure to drive in bearings and seals evenly and slowly with these tools to avoid damage.

Pinion Gear Removal

On 1965 and later units, unbolt and pull out the universal joint yokes from each side gear spline. On earlier units, remove the speedometer drive gear from the left-hand side of the differential carrier.

Remove the locking tab from each side of the gear adjusting sleeve and remove each sleeve with a spanner-type wrench or a bar across the wrenching slots. Remove the pinion gear adjusting sleeve with a similar tool. Push the ring gear to one side and pull out the pinion gear and bearing assembly.

Pinion Gear Disassembly

Remove the front and rear pinion bearings by pressing them off the shaft; as shown, support

Removing pinion bearings

the bearings directly under their inner races and press the shaft out of the bearing. If shim replacement is the only repair required on the pinion, remove only the rear bearing to get at the shim.

If required, replace the shim with another (thicker or thinner) shim to correct pinion gear depth. Install the shim (with an oil seal, for an automatic transmission unit).

Inspect the pinion bearings for damage and

REAR AXLE AND SUSPENSION

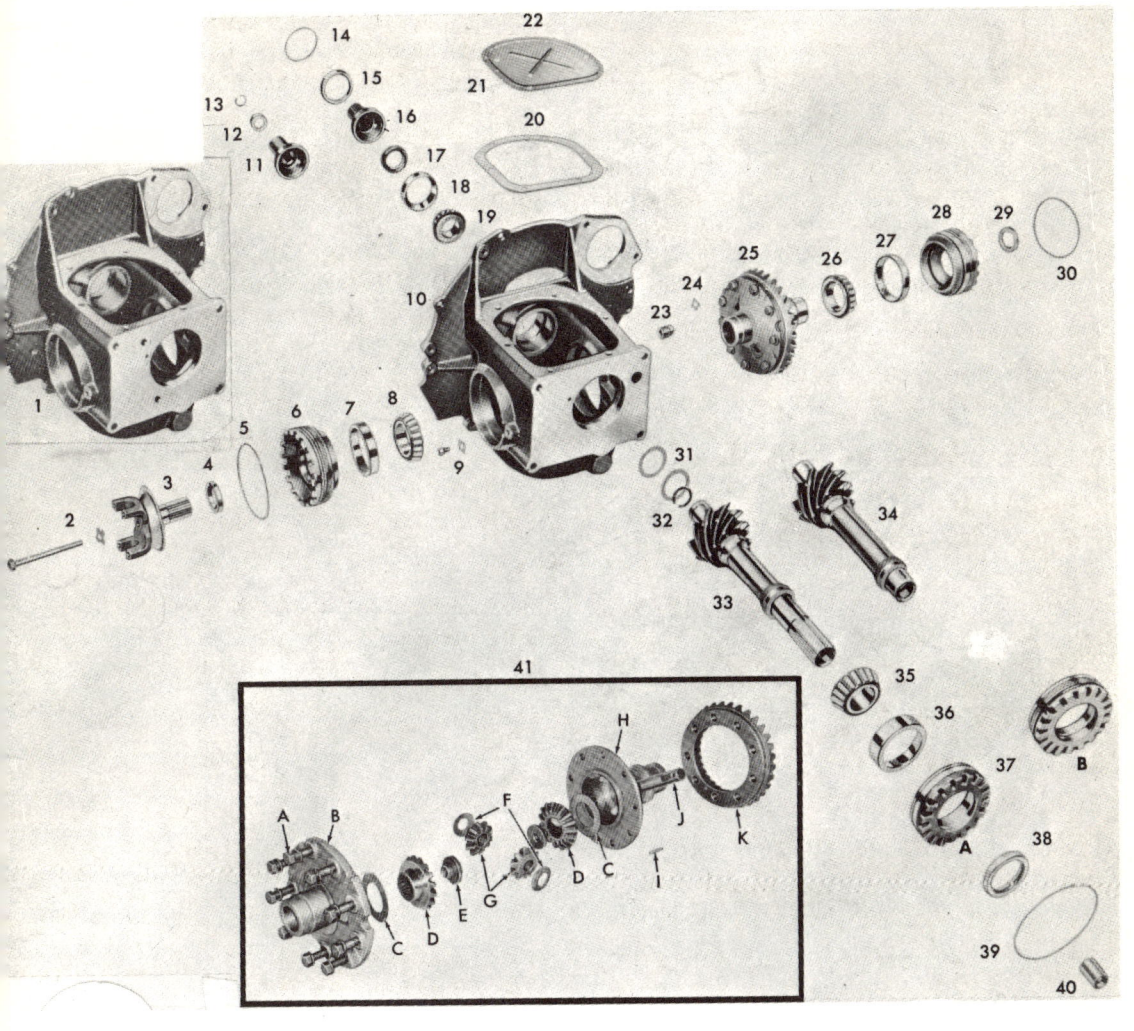

Differential carrier, exploded view

1. Differential carrier (manual transmission)
2. Yoke attaching parts (later production)
3. Yoke
4. Side bearing adjusting sleeve
5. Side bearing adjusting sleeve seal ring
6. Side bearing adjusting sleeve
7. Side bearing race
8. Side bearing
9. Adjusting sleeve lock tab and bolt
10. Differential carrier (automatic transmission)
11. Clutch release bearing shaft (manual transmission)
12. Clutch release bearing shaft seal
13. Split ring (manual transmission)
14. Seal ring
15. Converter hub seal (automatic transmission)
16. Stator shaft (automatic transmission)
17. Pinion rear seal (automatic transmission)
18. Pinion rear bearing race
19. Pinion rear bearing race
20. Cover gasket
21. Carrier cover
22. Vent
23. Filler plug
24. Adjusting sleeve lock tab
25. Differential assembly
26. Side bearing
27. Side bearing race
28. Side bearing adjusting sleeve
29. Side bearing adjusting sleeve seal
30. Side bearing adjusting sleeve seal ring
31. Selective pinion depth shims
32. Pinion shaft seal ring (automatic transmission)
33. Pinion (automatic)
34. Pinion (manual)
35. Pinion front bearing
36. Pinion front bearing race
37. Pinion adjusting sleeve
38. Pinion front seal (automatic)
39. Pinion adjusting sleeve seal ring
40. Pinion shaft bushing (automatic)
41. Differential components:
   A. Ring gear bolts and washers
   B. Differential cover (standard unit)
   C. Side gear thrust washers
   D. Side gears
   E. Yoke retaining nut
   F. Pinion thrust washers
   G. Pinion gears
   H. Differential case
   I. Retaining pin
   J. Pinion shaft
   K. Ring gear

replace bearings that have flattened or scarred rollers.

NOTE: If race or roller damage to the pinion bearings necessitates replacement, the outer race must be removed from the threaded adjusting sleeve. Use a punch to catch the edge of the race from the outer side of the sleeve and drive it evenly from the sleeve. Install the race of the new bearing by tapping it evenly into place.

Press the new or serviceable bearings back into place on the shaft.

Differential Disassembly (Standard Unit)

Disassemble the differential if necessary to replace the ring gear, side gears, or pinion gears.

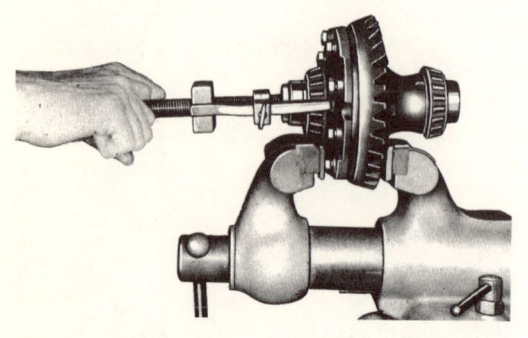

Removing differential side bearings

Remove the differential from the carrier after the side bearing sleeves have been removed (see "Pinion Gear Removal," above), and place the assembly on a bench.

Check the side bearings for damage (flattened or scarred rollers, scoring on the outer races,

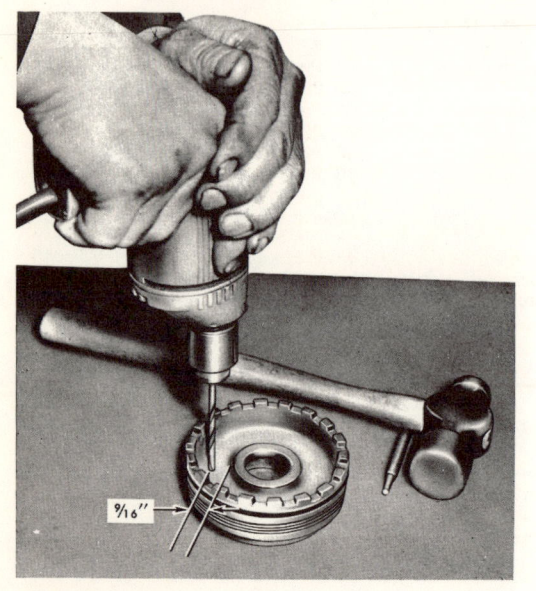

Drilling side bearing adjusting sleeve for race removal

etc.). Remove the bearings if necessary, using a locking screw-type puller such as that shown. Insert a block or disk over the end of the side bearing journal for counterforce. If the bearing is being replaced, its outer race must be replaced also; drill a 3/16" hole in the outer surface of the adjuster sleeve to expose the back of the bearing outer race. Use a small pin punch in the hole to drive the bearing race out. Deburr the hole at the inner side of the sleeve afterward and clean it thoroughly; install the new bearing outer race, tapping it evenly and squarely into place. Drive a lead ball or plug into the drilled hole to seal it.

Ring Gear Replacement

Remove the ring gear, if necessary, by unbolting it and tapping it off the case with a hammer. Install a new or serviceable gear by tapping it squarely into place on the case.

NOTE: Make sure the alignment marks on the cover and case are in alignment when the bolts are installed, as shown. Guide pins made

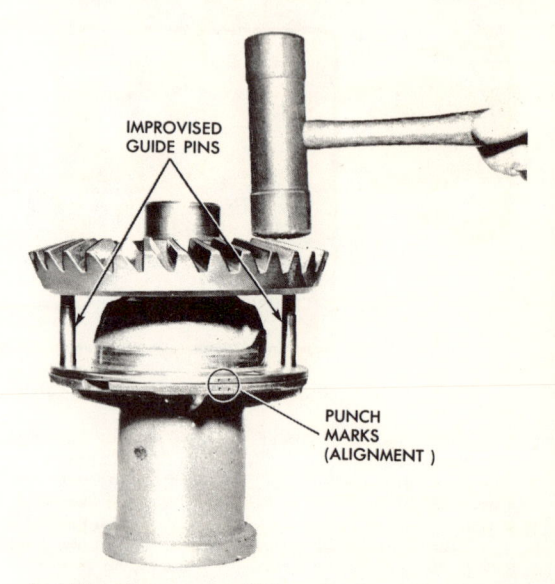

Installing ring gear on differential case and cover using improvised guide pins

from cut-off bolts may be used to guide the gear down squarely.

Install the cover bolts and torque them to 40-60 ft. lbs. in an alternate (diametrical) sequence.

Side and Pinion Gear Replacement

Remove the side and pinion gears by unbolting and separating the case and cover; one side gear can then be lifted out. To remove the other, drive out the lockpin securing the pinion

REAR AXLE AND SUSPENSION

shaft to the differential case and tap the shaft from the case, removing the pinion gears and thrust washers in the process. Remove the side gear from its recess in the case.

Install the gears in reverse order from the above, installing the side gear in the case and assembling the pinion gears (with their thrust washers) in the case with the pinion shaft through their centers. Drive the lockpin back into the shaft through the case to secure the shaft. Reassemble the case and cover and tighten the bolts to 40-60 ft. lbs. (be sure the case and cover alignment marks are in line).

Positraction (Limited Slip) Differential

This unit was offered as an option from 1962 on, and is shown. In this unit, a stack of preloaded clutch plates and discs allows one side of the drive line to slip, reducing loss of traction on the other side. The motion of one side gear is controlled by the friction of the "clutch pack," reducing the tendency of one wheel to get all the drive line's power in extreme cases.

Positraction differential, cross-section

Condition Check

Check the condition of the limited-slip differential while it is still in the vehicle by jacking up the vehicle and measuring the torque necessary to turn one wheel while a helper holds the other wheel to keep it from turning (back off the brake shoes on the wheel being measured to eliminate brake friction). This turning torque (the tension at which the clutch plates in the differential cover will slip) should be at least 50 ft. lbs. If it is below this limit, the unit should be overhauled.

Ring Gear Replacement

See "Ring Gear Replacement" for the standard unit, above.

Clutch Pack Disassembly

Mark the differential case and cover with alignment marks to make sure the parts are installed in the same position at assembly. Unscrew the cover bolts and separate the case from the cover.

NOTE: If the case and cover are secured with two flathead screws, remove them. It is not necessary to reinstall them.

Disassemble the case in the same manner as the standard unit (see above) if the gears or bearings need service.

The cover and "clutch pack" are shown disassembled. Remove the right-hand side gear from the cover, then remove the spacer and the clutch plates and disks. Inspect the plates and disks for damage such as cracks, scoring, or burn marks. If necessary, the clutch pack must be replaced as a unit.

Lubricate the clutch disks and plates lightly and assemble them in the order shown. The flat clutch plates and disks are installed nearest to the side gear. Install the preload spacer, chamfered side facing out. Install the side gear, mating its spline with the splines of both *clutch* disks.

Install the cover, lining up the alignment marks, and secure the cover and clutch pack assembly to the differential case. If the ring gear was removed, install it in the same manner as for a standard differential unit. Torque the cover bolts to 40-60 ft. lbs.

Checking Preload

Clamp the assembled limited-slip differential in a fixture and install a high-range torque wrench to measure the turning torque on the assembly's clutch plates. A universal joint yoke may be used to connect the wrench to the side gear, as shown. Check the torque required to turn the side gear; this torque should be at least 50 ft. lbs.

Assembly of the Differential

Install the differential assembly in the carrier and position the pinion gear assembly in mesh with the ring gear. With these assemblies held in position, install the side bearing and pinion bearing sleeves loosely. Tighten up the sleeves

REAR AXLE AND SUSPENSION

1 Differential cover
2 Clutch plates
3 Belleville clutch plate
4 Belleville clutch disc
5 Clutch disc
6 Preload spacer
7 Side gear

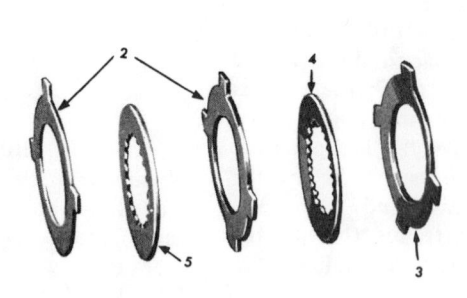

Positraction differential, exploded view

one by one until the right relationship of the ring gear to the pinion gear is obtained.

NOTE: Obtain the correct preload (turning torque) and backlash (measured by dial indicator), then make a dye check of the gear teeth as described above to be sure the gears are in correct mesh.

When the correct preload and backlash have been achieved, lock the side bearing sleeves with the lock tabs. Torque the tab bolts to 20-25 ft. lbs. On early-production differentials

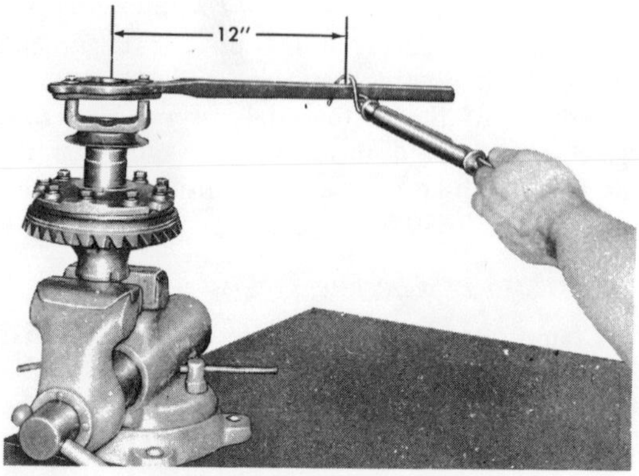

Checking clutch pack pre-load

(prior to 1965), install the speedometer gear and secure it with its locking bolt.

Replacement

Automatic Transmission Units

Make sure the front seal is in place to keep the differential lubricant from leaking into the automatic transmission.

Check the front end of the pinion shaft to be sure the original end play spacers are in place; if any change in pinion depth was made while rebuilding the differential, change the end play spacers to compensate for this change: if the pinion was moved forward (into the ring gear), decrease the end play spacers by that amount; if the pinion was moved rearward (out of the ring gear), increase the spacing.

NOTE: This spacing maintains a 0.025-0.045" clearance between the pinion shaft spacer surface and the end face of the planet hub of the automatic transmission.

Install the differential cover and torque the cover bolts to 130-230 in. lbs. Bring the differential carrier and transmission together on a level surface and install the transmission pump shaft through the pinion shaft as the assemblies

STATOR SHAFT
TURBINE SHAFT
FRONT PUMP SHAFT

Installing converter on transaxle

are brought together. Bolt the transmission and differential carrier together and install the governor on the transmission, meshing its drive gear with the gear on the pinion shaft. Install the turbine shaft from the rear of the carrier, over the pump shaft and through the stator shaft. Install the torque converter, being careful to engage all three splines, as shown.

Mate the transaxle with the engine and bolt the carrier to the flywheel housing flange. Bolt the torque converter to the engine's flex plate through the port in the flywheel housing. Torque the flex plate bolts to 20-30 ft. lbs.

Install the drive train in the vehicle as directed in Chapter Three.

Manual Transmission Units

Check to be sure the clutch release bearing seal is in place, held by its split ring. Assemble the transmission to the differential carrier, mating the spline of the transmission mainshaft with the inner spline of the pinion shaft. Install the clutch input shaft at the rear of the carrier, inserting it through the differential pinion and transmission mainshaft and into mesh with the clutch gear spline in the transmission.

Assemble the clutch fork and release bearing (see Chapter Six) and mate the transaxle to the engine. Bolt the differential carrier to the flywheel housing and torque the bolts to 20-30 ft. lbs. Install the drive train in the vehicle as directed in Chapter Three.

8 • Brakes

General

All Corvair vehicles are equipped with four-wheel hydraulic drum brakes. In 1962, self-adjusting brakes were introduced, and in 1967 a dual braking system was installed. A manual parking brake actuates the rear brake shoes.

Adjustment

The Corvair brakes use the conventional star-wheel adjustment system to move the shoes out toward the drums to reduce brake pedal distance. A port on either the outside of the drum or the inner surface of the backing plate allows access to the star wheel with a screwdriver or "brake spoon."

NOTE: From 1962 on, the adjustment hole is on the outer surface of the brake drum; previously it was on the backing plate. The later drum-port is closed at manufacture and must be driven out with a punch if it has not been punched out already. If this port is punched open, the drum must be subsequently removed and the metal punching removed to prevent its falling into the brake mechanism. On all models, the downward stroke of the screwdriver or brake spoon loosens the shoes and an upward stroke tightens them.

NOTE: On vehicles having self-adjusting brakes (1962 on), a screwdriver or brake spoon

Brake drum access hole—1962-69

Adjusting brakes—1960-61

BRAKES

alone will be sufficient to tighten the shoes, but the self-adjusting pawl (illustrated below) will not permit them to be loosened unless a thin screwdriver or punch is inserted in the access port to lift the pawl off the star wheel while another tool is used to move the star wheel.

Adjust the brakes by expanding the shoes until the wheel is stopped by their friction and can only be rotated with difficulty. Slack off the shoes until the wheel is free to rotate at least several times after a hard spin with the hand. Intermittent light rubbing of the shoe against the drum is permissible.

Bleeding the Brake System

If adjustment of the shoes is not sufficient to bring up the brake pedal and give quick, hard braking action, the trouble may be air in the hydraulic lines, and the system should be bled to expel the air.

Hydraulic fluid, being a liquid, is practically incompressible and gives firm pressure in the brake lines. However, air is compressible, especially under the conditions found in an automotive brake system. If air enters the system through leaks or through a dry fluid reservoir, this air will compress and give the brake pedal a spongy feeling and reduce or even destroy the braking efficiency. This air is bled out by opening a small valve on each wheel and applying pressure to the system to force out the air that is in the lines, together with some of the fluid. Either one of the following methods is suitable for this purpose.

With Pressure Bleeder

The Corvair brake system is designed to allow "pressure bleeding"—the pressurization of the system by means of an external air source. With this method, compressed air is introduced over the brake fluid supply in the reservoir to force the fluid down and through the lines, forcing trapped air out of the lines through the open bleed valves.

A device similar to that pictured is required to seal the top of the brake fluid reservoir (located in the front luggage compartment) and to provide a fitting for a compressed air source.

Remove the reservoir cover by flipping the cover bail to one side. Check the reservoir (both reservoirs in the dual system) and make sure that it is approximately half full of fluid.

NOTE: Remember that absolute cleanliness is essential around a brake system. Any dirt introduced into the hydraulic system will result in damage to the internal valve and piston surfaces and possible brake failure. Be extremely

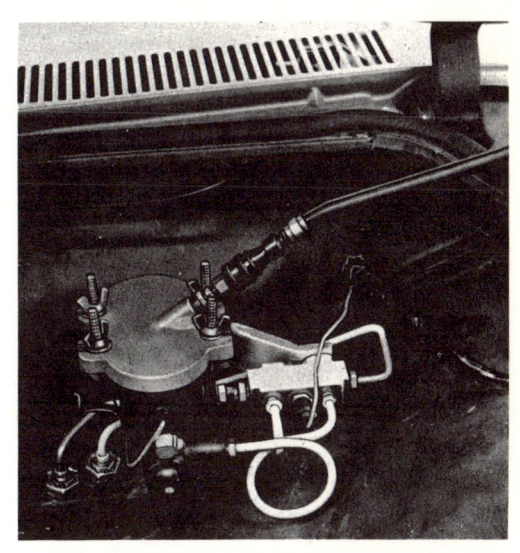

Brake bleeder adapter tool, installed

careful when opening the fluid reservoir not to knock any dirt into the fluid, as this dirt will eventually find its way into the system. Attach a pressure cap (similar to that pictured) firmly onto the top of the reservoir. Attach approxi-

General Chassis and Brake Specifications

YEAR	MODEL	CHASSIS			BRAKE CYLINDER BORE		BRAKE DRUM	
		Overall Length (In.)	Tire Size	Master Cylinder (In.)	Wheel Cylinder (In.)		Diameter (In.)	
					Front	Rear	Front	Rear
1960-64	All, exc. below	180.0	6.50 x 13★	1.0	$7/8$ ①	$15/16$ ①	9.0	9.0
1965-66	All, exc. below	183.3●	6.50 x 13	1.0	$7/8$	$15/16$	9.5	9.5
1967-69	All	183.3	7.00 x 13	1.0	$7/8$	$15/16$	9.5	9.5

★—1961-64—1200 Series and Sports Wagon—7.00 x 14 and 7.00 x 13.
●—Greenbrier—179.7
①—1200 Series—$1 1/8$ front, 1.0 rear.

mately 18" of thin hose, such as neoprene fuel line, to the bleeder valve of the first wheel to be checked, and lead the other end of the hose into a jar of clean brake fluid so that the end of the hose is submerged in the fluid. This is to prevent air from being sucked back up the hose and into the wheel cylinder.

Bleed each wheel in the sequence shown. The principle of bleeding is that the longest brake line should be bled first, the next longest bled next, etc. Have a helper put air pressure into the cover on the reservoir by compressed air hose, hand pump, etc. The pressure should not exceed 30 - 50 lbs.; as a safeguard drape the master cylinder in heavy cloth and spread cloth under the reservoir to prevent damage to the luggage compartment interior in case brake fluid sprays out. While this pressure is being applied, open the bleeder valve of the first wheel cylinder with a brake bleeder wrench slipped over the hose until the valve opens and fluid flows out through the hose and into the jar. If the line being bled contains air, bubbles will be visible in the fluid as it is forced out. When the fluid is clear of bubbles, close the valve, remove the hose and wrench, and move to the next wheel.

NOTE: This operation can be performed on the ground, but raising the car on jackstands will make access to the wheel valves easier.

If a significant amount of fluid was expelled in bleeding a wheel, remove the pressurization cover from the fluid reservoir (after pressure

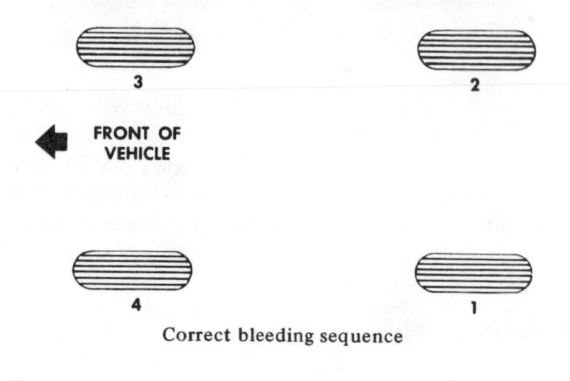

Correct bleeding sequence

has been safely released) to make sure there is still ample fluid left. (If the reservoir is pumped dry and pressurized air enters the system, the bleeding process will have to be repeated.) Bleed each wheel cylinder in this fashion, in the sequence specified. Afterward, add brake fluid to the reservoir and replace the cover and its seal.

Without Pressure Bleeder

With this method brake pedal pressure is used to force the fluid through the lines and out the bleeder valves. Bleed each cylinder in the same sequence and manner as before, except that now the pressurization must come from a helper stepping on the brake pedal each time a wheel cylinder is to be bled.

Bleeding brakes, using brake bleeder wrench

NOTE: Caution the helper not to release pressure on the pedal until the wheel cylinder valve is closed, or else air could be sucked into the system.

After bleeding is completed, add fluid to the reservoir to within 1/4" of the top and replace the cover and seal.

Master Cylinder Pushrod Distance

The master cylinder replenishes itself with fluid from the fluid reservoir through a port in the cylinder housing which is uncovered as the piston retracts. If for some reason the foot pedal does not return all the way up or if the piston sticks, this port may not be opened. Adjust the free travel of the pedal by loosening the locknut at the end of the master cylinder pushrod and threading the rod in or out until the pedal travel is as specified.

NOTE: This "free travel" is not to be confused with the "play" of the pedal between its return position and the point at which it pressurizes the cylinder. "Free travel" is measured in an upward direction.

Do not extend the pushrod as a means of

BRAKES

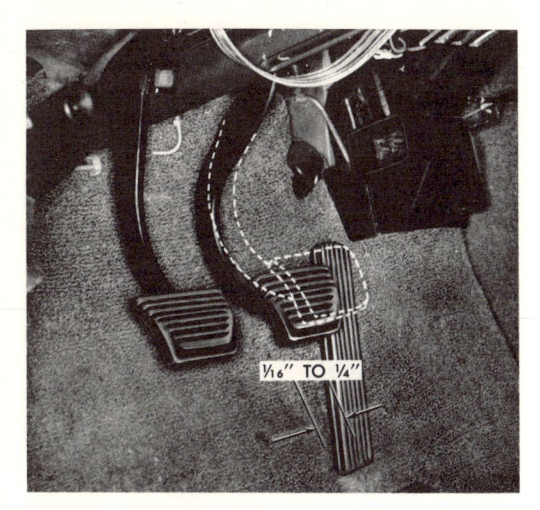

Brake pedal free movement

raising the pedal height when the brakes are low. A higher pedal will be gained for a short time, but if the compensating port in the master cylinder is closed by the piston being forced forward, the cylinder will not be able to replenish itself. Raise the pedal height by adjusting the shoes only.

Replacement of Brake Shoes

If adjusting the brakes does not relieve poor braking qualities or eliminate unusual braking noises, the linings of the shoes should be checked and the shoes replaced if necessary.

Jack up the vehicle and support it on jackstands. Do not attempt to support the vehicle with conventional auto jacks alone. Pull the front and rear brake drums (repack the front wheel bearings as described in Chapter Nine).

If the drums appear to "hang up" on the shoes on the way off the car, the shoes may be too tight, or they may have worn a deep groove in the drum so that a ridge has formed on the rear lip of the drum. In either case the shoes must be backed off to free the drum. Back off the shoes with downward strokes on the star wheel using a screwdriver or brake spoon until the drum is released. If the access port on the outer surface of the brake drum (on later production models) has not been opened up, remove the port cover by driving it inward with a hammer and a punch. If the brakes are of the self-adjusting type, the self-adjusting pawl will have to be held off the star wheel with one tool, while another moves the star wheel.

When the drum is off and the brake shoes are exposed, check the linings and wheel cylinders for general condition. The linings should not be worn down below 1/16" thickness at any point and should have an even, unglazed surface. The wheel cylinders should not show any evidence of fluid leakage; pull the rubber seals slightly away from their seating grooves on the ends of the cylinder to detect any leakage past the pistons. Cylinders with significant leakage should be replaced.

Remove the shoes by unhooking and removing the pull-back and hold-down springs.

Unhooking pull back springs

Keep the springs separate; they must go back in the same location they came from. Use only standard brake spring tools to remove the springs; pliers or a screwdriver can damage the springs, and using these tools may result in personal injury.

On self-adjusting brakes remove the self-adjusting pawl and spring as a unit. Push the bottoms of the shoes apart and pull out the star wheel and shaft. On the rear wheels, disconnect the parking brake lever from the brake shoe. Pull off the brake shoes carefully to avoid straining the wheel cylinder plungers. Clean the brake backing plate with compressed air.

NOTE: Once the brake drums are removed, do not push the brake pedal, or the wheel cylinder pistons will be pushed out of the cylinders.

Check the drums for condition. The inner surface should be smooth and even, with no deep circumferential scoring. Light polishing with emery cloth is permissible to clean up shallow grooving, but deep scoring must be repaired by turning the drum (boring it oversize), or replacing the drum. Linings 0.030" oversize are available for use with a drum bored 0.060" oversize

Removing hold down springs and pins

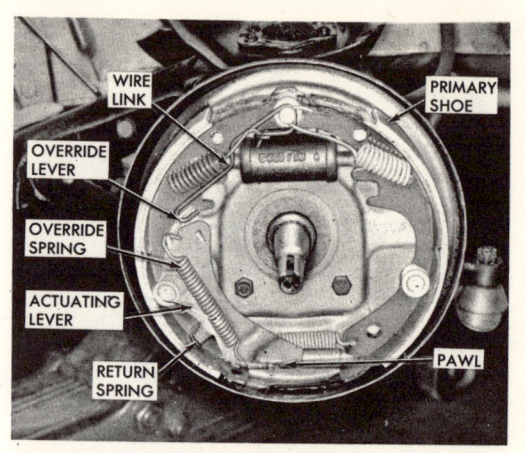

Self-adjusting brakes

in diameter. Certain local regulations forbid the machining of drums beyond a certain minimum wall thickness, and if this limit is exceeded the drums must be scrapped.

Install the new or serviceable shoes in their proper location on the backing plate, with the primary and secondary shoes in their proper places. Be careful to engage the piston actuating rods in the slots of the shoes. Install the adjuster and star wheel, positioned so that the star wheel is nearer to the secondary shoe and so will be accessible to the adjusting port in the drum or backing plate after assembly.

Install the springs, using standard brake spring tools to prevent damage. Install the self-adjuster mechanism, where used, and check it for free movement.

Check all parts for correct position.

Pre-set the brake shoes before installing the brake drums using one of the following methods.

Method 1: Back off the shoes with the star wheel until the drum can be made to slide on, then tighten the shoes until they almost touch the drum.

Method 2: Obtain a standard brake gauge, shown. Adjust the gauge to the inner diameter of the brake drum with the notched side of the gauge and lock the gauge with the adjusting screw. Invert the gauge without disturbing the setting and use the caliper side to set the required distance across the shoes.

Install the drums and seat them over the shoes and against the backing plate.

Wheel Cylinder Overhaul

A typical wheel cylinder unit is shown. It consists of opposing pistons forced out by hydraulic pressure to push on the actuating rods and force the brake shoes out. If excessively worn, the pistons will leak, causing loss of pressure and braking efficiency. A sign of excessive piston wear is brake fluid collecting behind the outer rubber seals at each end of the cylinder, or consistent presence of air in one

Using drum to brake shoe clearance gauge

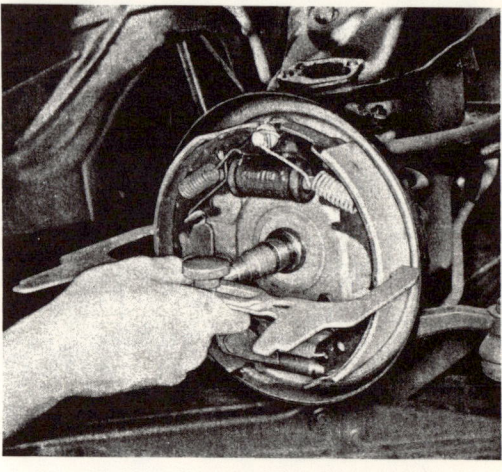

Checking brake shoe lining clearance

BRAKES

particular wheel cylinder, causing the brakes to have to be bled repeatedly.

Removal

Remove the brake drum and remove the brake shoe return springs leading to the stud above the wheel cylinder. On early models (1960 and 1961), the spring stud doubles as the fastener for the wheel cylinder. Unscrew the hydraulic line from the rear of the backing plate. Unbolt and remove the wheel cylinder

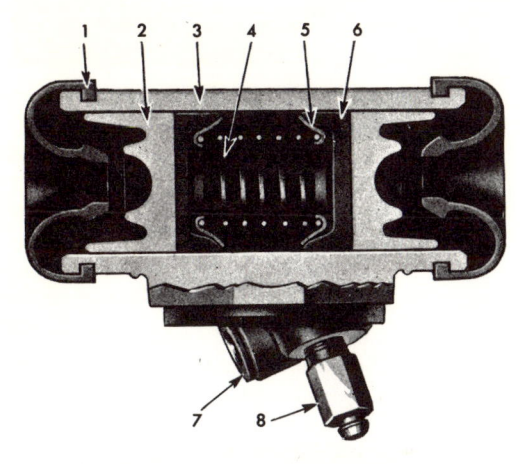

1 Pushrod boot
2 Piston
3 Housing
4 Spring
5 Piston cup expander
6 Piston cup
7 Fluid inlet
8 Bleeder valve

Wheel cylinder, cross-section

(unscrew the spring stud for certain types—see above).

Disassembly

Pull off the rubber seals and draw out the pistons, caps, and spring. Clean all parts in alcohol and keep them extremely clean. Inspect the bore of the cylinder for smoothness. The bore should be free of scoring or corrosion.

NOTE: The cylinder bore often becomes corroded at the outer ends because of exposure to the air and lack of protection from brake fluid (the pistons being farther in). Wear to brake parts, causing the pistons to move farther out,

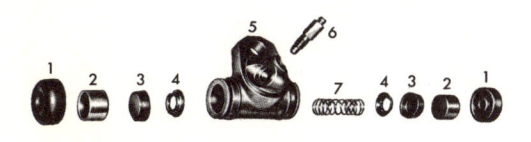

1 Pushrod boot
2 Piston
3 Piston cup
4 Piston cup expander
5 Housing
6 Bleeder valve
7 Spring

Wheel cylinder, exploded view

causes the cylinder to leak across the corroded surfaces.

Check the clearance of the pistons in the cylinder using a feeler gage. This clearance should be 0.002 to 0.004". If it exceeds this limit, replace the cylinder. Replace the rubber seals if they are distorted or damaged.

Assembly

Moisten all parts with brake fluid, keeping them clean and protected at all times. Assemble the cylinder from one side, installing a rubber seal at the other end to retain the parts; install a piston (recessed portion toward the seal), expander, spring, the other piston (recess outward), and a rubber seal. Replace the cylinder on the brake backing plate and tighten the bolts (or spring stud). Assemble the brake springs and replace the drum and wheel. Bleed the brake system as directed above.

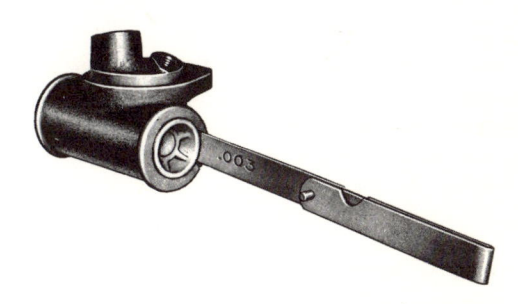

Checking wheel cylinder piston fit

Master Cylinder Overhaul

Poor braking action which cannot be traced to the wheel cylinders may indicate trouble in the master cylinder. This unit provides the pressure to actuate the brake system and consists of a horizontal piston which is forced against a column of hydraulic fluid when the brake pedal is depressed. From 1967 on, Corvairs were fitted with a dual brake system, in which two fluid reservoirs and two pistons in the same cylinder unit actuate the front and rear brakes separately. Failure of one system will leave the other intact, so that the vehicle can still be brought to a stop safely.

If bleeding the brake lines through the wheel bleeder valves does not keep air out of the master cylinder, remove it and disassemble it as directed below.

Removal

Remove all hydraulic lines to the master cylinder and plug them with clean plastic or rubber plugs, not cloth. Unscrew the nuts holding the cylinder to the luggage compartment

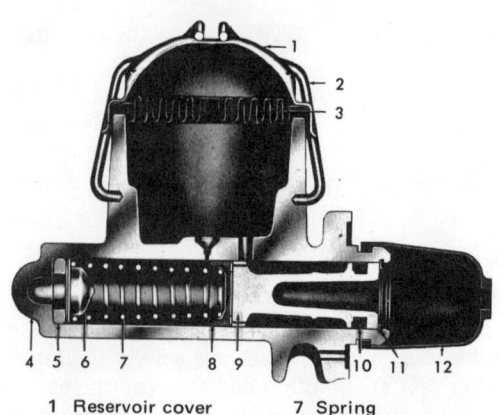

1. Reservoir cover
2. Bail wire
3. Seal
4. Body
5. Valve seat
6. Valve assembly
7. Spring
8. Primary cup
9. Piston
10. Secondary cup
11. Lock ring
12. Boot

Master cylinder 1960-66, cross-section

Remove the inner lockring, then pull the piston, cap, spring, valve and seat from the cylinder. Wash the metallic parts in *alcohol* (not gasoline or solvent).

Inspect the cylinder bore for corrosion or scoring. Check the compensating and bypass ports from the reservoir side to be sure they are clear. Check the piston-to-cylinder clearance with a feeler gauge, or with inside and outside micrometers. This clearance should be 0.001 to 0.005". Inspect all parts for condition (grooving, scoring, corrosion, etc.). The rubber caps and seals should not be swelled or distorted.

Assembly

Assemble the cylinder very carefully, installing the valve element correctly and without distortion. Wet all parts in new brake fluid and install the spring, caps, piston and lockring. Check the position of the piston with a wire to be sure that when retracted the piston is clear of the compensating port, as shown.

Check the operation of the cylinder by partially filling the reservoir with brake fluid and the piston with a rod inserted in the rear of the piston. Fluid should be expelled from the outlet port, with no suction when the piston retracts. The cylinder should be observed to replenish itself from the reservoir.

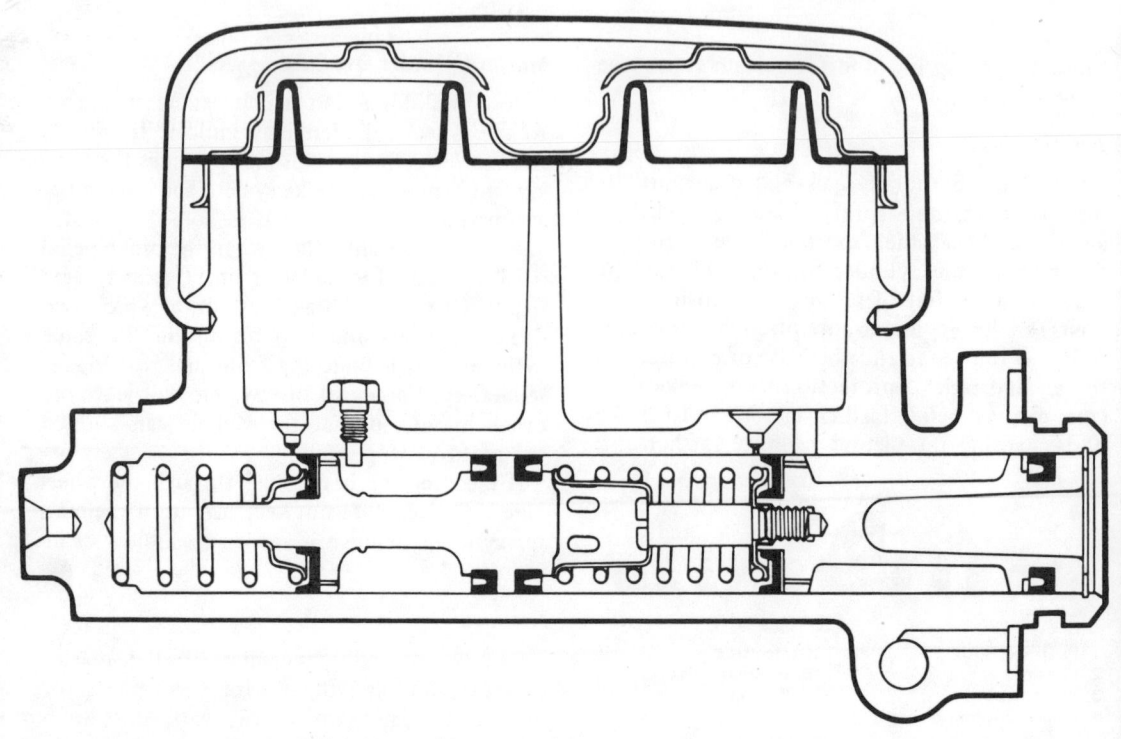

wall and pull the cylinder straight off to clear the push rod. Keep the cylinder upright until the reservoir has been emptied.

Disassembly – 1960-1966

Remove the rubber cap from the push rod entrance port. Flip the reservoir cover bail to one side and remove the cover and seal. Empty the reservoir.

Split brake system master cylinder 1967-69, cross-section

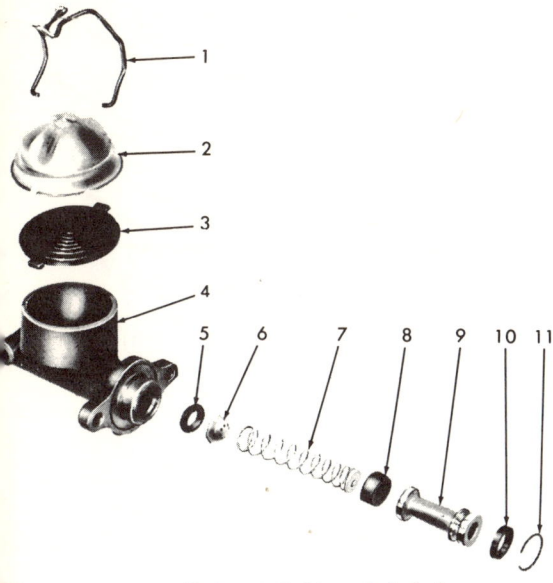

BRAKES

Master cylinder 1960-66, exploded view

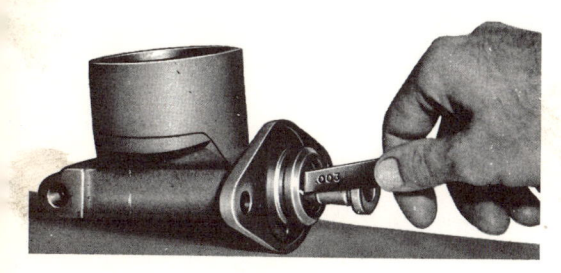

Checking piston fit

Installation

Install the cylinder on its studs on the wall of the luggage compartment, over the pushrod. Connect the hydraulic lines and fill the reservoir to within 1/4" of the top. Check the free travel of the pedal (see above) and bleed the entire brake system.

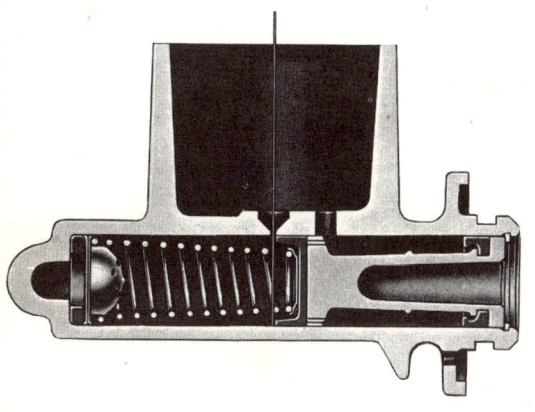

Checking compensating port clearance

Disassembly—1967-1969

Flip the reservoir cover to one side and remove the cover and seal. Empty both reservoirs. Using a small socket wrench, remove the stop plug from the front reservoir, allowing the front piston to be removed. Remove the rubber seal and the retaining ring and pull the secondary piston and associated parts from the cylinder. Remove the primary piston and associated parts.

NOTE: If the primary piston is difficult to remove, hook it out with a wire, or blow air into the front reservoir to push it out.

Check the cylinder bore for damage and corrosion. Look down into the reservoir, with a strong light shining into the cylinder bore, to be sure the compensating ports are clear. Check the pistons and seals for wear or damage.

NOTE: The master cylinder outlets are equipped with check valves which prevent suction of fluid back into the cylinder after the pistons retract. These can only be removed by drilling out the seats and pulling them out with a screw. If a test of the assembled cylinder shows that these valves allow suction of fluid back into either chamber of the cylinder, remove the faulty valve and press in a new one.

Assembly

Assemble the cylinder by assembling the primary spring, retainer, seal, and seal protector, and the primary piston and seals, and installing them in the cylinder bore. Thread the piston extension screw completely into the secondary piston through the stop, spring, retainer, seal, and protector. Install the seals on the secondary piston and install it in the cylinder bore with its spring. Push on the secondary piston to move both pistons forward in the bore far enough so that the primary piston stop screw can be installed through the bottom of the front fluid reservoir. Fill the reservoirs with fluid and check the operation of the pistons by cycling them several times. Check for correct check valve operation by inspecting for suction through the valves as the pistons are allowed to retract. Install the diaphragm seal and cover and secure the bail over the cover.

Installation

Install the pushrod in the cylinder and install the rubber seal over the end of the cylinder. Fasten the cylinder to the wall of the luggage compartment with a new or serviceable gasket. Connect the hydraulic lines and connect the pushrod to the brake pedal. Bleed the entire brake system.

BRAKES

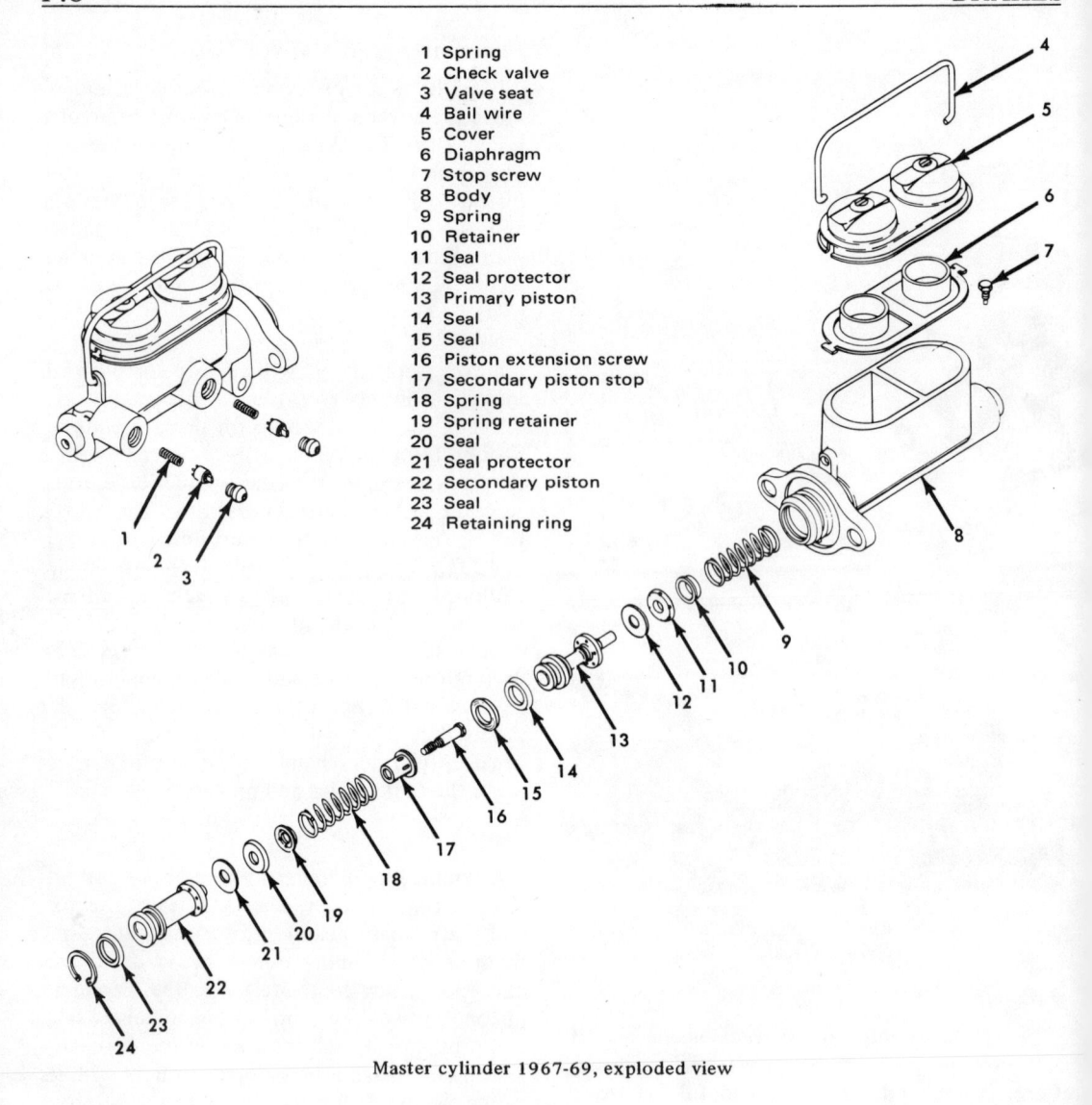

1 Spring
2 Check valve
3 Valve seat
4 Bail wire
5 Cover
6 Diaphragm
7 Stop screw
8 Body
9 Spring
10 Retainer
11 Seal
12 Seal protector
13 Primary piston
14 Seal
15 Seal
16 Piston extension screw
17 Secondary piston stop
18 Spring
19 Spring retainer
20 Seal
21 Seal protector
22 Secondary piston
23 Seal
24 Retaining ring

Master cylinder 1967-69, exploded view

9 • Suspension and Steering

Front End

The Corvair front suspension is of the short-upper, long-lower arm type with the steering arms and knuckles connected by ball-joints. Camber and caster are adjustable, and strut rods at each steering knuckle damp front end "brake dive." From 1964 on a stabilizer bar was fitted across the front suspension.

Coil springs are on each side, and a piston-type shock absorber is mounted through the center of each spring.

Each front wheel is mounted on double tapered roller bearings.

Front Wheel Bearings

Repack the front wheel bearings at least once a year and every time the front brakes are serviced (see Chapter Eight).

Front suspension, cross-section

SUSPENSION AND STEERING

Speedometer cable

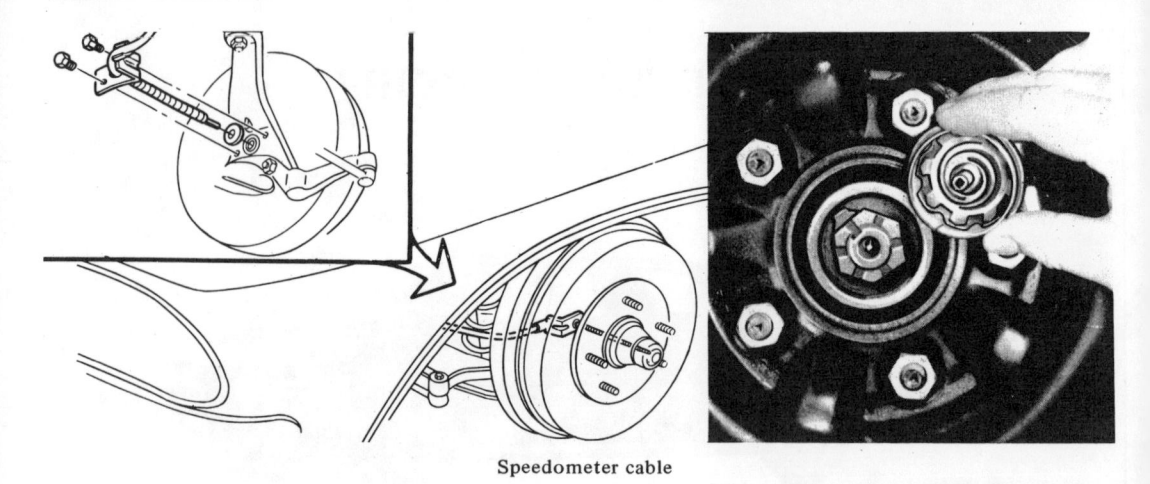

Jack up the front end until the wheels are clear of the ground and put sturdy jackstands under the front suspension. It is unsafe to support a vehicle on auto jacks alone. Pull off the grease cap on each wheel with water-pump pliers. Remove the cotter pin from the locknut and loosen the nut, backing it off about 1/4".

NOTE: From 1965 on the left front spindle contains the speedometer cable drive.

Be careful when removing the protective cap which contains the drive for this cable; pull the cap straight out and do not rock it or the drive may be damaged.

When the wheel locknut has been backed off slightly, grasp the front tire in two places to steady it and tug it straight off, toward the loosened locknut, and push it back again. This should push the outer wheel bearing out of its race in the hub and ease removal. Unthread the locknut completely and remove the outer wheel bearing from the spindle carefully with the fingers.

NOTE: Be careful with the bearing after removing it. Put it in a safe place until it is ready to be cleaned. Do not turn it around its inner race or let it get dirty.

Pull the tire and wheel straight off the spindle, to avoid scraping the spindle threads across the bearing races on the way off. Do not rap the threads on the bearing races, or allow the wheel and tire to hang, half-on, half-off the spindle.

Place the wheel and tire (inner side up) on the ground or on a bench. Carefully pry the oil seal out of the hub (or drift out from the outer side with a punch). Lift out the inner bearing with the fingers.

Clean both bearings from each wheel in clean solvent, carefully washing the old grease from between the rollers. Dry the bearings carefully and check the rollers for scratches, flat spots, blue-black burn marks, etc.

NOTE: Do not interchange bearings between wheels; each bearing is mated to its outer race in the wheel hub and one bearing cannot safely be installed in the race of another.

If the roller sufaces are flattened, burnt, or scarred, replace the bearing (inner race and outer race as a set). See the replacement procedure below.

Repack the new or serviceable bearings with a good grade of wheel bearing grease, either by working it in between the rollers with the fingers or by packing the bearing with a pressure packing fixture. Keep both bearings clean and protected at all times when they are out of the wheel.

Wipe out the inside of the hub and the bearing outer races. Check the races for damage (grooves, burning, intermittent flattening from faulty rollers, etc.) If the races are damaged, or if the mating bearing is to be replaced, drive the affected race evenly from its recess in the hub from the other side of the hub with a long punch and a hammer, tapping the inner side of the race where the retaining lip of the hub is cut away to allow this. Tap all around the circumference of the race until the race is pushed evenly from the hub. Wipe out the recess in the hub carefully, then tap the new bearing race into place (conical bearing surface facing outward), using a block of wood or a soft (brass) drift to protect the race. When the drift is felt to rebound when struck with the hammer, the race is fully seated.

NOTE: Do not attempt to interchange old and new bearing parts, or parts from different wheel assemblies, as rapid bearing failure will result.

Clean the wheel spindle with a rag to remove

SUSPENSION AND STEERING

old grease and dirt. Wipe the surface of the spindle lightly with wheel bearing grease to aid installation of the wheel assembly.

Check the brake linings and service the lining and the wheel brake cylinders if necessary (see Chapter Eight). Back off the shoes slightly to aid installation of the brake drum.

Fill the inner cavity of the hub (between the bearing races) with a thick coat of bearing grease to act as a dust seal when the wheel is back on the spindle. Install the repacked inner bearing in its race at the inner side of the hub and install a new grease seal over it, tapping the seal carefully and evenly into place with a block of wood and a hammer.

Lift the wheel and tire and push it straight onto the spindle until the inner bearing is felt to "bottom" against the shoulder on the spindle. Install the outer bearing on the spindle and into its race in the hub and install the sealing washer and the locknut.

Adjust the locknut as follows:

1960 and 1961: Torque the locknut to 80 in. lbs. while rotating the wheel to center the bearings; back the nut off one flat and insert the cotter pin; if the pin cannot be made to line up with the spindle hole, it is permissible to loosen the nut 1/2 flat more to achieve alignment.

1962 to 1964: Torque the locknut to 100 in. lbs. while rotating the wheel to center the bearings; back the nut off one flat and insert the cotter pin; if the pin cannot be made to line up with the spindle hole, it is permissible to loosen the nut 1/2 flat more to achieve alignment.

1965 to 1969: Torque the locknut to 12 ft. lbs. while rotating the wheel to center the bearings; back the nut off one flat and insert the cotter pin; if the pin cannot be made to line up with the spindle hole, it is permissible to loosen the nut 1/2 flat more to achieve alignment.

Bend the tabs of the cotter pin in different directions, one end over the end of the spindle, and tap the grease cap back into place. Adjust the brakes (see Chapter Eight).

NOTE: On vehicles with the speedometer drive in the left front spindle, be careful to install the cap (with its drive insert) straight and even and tap it carefully into place to avoid binding or breaking the drive.

Speedometer Cable—1965-1969

If necessary, the speedometer cable may be replaced by removing the grease cap from the left front wheel and unbolting the cable bracket from the back of the steering knuckle.

NOTE: Ordinarily the cable itself, if broken,

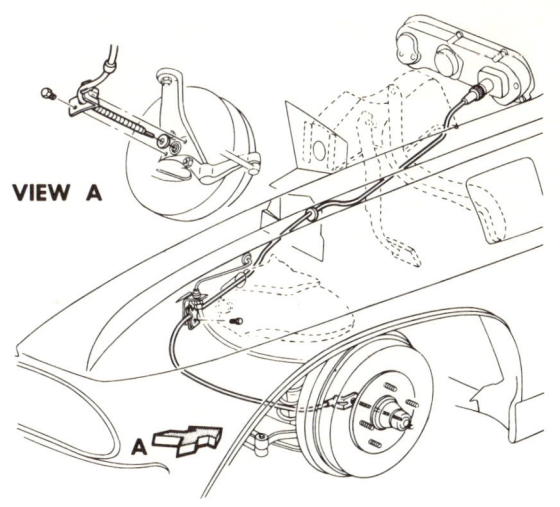

Speedometer cable

can be replaced by unscrewing the speedometer connection under the dashboard, removing the wheel spindle grease cap, and removing both pieces of the cable from each end of the sheath. Replace the cable, either with a stock item or with a "universal" cable carefully cut to fit. Lubricate the cable with graphite or light grease before installation.

Shock Absorbers

The Corvair front shock absorbers are positioned in the front spring towers. When the vehicle bounces on its front suspension with no damping effect from these units, they should be replaced with new units.

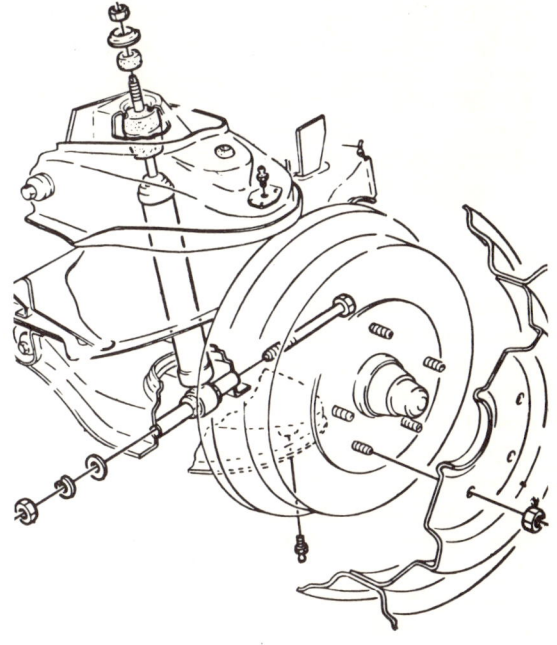

Shock absorber installation

Jack up the front of the vehicle so that the wheels are clear of the ground and support the vehicle on jackstands. Disconnect the upper end of the shock absorber (from inside the vehicle) by holding the flat stem with one wrench and unthreading the nut with another; disconnect the lower end by removing the retaining bolt in the lower control arm of the suspension. Pull the shock absorber down and out of the spring.

Install the new unit in reverse order: extend the new shock absorber so that its upper end protrudes through its upper mounting hole when in place. Insert it up into the spring from the bottom and secure the upper end and lower end with the nuts and bolts and new rubber bushings. Do not tighten the upper nut until the vehicle has been lowered to the ground.

Ball Joints

If, when the vehicle is jacked clear of the ground, play can be detected in the *upper* ball joints, the joints should be replaced.

NOTE: The lower ball joint is normally loose—this should not be confused with wear, but this joint also should be replaced when the upper joint is replaced.

Checking lower spherical joint

Make the following comparative measurement to check for ball joint wear: measure the distance shown on each steering knuckle, from the grease fitting to the top of the joint stud, in both the free (jacked up) and loaded (on the ground) state. More than 1/16" difference between the right and left sides indicates excessive wear. Burst grease seals, or difficulty in lubrication are also indications of poor joint condition.

Jack up the front end of the vehicle as far as is safe and practical and secure it on sturdy jackstands. If at all possible, use a lift and perform this work with the vehicle fully up in the air. Place an adjustable jack under the lower control arm of the first side to be serviced to take the tension of the coil spring. Remove the shock

Loop cable tool, installed

absorber (see above), then unscrew the lower ball joint stud nut and disconnect the stabilizer bar (1964 on) at the control arm. Lower the jack supporting the lower control arm, allowing the lower control arm to swing down.

With the lower control arm hanging free of the spring, remove the ball joint with a suitable screw-action ball joint pusher. Install the new joint by pressing it in place (or screw the early-production, threaded type in with a wrench).

To replace the upper ball joint it is usually

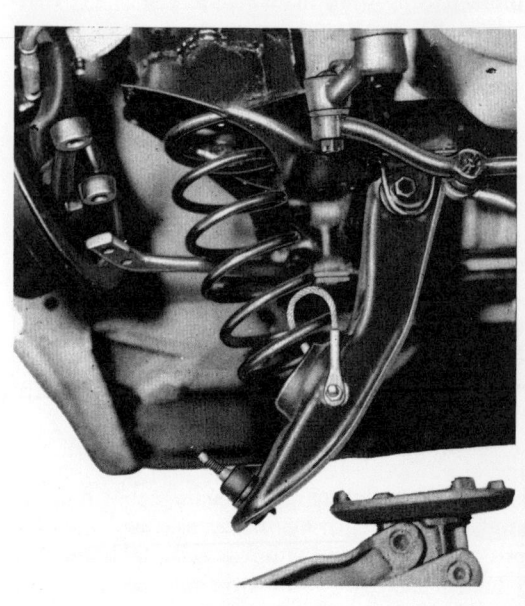

Spring relaxed

SUSPENSION AND STEERING

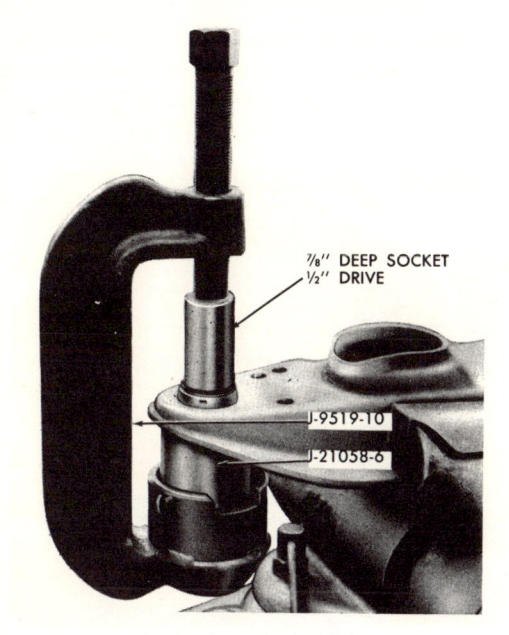

Removing spherical joint

necessary to remove the control arm, unless the joint has been replaced before; original joints are riveted to the arms, requiring some simple machining to remove them, but replacement joints are bolted. If the control arm must be removed, remove the cotter pin and nut from the ball joint stud and remove the stud, tapping it with a hammer if necessary. Remove the nuts securing the control arm to the front crossmember, after removing the coil spring. Remove the control arm downward, being careful to note and save any caster-adjustment shims found at this location.

If an upper control arm has its original ball joint, the joint will be riveted in place; carefully drill out these rivets and remove the joint.

Install the new joint and secure it with bolts in the old rivet holes torqued to 20-25 ft. lbs.

If excessive play was noticed in the control arms at their attachment to the frame, press out the bushings from the ends of the arms (with the arms off the vehicle) and press in new ones.

NOTE: Be careful to support each end of the arm well when pressing bushing in or out; do not press a bushing into one leg of an arm while supporting the arm at the other leg, as this will distort the arm.

Install the control arms on the vehicle, replacing any shims found between the upper crossshaft and the frame at removal. Install the ball stud through the upper ball joint and torque its nut to 30-40 ft. lbs. Lock it with a cotter pin.

Install the lower ball joint stud in the joint. Install the lower control arm and coil spring,

then, making sure the spring is seating correctly, jack the lower control arm up with the floor jack until the lower joint stud can be engaged through its mating steering parts, then install the stud nut and tighten it to 30-40 ft. lbs.

Replace the shock absorber as directed above. Service the other side of the front end in the same manner; always replace all the joints, not just one side, or the vehicle's riding characteristics will be affected.

Steering

The Corvair steering arrangement is by worm and ball-drive steering box to a pitman arm and relay rod, with ball-joint connections. Corvairs prior to 1965 featured an intermediary connecting rod and relay arm between the pitman arm and the relay rod, to provide for a steering box placed farther forward of the front wheel centerline.

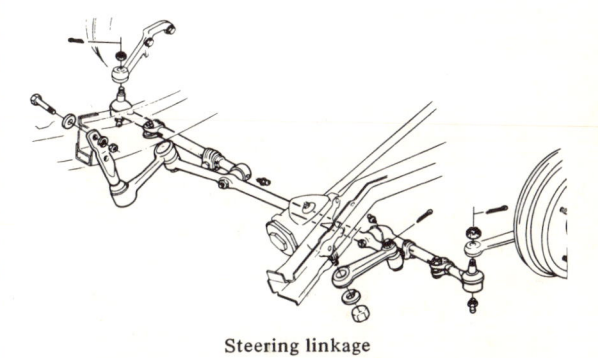

Steering linkage

Steering Box

The Corvair steering box is of the "recirculating ball" type shown. In this device a worm

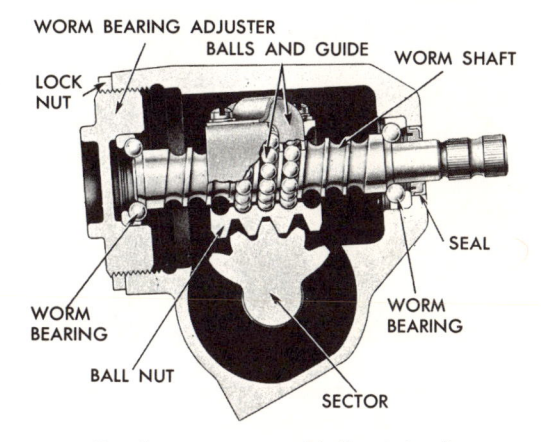

Steering gear worm and ball nut circuits

SUSPENSION AND STEERING

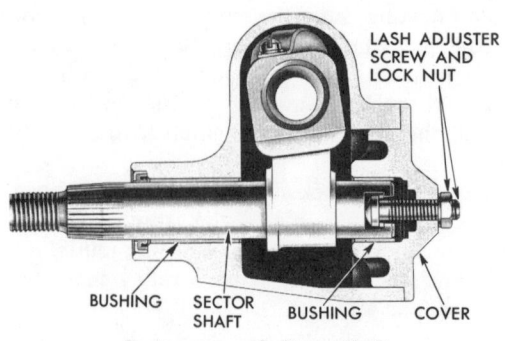

Sector gear and pitman shaft

gear moves a sector gear by means of a spiral row of ball bearings instead of by actual gear tooth contact. The sector gear engages the ball nut, containing the ball bearings, with beveled gear teeth, so that lash adjustment is possible by means of an adjusting screw.

The steering box incorporates a feature of "high load" in which the steering friction through the steering box is highest at the center, straight-ahead position and lowest during turns. This feature provides greater stability at normal road speeds, damping out "nervous" front wheel motion but keeping easy steering characteristics. Adjustment of the steering lash must take this high load characteristic into account, since the lash must be measured at this high point to be accurate.

Remove the horn ring from the steering wheel; at the steering box, unscrew the pitman arm nut and pull the pitman arm loose from the steering box with a suitable puller.

Removing pitman arm

Establish that the worm gear is properly adjusted by slacking off on the lash adjuster nut to eliminate sector gear friction, then measure steering torque with a torque wrench on the steering wheel hub. Adjust the worm adjuster nut until the steering turning force is 3 1/2-4 1/2 in. lbs.

Checking steering gear turning torque

Find the center "straight-ahead" position of the sector gear by counting turns from lock to lock at the steering wheel and dividing them by two. With the gear at this center position, remove all lash by tightening the lash adjuster screw, then lock the screw with its locknut. The steering torque through the "high point" should be 8-10 in. lbs. over the free torque measured previously, but no more than 14 in. lbs. in any case.

After this adjustment the relation of the wheels to the steering gear may have changed; "straight ahead" as registered in the "high point" of the steering box may not be "straight ahead" on the wheels. Replace the pitman arm

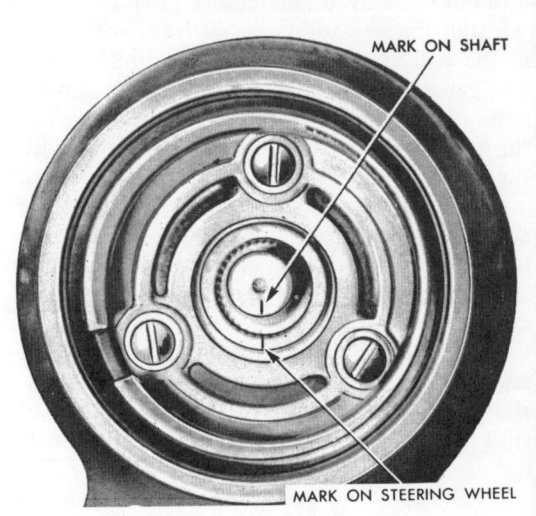

Steering wheel alignment marks

SUSPENSION AND STEERING

and tighten its nut to 80-105 ft. lbs., taking care that the front wheels are pointing as straight ahead as possible when doing this. Roll the vehicle for a few yards to establish that the wheels are pointing straight ahead.

Look at the mark on the steering shaft in the steering wheel hub; the mark on the shaft indicates the high point for the steering box and should be at the 12 o'clock position after "straight ahead" has been established by rolling the vehicle. If it is out of alignment, adjust both tie-rod sleeves on the outer steering linkage to move the wheels around to the same "straight ahead" attitude as that for the steering box.

NOTE: Be sure to adjust *both* sleeves, or the toe-in adjustment of the front wheels will be lost.

Steering Box Overhaul

Ordinarily the steering box will not have to be serviced beyond adjustment, but it may be disassembled and checked if the worm bearings seem worn or if the lash adjustment does not correct poor steering qualities.

Remove the pitman arm as directed in the lash adjustment procedure above, using a screw puller. Unbolt the steering box from the frame and disconnect the coupling to the steering shaft.

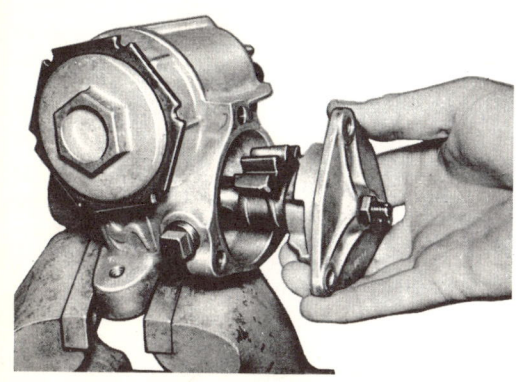

Removing pitman shaft

NOTE: It may be necessary to cut a two-inch access hole in the fender well in order to reach the shaft coupling to disconnect it.

Loosen both the worm bearing and lash adjustment screws and unbolt and remove the sector gear and cover. Remove the worm bearing nut and remove the worm and ball nut. Disassemble the ball nut if necessary and clean all parts thoroughly. The steering box is shown fully disassembled.

Check the worm bearings for wear or damage after they have been cleaned thoroughly. Check

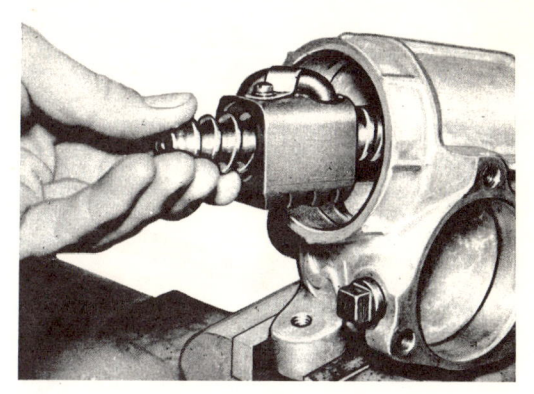

Removing wormshaft and ball nut

that all 48 balls are present and that they are not scratched or marred. Check the wormshaft for wear which could contribute to poor steering, such as worn grooves or damage to either end of the worm from the ball nut striking either end of the worm track.

Assemble the steering box by rebuilding the major groups, such as the worm and ball nut, the housing, and the pitman shaft and cover. Install the ball nut on the wormshaft, about

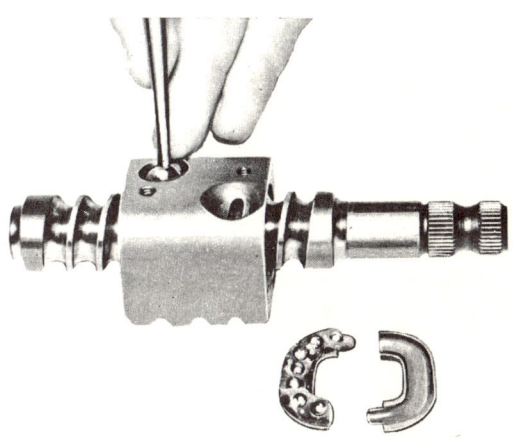

Placing balls in nut

midway on the shaft, and install the balls in the ball nut until they fill the entire inner track of the nut, as shown. Fill the two ball guides with

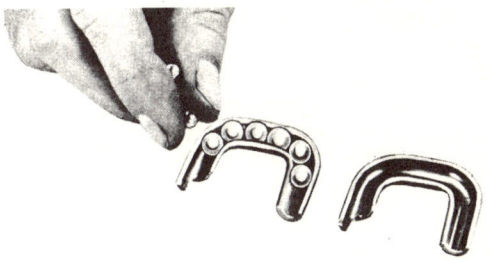

Filling ball guides

SUSPENSION AND STEERING

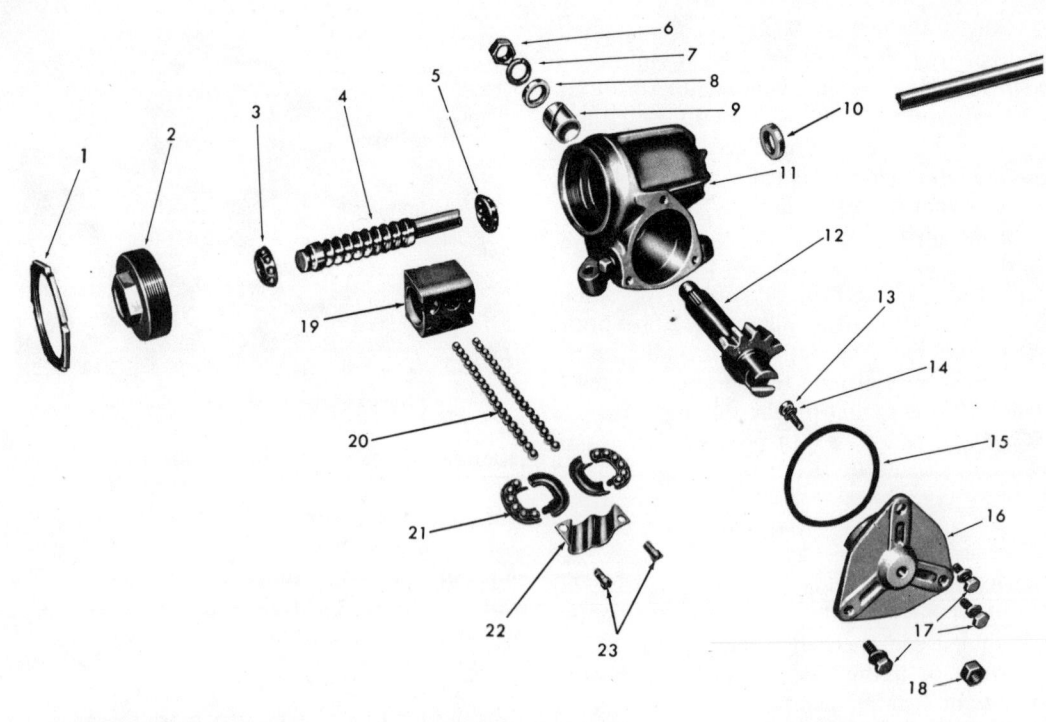

1. Wormshaft bearing adjuster locknut
2. Wormshaft bearing adjuster
3. Wormshaft bearing
4. Wormshaft
5. Wormshaft bearing
6. Pitman arm nut
7. Pitman arm lockwasher
8. Pitman shaft seal
9. Pitman shaft bushing
10. Wormshaft outer seal
11. Steering gear housing
12. Pitman shaft
13. Lash adjuster screw
14. Lash adjuster screw shim
15. O-ring
16. Side cover
17. Side cover screws and lockwashers
18. Lash adjuster screw locknut
19. Ball nut
20. Balls
21. Ball guides
22. Ball guide retainer
23. Ball guide retainer screws

Steering gear, exploded view

the remaining balls and secure the guides to the top of the ball nut with the retainer. Lubricate the wormshaft with chassis grease and turn it back and forth to move the lubricant under the ball nut surfaces. Assemble a new oil seal and wormshaft bearing on the wormshaft and install the shaft and ball nut assembly in the housing. Position the second bearing in the recess of the worm adjuster nut and install the nut on the housing, being careful to position the end of the worm in the bearing.

Assemble the pitman shaft and its lash adjuster and shim and check under the inner head of the adjuster screw (with the shim in place) for 0.002" minimum clearance between the adjuster screw head and the base of the slot. Select new shims as necessary.

Install the pitman shaft, with its screw and shim, in the cover and thread the locknut on the screw loosely. Install the cover and shaft into the housing, meshing the gear and the ball nut and checking to be sure that no interference exists. Slack off on both adjuster screws as necessary. When the cover is in place, fill the steering box with chassis grease and turn the wormshaft repeatedly to work the grease onto all moving surfaces. Set up the steering box adjustments (lash, "high point," etc.) after installing the assembly in the vehicle. See the procedure above for adjusting the installed steering gear.

Bolt the steering box back in place and torque the mounting bolts to 25-35 ft. lbs. Adjust the lash and turning torque as directed above, after the steering shaft has been connected.

Front End Alignment

The front wheels of Corvair vehicles are fully adjustable for caster, camber, and toe-in. See illustration for a diagram of these characteristics of steering geometry.

SUSPENSION AND STEERING

Wheel Alignment

YEAR	MODEL	CASTER Range (Deg.)	CASTER Pref. Setting (Deg.)	CAMBER Range (Deg.)	CAMBER Pref. Setting (Deg.)	TOE-IN (In.)	KING-PIN INCLINATION (Deg.)	WHEEL PIVOT RATIO Inner Wheel	WHEEL PIVOT RATIO Outer Wheel
1960	All Models	2½P to 3P	2¾P	0-1P	½P	3/16 +0 -1/16 ●	7 ± ½	20	18
1961	500, 700, 900	1½P to 2P	2P	0-1P	½P	3/16 +0 -1/16 ●	7 ± ½	20	18
	1200 and 95	2¼P to 2¾P	2½P	0-½P	¼P	1/8 ●	—	—	—
1962-63	500, 700, 900	1½P to 2P	2P	0-1P	½P	¼-3/8 ●●	7 ± ½	20	18
	1200 Panel, P.U.	1P to 1½P	1¼P	¼N-¼P	0	1/16-3/16 #	—	—	—
	1200 Greenbrier	2P to 2½P	2¼P	¼P-¾P	½P	1/16-3/16 ##	—	—	—
1964	500, 600, 700, 900	1½P to 2P	2P	½N-½P	0	¼-3/8 ●●	7 ± ½	20	18
	1200	-----Same as 1962-63 Specifications-----							
1965-66		1½ to 2½P▲	2P	½P to 1⅓P■	1P	¼ to 3/8 ★	7	20	18
1967-69		1¾P to 2¾P	2¼P	½P to 1½P■	1P	3/16 to 5/16 ★	6½	20	18

●—Rear toe-in 0 to ¼, with non-adjustable camber—2°N ± ½°.
●●—Rear toe-in 1/8 to 3/8, with non-adjustable camber—1°N ± ½°.
★—Rear toe-in 1/8 to 3/8, camber—1°N to 0.
▲—1966—2½ to 3½P.
■—Rear wheel camber 0 to 1N.

N—Negative.
P—Positive.
P.U.—Pickup truck.
#—Rear toe-in 1/16-3/16, rear camber 4⅝°N.
##—Rear toe-in 1/16-3/16, rear camber 3½°N ± ½°.

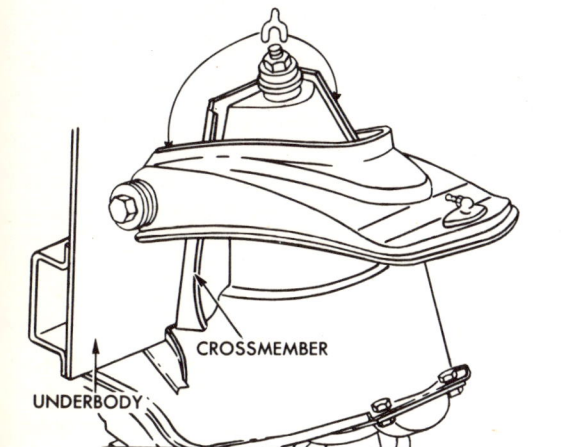

Camber shims

Camber—1960-1964

Adjust camber by installing shims between the upper control arm inner shaft and the frame crossmember, as shown. The shims are fork type (open-ended) and the bolts only need to be loosened, not removed. Adding shims will decrease the camber angle; add an equal number of shims to the forward and rearward bolt location so as not to affect the caster or toe-in. Remove the wheel on the affected side to ease access to the steering knuckle.

Camber—1965-1969

Adjust camber by loosening the cam bolt on the lower control arm pivot on the affected side, and turning the cam to move the wheel in or out as required.

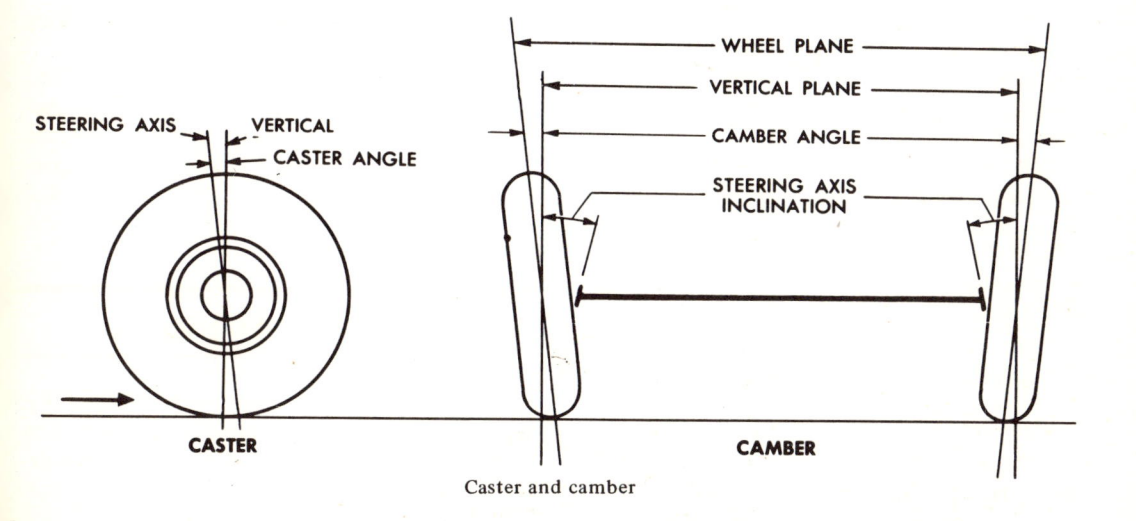

Caster and camber

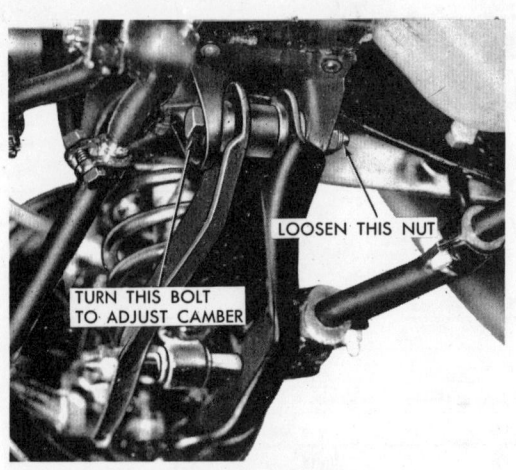

Camber adjustment

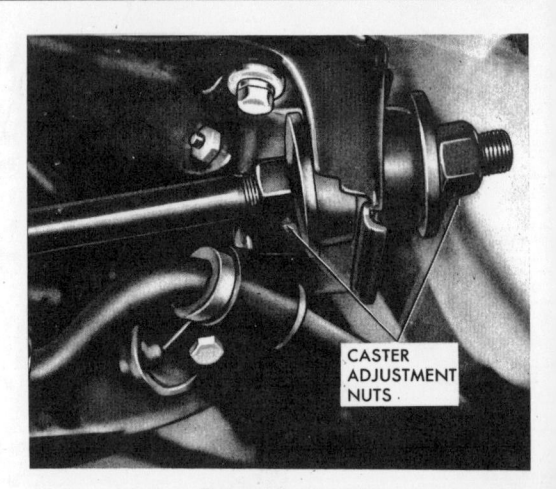

Caster adjustment

Caster

On all models, adjust caster by shortening or lengthening the strut rod on the affected side. Tighten the nuts against each other after the adjustment is complete; lengthening the rod increases caster and shortening it decreases caster.

Toe-In

Adjust toe-in last, after the caster and camber have been set. Adjust the steering tie-rod sleeves for each side to turn each wheel inward or outward as required. Make this adjustment with the wheels in the straight-ahead position; adjust the steering, if necessary, to bring the "high load" point in the steering box in line with the straight-ahead position on the wheels. See "Steering" above.

Steering Axis Inclination

Steering axis inclination is a designed-in deviation of the axis of rotation of the steering knuckle from an ideal vertical; it is non-adjustable and the limits are given here as an index of steering component condition. Front end parts which contribute to a steering axis out of specification should be replaced.